The Politics of Futility

The General Jewish Workers Bund of Poland
1917–1943

THE POLITICS
OF FUTILITY

*The General Jewish Workers
Bund of Poland, 1917-1943*

By BERNARD K. JOHNPOLL

State University of New York at Albany

Cornell University Press

ITHACA, NEW YORK

CORNELL UNIVERSITY PRESS

First published 1967

Library of Congress Catalog Card Number: 67-13044

PRINTED IN THE UNITED STATES OF AMERICA
BY KINGSPORT PRESS, INC.

To Nicholas Kirtzman
1896–1963

Preface

THIS book is the culmination of more than twenty years of work—and procrastination. It had its origins in Britain during the early 1940's, when I was a young seaman, just returned from the Soviet Union. During a four-month stay in that "Workers' Fatherland," I had become disillusioned with socialism. I discussed my experience with the late James Maxton, M.P., who suggested that I might study the difference between revolutionary democratic socialism and the totalitarianism practiced in Soviet Russia, which labels itself Socialist.

A few days after my visit with Jimmy Maxton, I met Arthur Zygelboym, the Bund representative in the Polish Parliament-in-Exile, who was, like Maxton, a revolutionary democratic Socialist. He also warned me against equating the Soviet system with socialism.

My interest in socialism was rekindled by these two meetings, and I began research into the Socialist movements of the interwar period. This volume is the first product of that research. I hope to follow it with studies of other democratic Socialist parties, particularly those of Sweden, the United States, Canada, Poland, Austria, and the Zionists. Each of these parties represents an aspect of the Socialist movement. The success or failure of each sheds new light on Socialist doctrine, on party theory, and on other aspects of political science.

My object in this study is to explore the workings of a particular political party in a specific setting—to examine the party's approach to problems as they arose and the solutions that were suggested. Primarily, the study has been limited to an investigation of the basic questions that confronted the

General Jewish Workers Bund of Poland (commonly called the Bund) as a party of the Jewish working people in interwar Poland. The work investigates the basic questions that confronted the Bund and the way the Bund answered these questions. Purely empirical in its approach, the study makes no claim to being a philosophic analysis; it is not a history of the Jews in interwar Poland, nor is it a study of Social Democratic philosophy, but a survey of the Bund and the conditions under which it existed.

From this analysis it is hoped that some new insight into political parties may develop; but my intention is not to propose any sweeping new theories or to disclose any new evidence of the difference between revolutionary socialism (as the Bundists labeled their myth) and Communism. This difference has been well documented previously. Any new evidence that may appear will be peripheral to the study itself.

As an investigation of a single party within the context of the broader problems inherent in any research involving Socialist theory, party theory, and comparative government systems, this study proposes to examine the twenty-six-year life of the Bund and to find through that investigation some answers to problems confronting political scientists. Chief among these questions is: What can be the role of a political party that is by nature precluded from actual state power? This was the major problem confronting the Bund, whose constituency was less than 10 per cent of the population of Poland.

Peripherally, three related questions will be considered: (1) In view of Marx's failure to deal with the nationality question in a positive manner, how does a party that labels itself Marxist propose to solve the nationality problem while remaining true to what it considers Socialist internationalism?[1] (2) What is the driving force of such a party? What is its

---

[1] Internationalism, in the sense used here, might better be labeled multinationalism. Unfortunately, Marxists persist in calling it internationalism.

mystique or myth? (3) How does a party adapt itself to the semi-illegality imposed on it by a series of authoritarian governments?

This inquiry may not find all the answers it seeks, nor can final answers be made without the study of other, similar parties. But such an undertaking can break new ground, suggest some partial and tentative solutions, and throw light upon areas that are now in almost total darkness.

The Bund was a party that limited its constituency to a persecuted national minority, and that had a political doctrine from which it refused to budge—a self-proclaimed Marxian party dedicated to a new social, political, and economic order. There were other Socialist parties made up of national minorities in independent Poland between 1917 and 1943. No serious investigation of these parties has been undertaken. The Ukrainian, German, and Byelorussian Socialists of interwar Poland represented constituencies whose problems were in many ways similar to those faced by the Bund, though not as sharply defined. These parties represented national minorities within specific geographic areas; the Jews, on the contrary, were dispersed through Poland and had to acclimatize themselves to remaining a permanent minority. The other minorities could speak of an ultimate goal of territorial integrity as nation-states; but this was precluded for the Jews.

From the point of view of scientific investigation it is fortunate that the Bund existed as a Polish political party for a relatively short period—1917 to 1943. For within this twenty-six-year period the issues were clearly delineated. Those issues are investigated here in their historical setting and without the use of any mathematical formulas. History must, in this case, serve as the vehicle for investigating basic political issues scientifically. The struggles within the party, the search for partners among the Socialists of other nationalities within Poland, and the relations with other parties within the Jewish community are studied in the hope that some broad generalizations may emerge.

If I appear to be too harsh in my treatment of the Bund in

this book, I am genuinely sorry. Had I been a Jew in interwar Poland, and even had I known then what I claim to know today, I should nevertheless have been a member of the Bund. My criticism is based purely on my personal theory of politics—a theory which holds that politics is the study of power and that a successful political party is one which can influence the structure and operations of the state. On the basis of ethical theory or moral philosophy, I am still in agreement with the Bund.

SOURCES

Research into the Bund was made possible by the ready availability of materials. The Bund's members had a sense of history. They therefore made over the years a collection of materials, the Bund Archives, which are invaluable to any scholar in East European or Jewish politics, history, or culture.

The Archives have an unusual history. Begun about the turn of the century by John Mill, one of the founders of the movement, they were housed in various cities throughout Western Europe, and finally came to Berlin after the end of World War I. When Hitler rose to power, the Archives were moved to Paris lest they be destroyed by the Nazis. After the fall of Paris in 1940 the Archives were seized by the Nazis, though for reasons as yet unexplained they were not moved to Germany but were left in Paris. As the Allied armies moved toward Paris, the Germans attempted to destroy the Archives by throwing them into a garbage dump. Fortunately, they were discovered there by a sympathizer with the Bund, and most of their contents were saved. After the war they were moved to New York. Unfortunately, some valuable material had been lost in the meantime. Almost all the brochures, many books, and files of most of the journals and newspapers published by or relating to the Bund, together with numerous personal papers and letters, are kept in the Bund Archives at

25 East 78th Street in New York. They were made available to me, and much of my research was done there.

Another extremely valuable collection for students of East European Jewry is in the library and archives of the YIVO–Institute for Jewish Research. Originally established in Vilno, the YIVO moved to New York during the late 1930's. Many of the materials relating to the Bund in the YIVO and the Bund Archives duplicate one another. Some items in each of the collections, however, are unique.

A complete file of the most important newspaper of the Polish Bund, the daily *Folkscajtung* [2] of Warsaw, is available on microfilm in the Jewish section of the New York Public Library. Other major Warsaw dailies in Yiddish are also available there. Some Bund materials in the library, particularly those concerned with the Russian Revolution of 1917 and with the early 1920's, are, however, in extremely poor condition. Some material of a theoretical nature was also found at the Tamiment Institute in New York. The concentration of all these collections in the city of New York simplified the task of research.

Other materials are not available in the United States. Many of these are in the British Museum in London—particularly such newspapers as *Arbeiter Sztyme* of Warsaw and *Der Emes,* the official Yiddish organ of the Communist Party in Soviet Russia.

The Soviet Embassy's cultural attaché in Washington was helpful in making available rare materials that are to be found only at the Marxism-Leninism Institute in Moscow.

Despite this wealth of sources, for some areas—particularly the early years of the Bund in independent Poland—archives are no longer available. These were mostly destroyed by the anti-Semitic government then in power. Some of the material disappeared when the Bund Archives were being moved from Berlin to Paris, or was destroyed when the Germans fled the

[2] *Folkscajtung* is the Polish spelling as it appeared on the masthead of the newspaper. See "A Note on Languages," which follows.

French capital. A search in all available collections of materials in Yiddish, Russian, Polish, German, and English has failed to uncover any of the missing archives. Although these might have enriched the study, I do not believe they would have changed its basic thesis. Interviews with surviving Bundists have helped fill the gap.

So far as possible this study has been based on original materials. Personal papers, letters, messages, journals, newspapers, and brochures were consulted wherever they were available. Memoirs of persons directly involved have also been used to a great extent. Secondary sources have generally been avoided except where no others were extant.

A NOTE ON LANGUAGES

Most of the material on which this study is based is in Yiddish, the dominant language of East European Jewry. This language is basically Germanic, although the vocabulary, grammar, and alphabet are distinct. The alphabet of Yiddish is a modified form of the Hebrew, and unfortunately there are no established forms for transliterating from Yiddish to English. So a serious problem in transliteration is encountered here. Because the Yiddish alphabet differs from the Latin, it has been necessary to transcribe phonetically. The exceptions are certain Yiddish words that are spelled with Latin letters in the original material; these spellings have been retained. Many of these are names of Yiddish journals published in Poland. Thus, the name of the Bund journal was written *Uncer Cajt* while it was published in Poland, but was changed to *Unser Tsait* after it was moved to New York. Some Yiddish publications follow the German spelling of their names: two such are *Der Wecker* and *Zukunft*, both published in New York. For these, the publisher's spelling has been retained. Where Russian material has been transliterated, the accepted spelling in the Latin alphabet has been employed. The original spellings have been used for Polish and German words.

Although the titles of publications in Yiddish, Polish, Russian, and German are cited in the original only, translations will be found in the bibliography. In those few instances where linguistic peculiarities made literal translation impossible, translations are as nearly exact as linguistic dissimilarity will allow.

Proper names, particularly of persons, constitute an exceptionally serious problem in transliteration. Even where an English spelling or an Americanized form of a person's name existed, the spelling used by the person himself has been employed. Thus Arthur Zygelboym's family name could have been transliterated to Siegelbaum, a spelling preferred by most American Jews bearing that name. Zygelboym, however, kept the spelling as it appears here.

GUIDE TO TRANSLITERATION

The list which follows has been selected as a guide to Yiddish and Polish spelling and pronunciation.

YIDDISH

Letter	*Equivalent in English*
a	as in *mop*
ay (ai is somewhat softer)	as in *high*
ey	as in *pay*
u	as in *broom*
ch	as in German *ach*
kh	harder version of *ch*
zh	as in *gendarme*

(All other Yiddish transliterations are spelled phonetically.)

POLISH

Letter	*Equivalent in English*
a	as in *hot*
e	as in *get*

i	as in *free*
o	as in *cost*
c	as in *hats* or *its*
u	as in *scooter*
ć, ci, or cz	as in *ouch*
dź, dzi, or dz	as in *just*
g	as in *go*
ch	as in German *ach*
j	as in *young*
aj	as in *height*
y	as in *big*
s, si, or sz	as in *short*
z, z, zi, or rz	as in *gendarme*

The Polish government required the title of every Yiddish newspaper and periodical to appear transliterated into Polish on the masthead. Thus the following titles follow the Polish spelling style: *Arbeiter Sztyme, Dos Fraje Vort, Folkscajtung, Hajnt, Jugnt Vecker, Socialistisze Bleter, Uncer Cajt, Uncer Sztyme,* and *Warszawer Radio.*

ACKNOWLEDGMENTS

Many people aided me in the preparation of this study. I could not possibly list all who have helped me to learn the four languages—Russian, Polish, German, and particularly Yiddish—which were essential to carrying on this work. Nor could I mention by name the legion of librarians at the New York Public Library, the Tamiment Institute, YIVO–Institute for Jewish Research, the British Museum, Columbia University, Ohio State University, the University of Minnesota, the University of Chicago, the University of Wisconsin, and Rutgers, the State University of New Jersey, whose assistance I found invaluable.

My greatest debt is to the National Foundation for Jewish Culture, particularly to its director, Dr. Judah Shapiro. A grant from the Foundation made it possible for me to complete the project. I am also deeply indebted to my late father-in-law, Nicholas Kirtzman, to whom the book is dedicated. His moral and financial support allowed me to continue research and writing during extremely trying periods.

For aid in locating documents and publications I am most particularly indebted to Hillel Kampinski, of the Bund Archives. Although he knew that he could expect to disagree with my conclusions, he cooperated by making available obscure and rare materials which were of immense value.

Among my fellow academicians I am particularly grateful to Professors Benjamin Baker, Ardath Burks, Michael Curtis, Eugene J. Meehan, and Abraham Yesselson of Rutgers, the State University, in New Brunswick, New Jersey; Dr. Webb Fiser, vice president for academic affairs at the State University of New York at Albany; Professors James Riedel, Fred Tickner, and Lewis Welch at the Graduate School of Public Affairs, State University of New York at Albany; and Professor Edgar Eddins of Hartwick College, Oneonta, New York.

For typing a manuscript that required extreme patience I am obligated to Mrs. Nadine Hunt and Miss Sandra McGee, of the University of Saskatchewan, Regina Campus.

The editorial staff of Cornell University Press did an excellent job of preparing the manuscript for publication. George Krycuk of Rensselaer Polytechnic Institute, and Dr. A. Joachimowski, of the University of Saskatchewan, Regina Campus, did yeoman service in checking my Polish for errors.

I would be remiss if I did not mention my long-suffering wife Lillian, and the rest of my family. To my mother and father, whose decades-long devotion to the cause of democratic socialism is at the root of my interest, I also desire to express my sincerest thanks.

Although all of the persons mentioned aided me, I am alone responsible for any errors or omissions.

B. K. J.

Albany, New York
July 1966

Contents

The Politics of Futility

The General Jewish Workers Bund of Poland

1917–1943

Introduction

A POLITICAL party must be studied in the context of the political and social system in which it arises; "the peculiar character of each party must be defined in terms of the political order of which it is an integral part." [1] Thus any attempt at studying a party requires some discussion of the system in which it existed and the problems that confronted it. This is particularly true of the General Jewish Workers Bund of Poland, which met with problems such as rarely confront other parties.

The Bund was only one of a multitude of doctrinally oriented parties competing for power. Moreover, it was a party with a limited constituency—Poland's Jewish minority —representing, at most, 10 per cent of the population of Poland. Even within that limited constituency it was competing with other parties, at least one of which also considered itself to be Socialist.

PERMANENT MINORITY STATUS

Edmund Burke, in the middle of the eighteenth century, defined a political party as an organization whose goal was the control of state power. He wrote:

Party is a body of men united for promoting the national interest upon some particular interest in which they are all agreed. . . . Therefore every honorable connection will avow it is their first purpose to pursue every just method to put the men who hold their opinions into such a condition as will en-

[1] Sigmund Neumann, *Modern Political Parties* (Chicago: University of Chicago Press, 1956), p. 395.

I

able them to carry their common plans into execution with all the power and authority of the state.[2]

What of the party which can never hope to attain state power, at least by itself? This was the situation of the Bund. Even assuming that it won 100 per cent of the vote of its limited constituency, it could claim only 10 per cent of the total vote of Poland. How could it hope to achieve its aims? In the United States and the United Kingdom, minor parties that had no hope of gaining power were able to influence policies of the major parties. Much of the progressive legislation of the United States was first put forward in the platforms of such minor—and often transient—parties as the Populists, the Progressives, the Socialists, and the Free Soilers. These parties functioned, in a sense, like pressure groups, winning popular support for some of their doctrines but failing to assume the power and responsibility of government.[3]

The Bund, however, was precluded from being an effective pressure group. The minority it represented was despised by a great portion of the population in Poland. Its support of a position might have the reverse effect, and prevent consideration.

It was, by the very nature of its position on the nationality problem, irrevocably tied to operating within Poland, and as a party of a limited constituency. Yet there were alternatives available to the Bund, alternatives it debated endlessly. It could, for example, have merged into the Polish Socialist Party (*Polska Partja Socjalistyczna*, hence PPS) as a separate constituent part. Such a merger would have required the acquiescence, at least, of the Polish party. Acquiescence was, however, not forthcoming.

[2] Edmund Burke, "Thoughts on the Cause of the Present Discontent," *The Works of the Right Honorable Edmund Burke* (Boston: Little, Brown and Co., 1865), I, 530.

[3] See, for example, Howard R. Penniman, *Sait's American Parties and Elections* (New York: Appleton–Century–Crofts, 1952), pp. 221–239; V. O. Key, *Politics, Parties, and Pressure Groups* (4th ed.; New York: Crowell, 1964), chap. x.

The Bund might have dissolved, recommending that its members enter the PPS. It is true that entry into the PPS would have meant the death of the Bund, a matter of great concern to most Bundists, but it would have placed the Bundists in a strong position within a major Socialist party which did have the potential for forming a government. The Bund might also have been instrumental in forming a coalition with the PPS and the Socialist parties made up of the other minorities. This possibility, more than any other, was debated by the Bundists. That no coalition was ever formed was as much the fault of the PPS as of the Bund, although the latter refused until it was too late because it would not compromise its doctrines.

In the first years after the Russian Revolution, the Polish Bund might have gone into the Communist Party, as its Russian counterpart did, and as some of its members desired to do. This possibility was considered seriously by the Bundists between 1919 and 1921. That it did not come about is attributable more to the Communists' insistence on total obeisance than to the Bund's unwillingness.

SOCIALISM AND NATIONALITY

Marx did not consider nationality a vital issue. In his one major work on the Jewish problem, he showed a failure to understand the Eastern Jews' insistence that they constituted a distinct nationality with a cultural and historical identity of its own.[4]

Moreover, Marx considered nationalism to be a dying attribute of capitalism. He refused to concede that nationality might have as strong a claim as class on the workers' loyalty. In his most popular work, *The Communist Manifesto*, Marx laid down the dictum that the working man had no nation.

---

[4] Karl Marx, "Zur Judenfrage," in *Historisch-Kritische Gesamtausgabe, Erste Abteilung* (Berlin: Marx-Engels Verlag G.M.B.H., 1927), I, 576–606. See also Karl Marx, *A World Without Jews* (New York: Philosophical Library, 1959).

He said the workers' only struggle was for political, and thus economic, power. National liberation, Marx insisted, was of no interest to the workers. He wrote:

> National differences and antagonism between people are daily more and more vanishing, owing to the development of the bourgeoisie, to freedom of commerce, to the world market, to uniformity in the mode of production, and in the conditions of life corresponding thereto.
> The supremacy of the proletariat will cause them to vanish still further. . . .
> In proportion as the exploitation of one individual is put an end to, the exploitation of one nation by another will also be put an end to. In proportion as the antagonisms between classes within the nation vanishes, the hostility of one nation to another will come to an end.[5]

Marx was wrong. The nationality question could not be brushed blithely aside in the hope that once the working class had achieved power all national antagonisms would vanish. The problem plagued the Socialist movement for many generations after Marx's death. It is still a problem with which Marxists must cope.

It was this issue which separated the Bund from the other Socialist parties of Poland. And it was this issue which divided the Jewish Socialist movements as well.

THE MYTH

That the Bund existed in Eastern Europe for as long as it did—from 1897 to 1943—is one of the minor miracles of Socialist politics. Why did the Bund refuse to dissolve into the Communist Party of Poland in 1918? The Bund was as revolutionary a group as at least one of the two parties which merged into the Communist Party of Poland. Many Bundists

---

[5] Karl Marx, *The Communist Manifesto*, Centennial edition, with introduction by Harold Laski (London: George Allen and Unwin, 1948), pp. 142–143.

—a majority between 1919 and 1921—were prepared to accept the Communist principles and tactics. And why did a vast majority of them refuse to join the Communist International (Comintern) on the Comintern's conditions in 1921? Even in refusing to join, the Bund proclaimed its adherence to the Comintern's program.

Why did the Bund continue to defy the anti-Semitic, anti-Socialist governments that ruled Poland for most of its twenty-one years of independence between the two wars? Its members faced death, imprisonment, and repression, and still they refused to concede that the Jews would be better off if they emigrated to a less hostile national home. What led the Bund to take the lead in organizing the obviously futile—though heroic—Battle of the Ghetto?

Georges Sorel, the erratic *ex post facto* philosopher of syndicalism, has described the myth thus:

> Experience shows that the framing of a future, in some indeterminate time, may, when it is done in a certain way, be very effective, and have very few inconveniences; this happens when the anticipations of the future take the form of those myths, which enclose with them, all the strongest inclinations of a people, of a party, or of a class, inclinations which recur to the mind with the insistence of instincts in all circumstances of life; and which give an aspect of complete reality to the hopes of immediate action by which more easily than by any other method, men can reform their desires, passions, and mental activity. We know, moreover, that these social myths in no way prevent a man profiting by the observations which he makes in the course of his life, and form no obstacles to the pursuit of his normal aspirations.
>
> The myth must be judged as a means of acting on the present; any attempt to discuss how far it can be taken literally as future history is devoid of sense. *It is the myth in its entirety which is alone important:* its parts are only of interest in so far as they bring out the main idea.[6]

[6] Georges Sorel, *Reflections on Violence* (New York: Collier Books, 1961), pp. 124–126. Italics in original.

The revolutionary myth was what allowed the Bund to exist for so long, enabled it to overcome serious obstacles, and turned it into a devout band, an *ecclesia militanta.*

No question raised more debate within the Bund than the issue of international affiliation. The Bund had, at various times during its existence as a party in independent Poland, applied for affiliation with three international bodies, the Communist International (1920), the Paris-based Bureau of Revolutionary Socialist Parties (1923), and the Labor and Socialist International (1930). The Bund never became a member of the Communist International; it did, however, affiliate with the Bureau of Revolutionary Socialist Parties (1923–1930) and with the Labor and Socialist International (1930–1943).

Socialist Internationals have had a long and involved history. The first, The International Working Men's Association, was organized in 1864, with headquarters in London. It was a loose association with individual members as well as affiliated organizations. By 1872 the First International, as it has since come to be known, had disintegrated in a struggle between the Bakhunin anarchists and the Marxian Socialists. Several attempts were made to resurrect the International between 1872 and 1889, but none succeeded.

In 1889 the Socialist parties of Western and Central Europe formed the Socialist (or Second) International. Parties from all of Europe and from North America affiliated with it. By 1914 significant Socialist parties in more than a dozen nations were members of the Second International. World War I led to its demise, however.

The Second International was doomed when the German Social Democratic Party (SPD), the largest Socialist party, decided to support the war. The decision led to a serious split within the party itself, and divided the world Socialist movement into three camps: pro-German, pro-Allied, and antiwar. Except for rare individuals, Socialists generally belonged to the camps in which their countries found themselves. The only exceptions of note were the American Socialist Party, the internationalist wing of the Russian Mensheviks, the Bund, a segment of the Russian Bolsheviks, the Polish Socialist Party (both factions) in the Russian portion of Poland, and the Independent Socialists of Germany.

Conferences of Socialists in the Allied countries were held during the war, but not until 1920 was the Second International resurrected, and then only for a short time (until 1923). The resurrected International was dominated by those Socialist parties which had participated in coalition governments and had officially supported their governments' positions during the war: the British Labour Party, the Social Democratic Party of Germany, and the Belgian, Danish, Dutch, and Swedish Socialist parties.

In March 1919 the Communist International (generally called the Comintern or the Third International) was founded in Moscow. It attracted most of the Socialist groups that still considered themselves revolutionary. The Comintern insisted, however, upon total obeisance and the purge of non-Communists. This insistence caused splits in most of the Socialist parties.

A third group, which included the more radical non-Communist parties, refused to support either the Second or the Third International and formed its own organization at a conference in Vienna in February 1921. The new International, the International Working Union of Socialist Parties (commonly called the Two-and-a-Half International), included the Austrian party, the Swiss, and a segment of the French (the other segment of which joined the Comintern), the Independent Socialist Party of Germany, the Independent Labour Party of Great Britain, and the Russian Mensheviks and Social Revolutionaries.

But when the German Independent Socialists returned to

the Social Democratic Party in 1923, and disillusionment with the Russian Revolution had begun to develop, the Second and the Two-and-a-Half-Internationals united at a joint conference in Hamburg to form Labor and Socialist International (LSI) which existed throughout the interwar period. A small group of parties in the Two-and-a-Half International, headed by the left-wing German Socialist Georg Lederbour, refused to enter the LSI and founded their own Bureau of Revolutionary Socialist Parties with headquarters in Paris. The Bureau was composed of tiny doctrinaire groups plus the Norwegian Labor Party, which withdrew in 1927, and the Bund, which withdrew in 1930 and then joined the LSI.[7]

LEFT, RIGHT, AND CENTER

The use of the terms left, right, and center in this study follows whatever sense was intended by those who so labeled themselves. It should be noted that these terms had distinct meanings within and outside of the Bund.

In the Bund the left wing would have to be defined as the group who had an affinity for the philosophy and tactics of the Communists while remaining within the Bund. This group represented the majority of the Bund for only two years—1919 to 1921—but it was supported by a sizable minority within the Bund for the rest of its existence.

The left wing considered itself the revolutionary faction of the Bund; that is, it was less interested in the use of legal democratic means than it was in obtaining power per se. It opposed the right wing's insistence that the Bund limit itself to democratic, nonviolent tactics. The left wing of the Bund differed from the Communists, however, in its distaste for

[7] For a full discussion of the Socialist and Communist Internationals prior to World War II, see G. D. H. Cole, *A History of Socialist Thought* (London: Macmillan, 1958), especially Vol. IV, pp. 287–342 and 680–714. See also John Price, *The International Labour Movement* (London: Oxford University Press, 1945), pp. 10–25.

monolithic control of the party by its leadership, and its rejection of the principle of totalitarian state rule as a prerequisite for socialism.

The left wing and the centrist factions of the Bund agreed that in all probability socialism could not be achieved by peaceful, democratic means. They also agreed that the new Socialist order ought to be achieved with as little sacrifice of life and liberty as possible. Likewise they were in agreement (as was the right wing) on the solution to the Jewish question; all favored national cultural autonomy.

Essentially the centrists were interested in bridging the chasm between the two other factions. They supported one or the other of the more stable wings during the early years of the period covered in this study. From 1924 onward they supported the right wing on almost all issues, and by 1930 they no longer constituted a distinct faction.

The right wing of the Bund, unlike the two other factions, was insistent on parliamentary democracy as a necessary concomitant for socialism. It rejected the whole idea of a cataclysmic overthrow of the capitalist state structure. It favored, instead, a gradual transformation of the state, from capitalist to Socialist, under a parliamentary, democratic form of government. It was, in sum, the Social Democratic faction.

Although the right-wing leaders would have denied any debt to the German Socialist theoretician, Eduard Bernstein, who revised Marxism at the turn of the century, and although they never accepted all of his philosophic and economic views, they owed much of their political outlook to him. Bernstein wanted the Socialists to recognize that they were a "democratic, Socialist party of reform." He considered dictatorship, even of the proletariat, to be a throwback to an earlier age. In his view, parliamentary democracy was "not only the means but also the substance" of socialism. He recognized that democratic methods might not always be available to Socialists, but he insisted that parliamentary democracy be used wherever possible to bring about a gradual transition from capitalism to socialism. He considered violence barbarian, and opposed it vehemently.[8]

The outlook of the right wing was closely related to that of the major Social Democratic Parties of Europe. Although it opposed coalitions between Socialist and non-Socialist parties, its position apparently was influenced by the fact that the Bund was never in a position to be considered for partnership in such a coalition. It was opposed on principle to working with the Communists, preferrring instead to reach a *modus vivendi* with the Polish Socialist Party. The right wing recognized and opposed the nationalist tendency in the PPS, but it assumed that the PPS would in time become more internationalist.

Of the several issues on which the right and left wings disagreed, the most persistent was the question of international affiliation. The right wing favored joining the Labor and Socialist International, which included almost all of Europe's Socialist parties. The left wing preferred to remain unaffiliated unless the Communist International were to be reformed, at which time it proposed to enter the Comintern. The centrists' position on this issue shifted over the years from

[8] Eduard Bernstein, *Evolutionary Socialism* (New York: Schocken Books, 1961), particularly pp. 146–147, 166, and 197; Peter Gay, *The Dilemma of Democratic Socialism* (New York: Columbia University Press, 1952), particularly chaps. viii, xii. Bernstein attempted to give the philosophic base of Marxism a Kantian rather than a Hegelian cast. He also rejected Marx's contention that under capitalism class tensions would mount, the working class would be further pauperized, and the middle class would shrink and finally vanish, and that a greater centralization of industry was inevitable. Instead, Bernstein maintained that there was a tendency toward greater class tranquillity, that wealth was being more equitably distributed, that there was a tendency toward more widespread ownership of property, and that the trend toward a concentration of industry was slowing down. See, for example, George Lichtheim, *Marxism: An Historical and Critical Study* (London: Routledge and Kegan Paul, 1961), p. 289. Bernstein's theories are merely sketched here. A reading either of Gay or of Bernstein's short work would be required for a full comprehension of his position and influence.

left to right. The left wing also considered the PPS an un-reformable party of nationalism parading under the colors of socialism. The left wing's position was thus almost dia-metrically opposite to that of the right wing. The centrists were generally more sympathetic with the right wing on this issue. In 1919 the left wing opposed participation in the national elections, which the right and center wanted to contest. There were other issues on which the factions dis-agreed. But no issue more persistently dramatized the sharp cleavage between them than did the question of international affiliation.

Although the factions were not separate organizations, they were given tacit recognition within the Bund. Each faction ran separate slates at the elections of delegates to national conventions; and the number of delegates was on the basis of proportional representation. At each conference the factions were distinctly labeled: the *Aynser* (first) represented the majority, who were generally the right wing; the *Tsvayer* (second) represented the minority, who were generally the left wing; and where necessary, the *Drayer* (third) repre-sented a lesser minority, who were usually the centrists. Representatives of each faction were included on the central committee and on the editorial boards of all official Bund publications in proportion to the number of delegates to the last convention.[9]

THE POLISH PARTIES

The Polish right, left, and center were considerably dif-ferent from those within the Bund. Essentially, the right

[9] For a discussion of the left wing of the Bund see Leon Ohler, "Di Tsvayer in Poylishn Bund," *Unser Tsait*, XVII (November–December 1957), 52–54, and files of *Kegn Shtrom*, organ of the left wing, 1930–1935, in the Bund Archives. Concerning the right wing see the works of Vladimir Medem or Bernard Goldstein; also *Socialistisze Bleter* (one issue only), 1931. For the centrist position see works by Henryk Erlich or Victor Alter.

represented the conservative parties, the center the moderately conservative parties, and the left the more liberal or radical parties. Since these descriptions are themselves open to differing semantic interpretations, the blocs must be described separately, party by party.

The main parties of the right were the National Democratic, the National Christian, and the Christian Democratic. Besides these the National Radicals, a pro-Nazi party, emerged in the mid-1930's.

The National Democratic Party (Endek) was the largest as well as the oldest of the parties of the right, and the largest single party in most of the freely elected parliaments before Pilsudski's seizure of power in 1926. Its center of strength was within the middle class, especially the white-collar and professional groups in the cities. An anti-Semitic party, as well as an enemy of cultural and political equality for any of the other national minorities in Poland, it called for the absorption of the other minorities into the Polish majority and for the forced emigration of the Jewish population. It was anti-Socialist, and opposed most social legislation. In foreign policy it was anti-German and pro-French during the early years of Polish independence. Its later foreign policy vacillated with the tides of European politics; but it showed sympathy for Mussolini and Hitler in the years immediately preceding the outbreak of war in 1939. In its early years the Endek had been pro-Czarist and favored a Pan-Slavic confederation closely tied to the Russian rulers. After the Russian Revolution of 1917 it became increasingly more anti-Socialist and alienated from Russia. It also favored a close alliance between the dominant Roman Catholic Church and the Polish state.

The National Christian Party was a small organization which represented the so-called Leviathan, the Polish ruling industrial magnates, and the large landowners. It opposed all social legislation, particularly redistribution of land to the peasants. It was anti-Semitic to the extent of favoring expropriation of Jewish fortunes and the forced emigration of Jews from Poland.

The Christian Democratic Party was Church-controlled. Its program was simply "Poland for the Poles," by which it meant Poland for the Roman Catholic Poles. On social questions it was inconsistent: it opposed almost all social legislation while formally proclaiming its support for Pope Leo XIII's *Rerum Novarum*. It never became an important party in terms of popular support.

The centrist bloc was dominated by the Peasants' Party (*Polskie Stronnictwo Ludowe, "Piast"*), which had no policy except land reform. On this issue its stand was similar to that of the parties of the left—a call for distribution of the large estates among the peasants. It had no other political or economic interests of any significance until 1930, when under the pressure of Pilsudski's authoritarian rule it allied itself with the parties of the left. Its alliances before then had shifted from the left, in 1920, to the right, in the years from 1923 to 1926. Its stand on national minorities was also based on expediency. It was sympathetic to the aspirations of the Jews, Ukrainians, and Germans while it was allied to the left; but it was anti-Semitic during its coalition with the Endek in the mid–1920's.

The non-Communist left consisted of at least three parties, of which two were dominant.[10] The largest and oldest party of the left was the Polish Socialist Party, whose strength was primarily among the workers in the cities, although it had considerable support among the intellectuals. Since its organi-

[10] Other parties of the left represented non-Polish minorities. Of particular importance were the German Social Democratic Party in Poland, the Ukrainian Social Democrats, and the Jewish Socialist parties: the Bund, the Poale Zion, and the Territorialists. The Jewish Socialists will be discussed later in this chapter. The German and Ukrainian Social Democrats were similar in outlook to the PPS, except that they represented the national points of view of the minorities that made up their constituencies.

zation in 1892, the PPS had been more interested in Polish independence from Russia, Austria-Hungary, and Prussia than in socialism. In 1906 it split into two separate parties: a Socialist majority, the Lewica (Left), and a nationalist minority, the Frakcja (Revolutionary Faction), which until 1916 was led by Pilsudski. In 1918 the Lewica merged with the Social Democracy of the Kingdom of Poland and Lithuania (*Socialna Demokracja Krolestwa Polskiego i Litwy*, hence SDKPiL),[11] and formed the Communist Party. The Frakcja then became the PPS. Once Poland achieved its independence, the PPS became a moderate Social Democratic party, which was represented in several coalition governments. It was dedicated to parliamentary democracy, and to equality for all the national minorities in Poland. It favored full equality for the Jews, but it was inconsistent on the issue of autonomy. Many of its leaders either were Jewish or were married to Jewish women; for example, Herman Liebermann, leader of the anti-Pilsudski wing in 1928–1930, was Jewish, but he considered himself a Pole first and a Jew second.

Although the PPS considered itself a Marxian party—in part because Marx had supported the 1863 Polish revolution—it was not doctrinaire. Relations between the PPS and the Bund changed with changing conditions; these parties were generally hostile to one another prior to 1926, friendly from 1926 to 1930, estranged from 1930 to 1932, and fraternal again during the Bund's last decade of existence in Poland.

The second party of the left, the Wyzwolenie or Populist Party, was composed of poor farmers and agricultural workers. Its policies were similar to those of the PPS, except that it placed greater emphasis on agricultural land reform

---

[11] The SDKPiL was historically opposed to all forms of nationalism. It called for united action between the Polish and Russian working classes against the Czarist empire. Its leading figure, Rosa Luxemburg, did battle both with the PPS and with Lenin on the issue of national self-determination, which she opposed as un-Marxian. See Paul Frolich, *Rosa Luxemburg: Gedanke und Tat* (Paris: Editions Nouvelles Internationales, 1939).

than it did on socialism. Its stand concerning national minorities was the same as that of the PPS.

The third party of the left, the National Party of Workers (*Narodowa Partja Robotnicza*), was closely allied with the PPS, and its policies were almost identical except that it refused to call itself Marxian. It also had anti-Semitic tendencies. It considered itself a party of the organized workers, representing the trade-union aspirations in the political arena. But the trade unions, which were closely allied with the PPS, refused to recognize it as their political arm. Never a significant party, it generally supported the PPS in the Sejm. Its largest vote was 228,000 in 1928, as compared to 1,482,000 for the PPS.

Although the Communist Party (*Komunistyczna Partia Polski*, hence KPP) considered itself a party of the left, it was never accepted as such by the other parties in the group. It was a typical Communist party, subservient to the will of Moscow. Because it was illegal during most of its existence, its actual strength is hard to assess, but it did not have any significant following. It was dissolved by order of the Comintern in 1938 on charges of Trotskyism.[12]

THE JEWISH SOCIALISTS

There were three Socialist parties among the Jews: the Bund, the Poale Zion, and the Territorialists. The last of these dissolved during the early years of Polish independence and is not significant to this study. The Bund and the Poale Zion, however, were bitterly hostile rivals for the support of the Jewish working class.

The animosity between the Bund and the Poale Zion was due to their different approaches to the Jewish problem.

[12] For a fuller description of the Polish parties see Raymond Leslie Buell, *Poland: Key to Europe* (New York: Alfred A. Knopf, 1939), pp. 104–108. For the KPP see M. K. Dziewanowski, *The Communist Party of Poland* (Cambridge: Harvard University Press, 1959).

The Bundists proposed a solution within Poland; the Poale Zionists suggested that any answer to the Jewish problem required a national homeland. The debate and ensuing conflict went on continuously from 1897, when both the Bund and the Zionist organizations were born, until 1943, when the Jewish community of Poland was destroyed by Hitler.

At the time of its organization, and for eight years thereafter, the Bund offered no plan for solving the Jewish problem. It spoke of equality, and implied that the hope of the Jews was to be found in socialism alone. In 1905, however, the Bund adopted as its own the concept of national cultural autonomy first advanced in 1897 by Karl Renner, the Austrian Socialist leader, as a solution to the problem of multinationality within the Austro-Hungarian empire. National cultural autonomy did not become a crucial issue until the establishment of an independent Poland, although the idea had been the rallying cry of the Bund for more than a decade before. Since approximately 40 per cent of the population of Poland belonged to non-Polish national minorities, the proposal might have been seen as a solution to what became one of the thorniest of the country's problems.

The concept was spelled out in considerable detail by the Bund:

Each country undertakes certain cultural work; it builds schools, high schools, teachers' colleges, museums, libraries, and the like. Should we achieve national cultural autonomy this work would be turned over to each of the nationalities. Let us assume a country is composed of many nationalities—for example: Poles, Lithuanians, and Jews. Each of these nationalities would have to build a separate organization. All citizens on the lists of each nationality would have to join a special organization which would organize cultural assemblies in each area and a general cultural assembly for the country as a whole. These special assemblies would have special financial powers; each nationality would have the right to tax its own members, or the state would distribute, from its general fund, a proportionate part of its cultural budget to each of the nationalities.

Each citizen of the land would belong to one of these nationality groups; but the question of which nationality organization he should join would be a matter of personal choice, and no one would have any control over his decision. These autonomous organizations would work within the framework of general laws passed by the parliament of the country; but in their own sphere they would be autonomous, and none of them would have the right to interfere in the affairs of the other.[13]

The Bundists considered national cultural autonomy the only way to prevent persecution of one nationality by another. National cultural autonomy was thus the only hope they could see for tranquillity in a multinational state such as Poland.

The Bundists' position on the Jewish question carried with it certain basic corollaries. First, the Bundists rejected any theory of nationality that insisted on a geographic basis for a nation. They maintained that nation was a matter of heritage and culture, and not a matter of common geography. Secondly, the Bundists insisted that the Jews' cultural heritage was East European and not Middle Eastern. The Jewish home in Palestine had been dissolved too long ago to be considered the basis for the Jewish heritage. Therefore, the Bundists maintained, the language of the Jewish people was Yiddish and not Hebrew. They insisted that Yiddish was a language equal to any other, with a unique grammar and literature and with a history of its own.

The Poale Zion accepted the Zionist proposition concerning the Jewish question, which precluded any hope of a solution within the countries of the Diaspora.[14] It insisted

[13] *Lebnsfragn*, I, February 8, 1916.
[14] The Diaspora or dispersion of the Jews had its origin shortly after the beginning of the Christian era, when the Jews were ousted from Palestine by the Roman rulers and scattered throughout the world.

that the Jews needed a homeland of their own; and it limited the choice of homeland to the Jewish ancestral home, Palestine.

The Zionists maintained that autonomy within any of the states where the Jews were then living would be short-lived. They believed that tendencies toward national uniformity would grow, and that cultural autonomy would disappear. A national homeland would, on the contrary, be a radical transformation of Jewish life. It would, the Zionists argued, place the destiny of the Jews in their own hands. Palestine was chosen because there was, so the Zionists claimed, a historic and spiritual connection between the Jewish people and their ancestral homeland.

According to Zionists' basic argument,

> . . . in the Diaspora the development of the nation cannot but be abnormal . . . Its normalization requires the restoration of the people to its ancient homeland.
> . . . The very existence of a national minority that has lost its historic homeland stirs up feelings of dislike and enmity. At best the "intrusive" minority is tolerated, for the most part it is maltreated and persecuted. . . .
> . . . The homeless national minority, unable to settle upon the land, which the native population occupies, must live chiefly in the towns. It is thus excluded from basic sectors of the country's economy: from agriculture and the other primary stages of production . . . Having lost contact with the soil, the nation becomes more and more alienated from the life of nature. . . .[15]

The Zionists did not believe that all Jews would or should migrate to Palestine. They merely wanted Palestine to be the potential home for all Jews. This would have the effect, according to the Zionists, of offering all Jews a possible haven, and thus of eliminating the insolubility of the Jewish problem.

Another major point in the Zionists' proposal was a return

[15] Joseph Heller, *The Zionist Idea* (New York: Schocken Books, 1949), pp. 68–69.

to Hebrew, the language of pre-dispersion Palestine. They argued that Hebrew was the historic language of the Jews and that its revival was essential to a return to the national homeland, since the Hebrew spirit could only be conserved in a land where Hebrew was the language and where a Hebrew culture prevailed.[16]

Socialism and Zionism are not mutually exclusive. Moses Hess, a Socialist thinker and a contemporary of Marx, was also a believer in the basic tenets of Zionism. But his Zionism and his Socialism were not related. In the later nineteenth century, Nacham Syrkin based his Zionist beliefs on an Utopian Socialism.

The first attempt to link Marxian socialism and Zionism was made by Ber Borochov. In 1905 he suggested that the national struggle was waged not only, like the class struggle, for material possessions, but also for advantages shared equally by all classes, such as political unity, political institutions, culture, and language. The struggle for achieving nationhood—that is, the historic homeland—would unite the different classes. Once the struggle for the homeland was successfully completed, each of the classes would go its individual way and the class struggle would proceed. But before the Jewish proletariat could assume its rightful place in a class struggle it must have a homeland to which each of its members would feel an attachment.[17]

The Poale Zion's philosophy was an amalgam of socialism and Zionism. The Bund and the Poale Zion both favored the same basic economic-political system. But on the national question they took diametrically opposite views. Since both appealed to the same portion of the Jewish population, it was inevitable that a serious rivalry would develop.

[16] *Ibid.*, pp. 56, 58–59, 61, 66, 73–74.
[17] Ber Borochov, "The National Question and the Class Struggle," in Arthur Hertzberg, *The Zionist Idea* (Cleveland and New York: World Publishing Company, 1959), pp. 355–360. See also Arieh Tartakower, "Labor Zionism–Mapai," in Basil J. Vlavianos and Feliks Gross, *Struggle for Tomorrow* (New York: Arts Inc., 1954), pp. 53–57.

I

Prelude

POLITICAL organizations do not arise spontaneously, nor do they originate without consideration of their environment. Almost invariably these movements are caused by social and economic conditions; they are not exempt from the fundamental dialectic of history.

Thus the Bund did not arise in a vacuum, nor was its origin dissociated from the condition of the Jews in Czarist Russia; nor was the later Bund in independent Poland without an ecological base. The General Jewish Workers Bund of Poland, Lithuania, and Russia, and its successor, the General Jewish Workers Bund of Poland, were children of the hostile conditions in which they developed. The Bund was born of oppression, persecution, and strife; it warred first against the hated Czar and the persecutions and pogroms instigated by his regime against the Jews, and later against the Polish regime, that used the Jews as scapegoats for its own lack of viability.

There were Jews in Poland as far back as the ninth century A.D.; but the Jewish communities that existed in that early medieval period were extremely small. The first major Jewish influx into Poland began during the Black Plague at the end of the fourteenth and beginning of the fifteenth centuries, when the Jews were expelled from German cities and were "allowed to seek refuge in the Great Polish Empire." [1]

---

[1] Ismar Elbogen, *History of the Jews after the Fall of the Jewish State* (Cincinnati: Union of American Hebrew Congregations, 1926), pp. 108–110; *Jewish Encyclopaedia* (New York: Funk and Wagnalls, 1909), X, 561.

Although Poland was hospitable toward the Jews during the early years of their stay, anti-Semitism was already present among the population. Formal discrimination was almost unknown, however, until after the partition of Poland between Russia, Austria, and Prussia at the end of the eighteenth century. Discrimination then became particularly noticeable in the part of Poland that fell under the autocratic rule of Russia's Catherine. Her most notable action was the issuance of an ukase in 1794 limiting Jewish residence to the "Pale of Settlement," the four provinces of Poland under her rule—Great Poland, Little Poland, Volhynia, and Lithuania. The object of the ukase was to keep the Jews out of Russia itself, even though Jewish settlements already existed there by that time.[2]

Despite anti-Semitism among the Poles, the Jews considered themselves Polish patriots and fought with Tadeusz Kosciuszko in the 1794 rebellion against the Russians. Almost all of the Jewish soldiers who took part died at the ramparts of Warsaw; their leader Berek Joselevitch lost his life in a later battle. Jews also participated in the Polish nationalist uprisings of 1830–1831 and 1863. Their devotion to the cause of Poland did not, however, save them from persecution at the hands of Poles during the nineteenth and early twentieth centuries.[3]

Most of the Jews were artisans, and had been since the eighteenth century. They were thus the backbone of whatever middle class there was in Poland during the period of Russian rule. Moreover, the Jewish population grew, partly because of migrations from the east, so that in the early part of this century most of the 5,700,000 Jews in Russia lived in the area that had been the Kingdom of Poland. By the end of World War I more than 3,000,000 Jews lived within the

[2] Howard M. Sachar, *The Course of Modern Jewish History* (Cleveland and New York: World Publishing Co., 1958), p. 82.
[3] *Ibid.*, pp. 73–74; Elbogen, *op. cit.*, p. 181.

boundaries of the new Polish Republic, and made up 10 per cent of its total population.[4]

The Jewish labor and Socialist movement developed in the Czarist empire under conditions of persecution and oligarchic rule. The earliest rumblings came not from the working or artisan classes but from the intelligentsia, who in the 1870's organized a Socialist group under the leadership of Aaron Lieberman. This small organization studied and discussed socialism in theoretical terms and published a journal in Hebrew, a language that was rarely used by the mass of Jews in Eastern Europe. Toward the end of the 1870's, Lieberman went to London, where with the help of Jewish Socialists in Whitechapel he began the first Socialist activities in Yiddish, the usual language of Jews. By 1880 the Group of Jewish Socialists in Geneva, composed mainly of Jewish students barred from Russian universities, began publishing Yiddish propaganda on a broad scale. At about the same time, the first signs of labor organization began to be noticed in the Russian Pale. First to organize were the hosiery workers in Vilno, next the textile workers in Białystok, and then the brush-makers, who formed the first effective trade union. The Jewish unions were active in demanding shorter hours and decent wages—hours ranged from fourteen to sixteen for a daily wage of about thirty cents. Major strikes developed during the early 1890's, and by 1895 the textile union in Białystok was able to paralyze the city's industry with a strike of its 3,000 Jewish members.[5]

[4] *Ibid.*, p. 144; *American Jewish Yearbook, 1900–1901* (Philadelphia: Jewish Publication Society, 1901), p. 625; *American Jewish Yearbook, 1928–1929* (Philadelphia: Jewish Publication Society, 1929, p. 249.
[5] Gregory Aronson, "Der Bund in Rusland," *Unser Tsait*, XVII (November–December 1957), 16.

The Bund's immediate predecessor was the Jewish Social Democratic organization, which in the early 1890's had affiliates in Vilno, Minsk, Warsaw, and Białystok, and whose leaders included three of the men who were to become the outstanding personalities in the early years of the Bund—Arcady Kremer, Vladimir Kossofsky, and John Mill. By 1891 the Jewish Socialists had organized meetings in Vilno; by 1892 they were holding May Day rallies, and by 1893 they had begun publishing Socialist pamphlets. The first conference of the Jewish Socialists was held in Vilno in 1894, and the second in Minsk the following year.[6]

A turning point for the Jewish Socialists occurrred in 1895 when Lev Martov (Juli Ossipovitch Tsederbaum), an assimilated Jew, delivered an address to a group of Jewish Socialists in Vilno. In the speech, later published by the Bund as *The New Epoch in the Jewish Labor Movement*, the 22-year-old Martov said that Jewish workers had interests that were quite separate from those of the Russian workers; moreover, he maintained, the Jewish workers could not always trust the Russian workers to live up to the principles of international proletarian solidarity. The task of awakening the Jewish workers, he said, had to be along both class and national lines; to achieve this would require a separate Jewish labor organization.[7]

Almost immediately after the Martov speech, a movement began to create a Jewish Socialist organization which would use the Yiddish language. A Yiddish language publication,

[6] *Ibid.*, pp. 16–17.
[7] J. L. Keep, *The Rise of the Social Democracy in Russia* (London: Oxford University Press, 1963), p. 44; Abraham Patkin, *The Origin of the Russian Jewish Labor Movement* (Melbourne: F. W. Cheshire Pty., Ltd., 1947), pp. 130–132; Lev Martov, *Der Nayer Epoche in der Idisher Arbeiter Bavegung* (Geneva: Oyslands Komitet fun Algemayner Idisher Arbeiter Bund fun Poyln, Litte, un Rusland, 1904). Within five years after delivering the speech, Martov reversed his position and became an enemy of the Bund.

Der Idisher Arbeiter, appeared, and a new united Social Democratic organization was formed among the Jewish Socialists of Warsaw. In that year, too, Jewish Socialists were represented for the first time at a meeting of the Socialist International.[8]

By 1896 the Jewish Socialist movement was ready to unite into a single organization covering the entire Pale. The leading figure in the movement that produced this organization was Kremer, who had become a notable figure in the Russian Socialist movement because of a pamphlet he had written sometime earlier. Entitled *Og Agitatsye* ("On Agitation"), it discussed the methods for agitating for socialism among Russian workers but ignored the Jewish issues. Kremer was sent abroad by the Vilno organization and the St. Petersburg Russian Socialist group, which called itself the League of Struggle for Emancipation of the Working Class, to discuss with the leaders of the Russian Socialist movement abroad— Georgi Plekhanov, Vera Zasulich, and Pavel B. Axelrod—the possibility of their becoming international spokesmen for the two organizations. The three leaders suggested instead that the Jewish organizations unite before they attempt to get representation abroad. At their urging, Kremer called a meeting which was aimed at uniting the Jewish Socialist groups into a single organization.[9]

In 1897 the first conference was held in several small houses in Vilno during the Jewish High Holy Days, so as to hide the movements of the delegates and to keep from being conspicuous—for discovery could mean arrest, and arrest could mean long terms of Siberian exile. The thirteen delegates, representing organizations in Warsaw, Białystok, Minsk, Vitebsk, and Vilno, heard a fervent plea from Kremer for unity among the Jewish Socialists. He urged the use of

[8] Aronson, *op. cit.*, p. 17.
[9] Arcady Kremer, "Di Grindung fun Bund," reprinted in *Arcady* (New York: Ferlag Unser Tsait, 1942), pp. 358–359.

Yiddish as an expedient to help ensure "effective . . . development of a sector of the all-Russian proletariat." Because the new organization was to be based on working-class political considerations, national issues were to be treated functionally rather than ideologically. As proletarians, Kremer argued, Jews must seek political liberty; as Jews they must seek political equality. Autonomy was essential, he said, but only as a function of the practical revolutionary needs. Significantly, the language of the meeting was Russian rather than Yiddish, and the delegates ignored the Jewish problem.[10]

The founding conference did little more than formalize an already existing organization. Important issues were ignored while delegates debated the name of the new organization. Mill had proposed that it be called the Jewish Social Democracy, but this was rejected because it ignored the trade unions, which the delegates hoped would be the base of its organization. The name finally adopted was the General Jewish Workers Bund of Poland and Russia (Lithuania was added later).[11]

THE FIRST YEARS

Despite the inclusion in its name of the word "Jewish," the Bund spent much of its first year organizing non-Jewish workers, particularly Poles and Lithuanians. The Bund did not consider itself an organization interested specifically in the welfare of the Jewish workers as Jews, but rather as a working-class party interested in the Jewish workers as part of the working class. "The Bund was confronted with one concrete conscious aim—the Socialist idea. Socialism is the new era of

---

[10] *Ibid.*, p. 365; H. Shukman, "The Relations Between the Jewish Bund and the Russian Social Democratic Workers Party, 1897–1903" (unpublished D. Phil. dissertation, Oxford University, 1961), pp. 23–26; Patkin, *op. cit.*, p. 113.
[11] Kremer, *loc. cit.*, pp. 358–361.

human history, and the Jewish masses must enter the new Socialist world. . . . Socialism is the only means of Jewish liberation. . . . The Bund aimed to be the midwife at the birth of Jewish socialism." [12]

Its orientation led the Bund's leadership to work for the organization of a Russian Socialist party to unify the separate local Socialist groups that then existed in the empire. The problem of forming a Russian Socialist party took up most of the time of the central committee during the first six months of its existence. During this period the committee made almost all of the technical arrangements for the Minsk meeting in March 1898, at which the Russian Social Democratic Workers Party (RSDRP) was organized. Although they worked in cooperation with the Kiev League of Struggle for Emancipation of the Working Class, the Bund leaders were the prime movers in the organization. The Bund also gave the first RSDRP congress its only working-class representative; the other eight were middle-class intellectuals. And once the Russian party was organized, the Bund published all of the RSDRP's written material—in the Bund's own illegal publishing house in Bobruisk.[13]

The relations between the Bund and the Polish Socialist Party (PPS), the most important Socialist party in the empire, were strained from the outset. The PPS, which was nationalist in its orientation, had many Jewish members by the time the Bund was organized, and they resented what they considered the Russophile leadership of the new Jewish organization. The animosity was mutual, and one of the first brochures printed by the newly organized Bund was an attack on the Polish party which was accused of waging war against the Bund. In a series of polemical pamphlets issued by each side in the dispute, accusations of betrayal of socialism were among the less vituperative charges. The PPS accused the Bund of

[12] *Ibid.*, p. 363; I. J. Trunk (Bund historian) quoted in Patkin, *op. cit.*, p. 11.
[13] Kremer, *loc. cit.*, p. 373; Keep, *op. cit.*, p. 54.

opposing an independent Poland while trying to cloak its opposition with revolutionary phraseology. The Bund reciprocated by ignoring the PPS when it sent out invitations to the founding congress of the Russian Social Democratic Workers Party.[14]

Young students fresh from the religious schools went into the Bund; this accelerated the organization's change of position with regard to the Jewish question. Most of these young people spoke Yiddish and had at best a limited knowledge of Russian. Moreover, the inherent disabilities of being a Jew in the Czarist empire were of galling importance to them because of the *numerus clausus*, which prevented them from obtaining a secular education. A series of pogroms, particularly in Kishinief and Gomel, raised serious doubts whether the Russian workers—who participated in great numbers in the slaughter of the Jews—could be counted on to defend the rights of the Jews. The Bund reacted by organizing a corps of self-defense and began seriously to study the need for a specific Jewish policy apart from socialism.[15]

Mill from the outset had urged the Bund to adopt a program on the "national problem," to take a stand in favor of national rights as well as civil rights. His suggestions were generally ignored, and it was not until the Bund's fourth congress, in 1901, that any action was taken on the national question. Four more years elapsed before the program took final form in a demand for cultural autonomy. At its congress in 1901 the Bund called upon Russia to become a democratic multinational federal republic, and to repudiate anti-Jewish laws and the persecution of Jews. The Bund proposed further that the Jews be recognized as a nation with all of the inherent rights of membership in such a federation. Opposition within the Bund to the national program was sharp,

---

[14] Kremer, *loc. cit.*, p. 364; *Di Milkhome fun P.P.S. Kegn Bund* (Algemajner Idisher Arbeiter Bund, 1898); *A Clorer Entfer* (London: Polish Socialist Party, 1904), p. 2.

[15] Patkin, *op. cit.*, pp. 143–145; Aronson, *op. cit.*, p. 18.

half of the members objecting that the demand for national recognition was premature and that it might fan a national consciousness, "which can only dim the class consciousness of the proletariat and lead to chauvinism." [16]

THE SPLIT IN THE SOCIAL DEMOCRACY

The Czar's chief of secret police, S. V. Zubatov, recognized the revolutionary qualities of the Bund's leadership. The leaders of Jewish organization, he wrote, were especially distinguished for their "versatile experience and perfected underground techniques." His assessment was based on more than mere fancy; the Bund was publishing at least ten illegal newspapers and distributing them throughout the Jewish Pale.

Zubatov believed that the only way to destroy the Bund was to set up a competing organization, which would call for economic improvement but would refrain from political agitation. The spokesmen of Zubatov's Independent Jewish Workers Party asserted that it could win economic improvement for the Jewish workers, with the support of the regime, if they remained loyal subjects of the Czar and refused to become involved in political agitation. The new party failed to dent the Bund's hold on the Jewish working people within the Pale; most were openly hostile to the so-called Zubatov-chikes. Demonstrations by the Independent Party faced well-organized counterdemonstrations by the Bund, and many of its meetings were so thoroughly disrupted that they had to be adjourned almost as soon as they were called. The Zubatov movement soon collapsed; its life had been short, colorful, and insignificant.[17]

The interest of the police in the Bund became more intense as its activities, its audacity, and its membership increased. The

[16] *Ibid.*, pp. 18–19; Shukman, *op. cit.*, pp. 66–68, 70–73.

[17] Shukman, op. cit., pp. 62–63; *Di Geshikhte fun Idisher Arbeiter Bavegung in Rusland un Poyln* (Geneva: Algemajner Idisher Arbeiter Bund fun Rusland un Poyln, 1900), back page (no pagination); Keep, *op. cit.*, p. 104.

secret police followed the activities of the Bund in Russia and abroad with great energy, but apparently with little success. In Berditchev they searched for the Bund and discovered little, except for learning that there were separate Jewish and Russian Socialist organizations. In Vilno the secret police arrested a Ph.D. candidate named Gurevitch, and found in his possession a list of Bundists and their street addresses, but not the cities where they lived. In Odessa, according to a secret police report, a May Day manifesto was distributed in a synagogue by being dropped from the balcony at all three rites. Distribution of the leaflet, which was signed by the Bund, disturbed the services, but the worshipers were not particularly annoyed; on the contrary, they showed a marked sympathy for the Bundists and said that the act only proved their bravery.[18]

But the Bund had enemies in both the Jewish community and the Russian Social Democratic Party. Within the Jewish group the most persistent animosity developed between the Bund and the Zionists; it was a hatred which would last until the final demise of East European Jewry in 1943. As early as 1899, two years after its formation, the Bund published a pamphlet attacking Zionism. The author was a non-Bundist philosopher, Chaim Zhitlowski, who was at the time a member of the Social Revolutionary Party, a non-Marxist organization with a peasant-based ideology. A fist fight between Zionists and Bundists was reported by the Okhrana (secret police) in 1902, when the Bund not only printed an anti-Zionist manifesto, but trapped a Zionist leader into reading it. The only casualties were two policemen who were supposed to be protecting the synagogue where the scuffle occurred.[19]

The struggle with the non-Jewish leadership of the RSDRP

---

[18] Secret Police Files, Elias Tcherikower Archives, YIVO-Institute for Jewish Research: Special Department Police Reports #5435, August 27, 1902; #3580, April 15, 1903; and #298, March 18, 1903.

[19] Patkin, *op. cit.*, p. 153; Secret Police Files, Report #298, March 18, 1903; Chaim Zhitlowski, *Tsionism Oder Sotsialism* (Geneva: Idisher Arbeiter, 1899), no pagination.

was a direct result of the Bund's decision in 1901 to take a stand on the national question. Under the 1898 statutes of the RSDRP, the Bund had autonomy with regard to issues of a specifically Jewish nature. The Bund had its own central committee and dealt directly with Jewish labor groups throughout the Pale. Also, many Jews who went into the RSDRP directly were weaned away from the Russian group and became active Bundists. The leadership of the RSDRP became hostile toward the Jewish group and attacked it with venom in the Socialist journals, particularly *Iskra*. Plekhanov was an enemy of the Bund, and personally hated its representative in Geneva, T. Kopelsohn. Martov, the man who had originated the idea that gave birth to the organization, developed a violent antipathy toward the Jewish Socialists, and Lenin wrote vituperative attacks upon the Bund.

At the 1903 congress of the RSDRP held in Brussels and London, the Bund demanded to be regarded as the sole representative of the Jewish proletariat in all parts of Russia. This was an extension of the decision taken at its 1901 congress in favor of federalism. One of the Bund delegates at the RSDRP congress asked for the Russian party's support of the position that each citizen had the right to use his own language. The motion was opposed by Lenin and the entire *Iskra* group, and it was defeated in a tie vote of 23 to 23. The decision was based mainly on antipathy to the Bund rather than on opposition to the proposal.[20] The failure of the Bund to have its motion approved was in part attributable to the weighting of seats against it by the arrangers of the congress; any Russian Socialist group, however small it might be, had the right to send a delegate; the Bund, with tens of thousands of members, and many times larger than all the Russian groups combined, was allowed only five.[21]

[20] A similar motion by M. Zhordania, leader of the Transcaucasian Social Democrats, was passed. The Transcaucasian group was smaller and thus less of a threat to Lenin in the struggle for control of the party.

[21] Vladimir Kossofsky, "Farvos un Vi Azoy der Bund Hot Zikh

In addition, the Bund proposed the reorganization of the RSDRP into a federated party with the Bund as a constituent part. This demand had been formulated at the Bund congress that same year. The proposal was merely an extension of the 1901 demand for a federal republic in Russia. Mensheviks and Bolsheviks, who were then engaged in an internecine war of their own, united on this issue and defeated the proposal. Plekhanov, Martov, and Lenin labeled the Bund proposal "opportunist, nationalist, separatist." The Bund refused to remain within the RSDRP, and withdrew from the congress to become a completely independent body—a withdrawal that allowed Lenin to control the majority of delegates when the RSDRP itself split in two a few days later. The Bundists' position was almost identical with the Mensheviks' except on the issue of federalism.[22]

Despite the Bund's withdrawal from the RSDRP, the delegates had its help in evading the police on their way back to Russia, thanks to a network of its agents along the western border of the Russian empire, who were well trained in smuggling pamphlets and other material across the line.

The withdrawal of the Bund from the Russian party led to serious discord within the Jewish party, and some smaller units who opposed the federal idea actually dissociated themselves. But the loss was slight, and the splinter groups soon disappeared.[23]

THE 1905 REVOLUTION

The years immediately preceding the 1905 revolution were crowded with situations that tended toward crises, leading the radical parties into schisms and into romantic, and abortive,

---

Tseshpoltn," *Zukunft*, XXIV (1921), 38–39; Shukman, *op. cit.*, pp. 54–55, 163–190; Keep, *op. cit.*, pp. 110, 122; Secret Police Files, Report #315, March 12, 1903.

[22] Keep, *loc. cit.*, p. 110, 118; Kossofsky, *loc. cit.*, pp. 38–39; Aronson, *op. cit.*, p. 19.

[23] Keep, *op. cit.*, pp. 117–118; Kossofsky, *loc. cit.*, pp. 38–39.

attempts at terrorism. Although the Bund had looked askance at such activities, after the repressions by the Czarist regime had led to conditions which made it appear that no alternative existed, groups within the Socialist organizations began giving consideration to the use of terror. These groups called for "organized revenge" against the representatives of the Czar, whom they blamed for the anti-Semitic excesses and the repressions perpetrated by the regime. By 1902 fourteen sections of the Bund had formally approved the use of terror in the war against the Czar, although a vast majority of the Bund rejected it.[24]

The outbreak of war with Japan in 1904 greatly aggravated the situation. The radical elements opposed the war; and their opposition gained considerable support when with military defeat the corruption and inefficiency of the Czarist government became apparent. The government, being inefficient, responded by suppressing the revolutionary movements with even greater vigor than before; more than 4,500 Bundists were arrested during the war period, and many were exiled to distant areas of Siberia.[25]

The discontent caused by the inept handling of the Russo-Japanese War flared into open rebellion in 1905, when the economy collapsed under the strain of war. The Socialist groups were leaders in the revolt and the unaffiliated Bund played a vital role. The Bund was particularly important in the Polish provinces: it organized the March anti-Czar demonstrations in Warsaw, the strike and open rebellion in Łodz, and the uprising in Białystok. The general uprising in October was under the leadership of the Social Revolutionaries, the Social Democrats (mainly the Menshevik wing) and the Bund.[26]

---

[24] *Ibid.*, p. 39; Keep, *loc. cit.*, p. 79.
[25] Aronson, *op. cit.*, p. 18.
[26] For a full description of the Bund's role in the 1905 disorders see *Der Bund in Der Revolutsie fun 1905–1906* (Warsaw: Ferlag Di Velt, 1930).

The uprising forced the Czar to issue the October 17 manifesto, which pledged a constitutional government. But to many Czarist officials the manifesto was little more than a scrap of paper. They blamed the Jews for the uprising, and instigated pogroms throughout the Pale. The Bundists answered these new and bloody onslaughts with armed resistance by newly organized self-defense units. The Bund, repeating the tactic of 1903, publicized the atrocities abroad in open appeals to the non-Jewish intelligentsia and in messages to its members and followers outside Russia.[27]

There was, however, an easing of the political repression in the period after the uprising, when the first legal Bund publications began to appear, among them a daily in Vilno. Open elections were held for a quasi-parliament, the Duma. The Bund, however, boycotted the first election.[28]

AFTER 1905

The Bund was out of the RSDRP for only four years, 1903–1907, since the ties were too close for the two groups to remain long apart. By the time of the reconciliation, the membership of the Bund had increased to more than 25,000, and fifty-five delegates represented it at the 1907 Social Democratic congress. Significantly, there was considerable internal opposition to the return by a "hard" faction whose strength matched that of the "soft" faction who wanted to re-unite. Moreover, though the Bund finally united with the Mensheviks there was also considerable sentiment in favor of the Bolshevik faction, though no organizational link with it existed. The Jewish Socialists generally did not expect an early revolution and preferred to unite with the less rigid of the Russian factions. That the Bund did not split on this issue is one of the small miracles of Socialist politics and can be attri-

[27] *Ibid.* For earlier appeals and their effect, see Secret Police Files, Tcherikover Archives of YIVO, dated April 30, 1903.
[28] Aronson, *op. cit.*, pp. 14, 19–20.

buted primarily to loyalty to the idea of the Bund, which was based more on a history of struggle than upon any ideology.[29]

During the next seven years the Bund declined. Printing establishments had to be abandoned, literary work had to be curtailed sharply, and most of the organization's time and effort had to be spent in raising funds for strikes which had broken out throughout the Pale. Union activity was damaging the Bund seriously and was forcing it to lessen its political activity in favor of economic pressure. Between 1909 and 1910 the Bund led strikes in ten cities. These strikes consumed almost all of its time, and had results that were disastrous for the organization. They accomplished so little that by 1910 legal union organizations, limited to printers and other highly skilled trades, were found in only four cities—Białystok, Łodz, Riga, and Vilno—and those were weak. There were also a few illegal unions in a very few trades and industries. The total membership of the Bund unions was estimated by the organization itself at only 1,500.

The eighth conference of the Bund in 1910 demonstrated the extent of the decline. Delegates were limited to nine functioning organizations, representing only 609 members, of whom 404 were active. Most of the Bund's strength was centered in the area that was later to become part of Poland, while only two cities in Byelorussia, one in Lithuania, and one in Latvia were represented.[30]

Propaganda activities were limited mainly to study groups, which read Socialist books, discussed "simple" themes such as the class struggle, or held classes in Marxism.

The Bund's membership was not as yet reconciled to the nationalist wing of the PPS. There were doubts that an independent Poland would mean improvement for the con-

[29] John Mill, "Lenin un der Bund," *Naye Velt*, IX, February 20, 1920, p. 22; Aronson, *loc. cit.*, p. 20.

[30] *Barikht fun Der VIII Konferents fun Bund* (Geneva; Algemajner Idisher Arbeiter Bund fun Poyln, Litte, un Russland, 1910), pp. 7–8, 26. Bund organizations existed in Bobruisk, Białystok, Grodno, Dvinsk, Warsaw, Vilno, Łodz, Pinsk, and Riga. Five of these cities—with 463 members—were in the Polish sector of the Czarist empire.

ditions of the Jews in Poland; later events were to justify these doubts. "The Polish bourgeoisie . . . if it gets power, plans to oppress the other minorities," the Bund leadership insisted. The answer to the national problem was not to be found in a free Poland, or in a Jewish state; it was to be found in recognition of the national autonomy for the minorities within Russia.

"We are strongly opposed on principle to all territorial Utopias," the conference declared. The answer to the Jewish problem could be found, the Bundists said, in the recognition of Yiddish as an official language in Russia and in guarantees of full rights and cultural autonomy for all minorities. "The only guarantee that each citizen will receive an education is that his mother tongue will be officially accepted and that he will have national cultural autonomy." But even before cultural autonomy could be granted, the Bund wanted national schools in the mother tongue made available to each of the minorities, and most particularly to the Jews. And it wanted the Yiddish language to be recognized regardless of geographic location; wherever there were Jews, Yiddish was to be an official and legal language.[31]

By 1912 the Bund had in effect become an autonomous section of the Menshevik-led RSDRP organization, which by this time had accepted the idea of a federated organization.[32]

The war that was then approaching, the German occupation of Poland, the emergence of an independent Polish republic, and the Russian Revolution, were all to play a significant role in the development of the Bund into a Polish Jewish Socialist Party.[33]

[31] *Ibid.*, pp. 5, 67–69.
[32] Aronson, *op. cit.*, p. 20.
[33] A full study of the Bund will be found in *Di Geshikhte fun Bund* (New York: Ferlag Unser Tsait, 1963), and in Shukman, *op. cit.*, which is particularly strong on the early period. Patkin, *op. cit.*, and Keep, *op. cit.*, are also important studies. For the purposes of this study, which treats the interwar period of the Bund in Poland, the brief overview in this chapter will suffice to give the background.

II

The Bund During the German Occupation, 1915-1918

WORLD WAR I proved the emptiness of the Socialist slogan of international proletarian unity when it was in conflict with patriotism; it brought to power in Russia a monolithic sect, the Bolsheviks; it caused the Socialist parties throughout the world to divide into two hostile camps; it created new nations in which new political movements had to be built or old ones had to reorient their ideals and activities in the light of changed conditions.

The war and two great events it provoked—the Russian Revolution and the independence of Poland—turned the Bund, from the Jewish Socialist party of the Russian empire, into a Jewish Socialist party of the Polish republic, concerned with Polish problems as they affected the Jewish working-class population. The Bund's Russian section was absorbed by the revolution; its Lithuanian section vanished in the first blush of social upheaval; only the Polish section remained, and it became a totally new party.

END OF RUSSIAN RULE

It was apparent that the Jewish Pale would be a battlefield in any war between Russia and the Central Powers. The Jewish settlement was on the western frontier of the Czarist empire, directly in the path of a German-Austrian attack or Russian military movement. There could be no doubt that

the Jewish population in the westernmost portion of the Pale—
Poland—would be separated from the hinterlands in Byelorussia, the Ukraine, and probably Lithuania.

Faced with the prospect that its Polish organization would
be isolated from the center of leadership in St. Petersburg,
the Central Committee of the Bund appointed a separate
committee to direct activities in Poland. The organization of
the Committee of Bund Organizations in Poland, with headquarters in Warsaw, in November 1914, marks the beginning
of the Bund in Poland as a separate organization.

The committee was composed of four of the leaders of the
old Bund: Noah Portnoy, Victor Shulman, Lazar Epstein,
and Z. Muskat. As it happened, the leading intellectual of the
Bund, Vladimir Medem, was in a Czarist prison in Warsaw; he
was freed after the Russian withdrawal and was appointed to
the committee. Also added to the committee in 1915 was
David Meyer, leader of the Bund trade unions in Warsaw.[1]

There were now five separate Socialist organizations in
Poland. Three of these were Polish: The PPS Frakcja (Revolutionary Faction), the PPS Lewica, and the Social Democracy of the Kingdom of Poland and Lithuania, (SDKPiL).
The others were Jewish: the Bund and the Poale Zion (Socialist Zionists).[2]

The PPS, the largest of the parties, was more nationalist

---

[1] Victor Shulman, "Yorn fun der Ershter Velt Milkhome un
Daytsher Okupstsye," in A. Menes, Raphael Mahler, Jacob Shutsky,
and Victor Shulman, *Di Idn in Poyln* (New York: Committee for
Publication of "The Jews in Poland," 1946), p. 772 (Shulman was a
member of the Bund committee); A. Millman (a delegate), "Barikht
fun der Lubliner Konferents" (1917), Yiddish typescript in Bund
Archives; Emanuel Novogrodsky, "Der Bund in Umophengign
Poyln Tsvishn Bayde Velt Milkhomes," *Unser Tsait*, XVII (Novem-
ber–December 1957), 23; Emanuel Novogrodsky, "Ha Bund Bain
Shatai Milkhome Ha Ellem," *Entsiklopedea Shel Galut*, II (Tel Aviv:
Encyclopaedia of Jewish Life in the Diaspora, 1959), 71–72.

[2] For the sake of brevity, and to avoid confusion, the PPS Frakcja
will be called hereafter the PPS, the PPS Lewica will be called
Lewica, and the Social Democracy will be called SDKPiL.

than Socialist. It had split with the Lewica in 1906 on the issue of Polish independence; its former leader, Josef Pilsudski, had formed a Polish detachment to fight with the Austrian army against Russia, whom he considered Poland's worst enemy. The Lewica had opposed independence but offered no alternative; in ideology it was close to the Martov-Dan group of Russian Mensheviks. The SDKPiL opposed independence because, it argued, the Polish economy could not be divorced from the Russian. It favored autonomy within a federated, democratic Russian state. The SDKPiL was close to the Bolsheviks, although its leader, Rosa Luxemburg, had disagreed violently with Lenin over organizational and ideological issues. The Bund was divided on the issue of Polish independence; its leaders generally favored autonomy as a minimum.[3]

The Bund and the PPS had been hostile to each other for many years; the Bund considered the PPS to be a chauvinistic group more interested in Polish nationalism than in socialism. The Bund's leaders had long maintained that the PPS was Socialist in name only, that it was "leading the workers into the trap of bourgeois nationalist politics." [4]

The Bund had long acknowledged that it would remain a helpless minority unless it could form an alliance with one of the national parties. In Imperial Russia it had, therefore, been a constituent part of the Russian Social Democratic Workers Party. Under the new conditions it sought alliance with the Polish Socialists. It could not form such an alliance with the PPS because of the latter's nationalistic position. The Bund thus turned to the Lewica and SDKPiL, with whom it formed an all-inclusive Rahde (action committee) in Warsaw. The Rahde's activities were limited to opposition to the war; its formation did not indicate a trend toward merger or permanent alliance.

[3] P. Minc [Alexander], *Di Geshikhte fun a Falshe Iluzie* (Buenos Aires: Union Central Israelita, 1954), pp. 15–17.
[4] *Tsvai Konferentsn* (Warsaw: Algemajner Idisher Arbeiter Bund, 1918), pp. 12–13.

The three parties in the Rahde were united in their opposition to the war. Unlike the PPS, they rejected the thesis that Poland, by supporting Austria, could take advantage of the war to achieve its independence. The war, they maintained, was a product of capitalism and should be opposed as a matter of Socialist principle. Even before the war began, the Rahde called in vain for a general strike against the mobilization. "Down with the war! Down with Czarism!" the Rahde proclaimed. "Long live the forthcoming democratic republic! Long live the revolution!" [5]

No sooner had the Czar declared war on the Central Powers than the alliance issued a call for a Socialist revolution —a call that went unheeded.

> The proletariat declares war against his government and his oppressors! The birth of the workers' revolution draws nigh! The revolutionary march of the working class is already heard throughout the land as it assaults the fortress of the present capitalist order.
>
> The proletariat must remain an independent force against capitalism and the government.[6]

Although the Bund joined in the call for a revolution against the war and the regime, it was not ready to support the Leninist thesis of turning the "imperialist war into a civil war." Its position was closer to that of the internationalist Mensheviks, who took a near-pacifist stand, urging an end to the war and to the death and starvation that were its inevitable concomitants. The Bundists blamed the war on the capitalist method of production; on the imperialist designs of the bourgeois rulers; on the colonial policies of the governments on

---

[5] Shulman, *op. cit.*, p. 772; *Oyfruf Vegn Der Mobilizatsie* (Warsaw: National Committee of the SDKPiL, Central Workers Committee of the PPS Lewica, and Central Committee of the Bund, July 1914); original of proclamation in the Bund Archives, *Historishe Zamlbukh* [Historical Scrapbook].

[6] *Nider mit der Milkhome! Zol Lebn der Sotsialism,* (Warsaw: National Committee of the SDKPiL, Central Workers Committee of the PPS *Lewica,* and Central Committee of the Bund, August 1914); original in Bund Archives, *Historishe Zamlbukh.*

both sides; on aggressive external politics, furthered by secret negotiations and diplomatic intrigues; on the huge armies and navies, and "the powerlessness of the broad working masses regarding the external policies of their governments." The answer, said the Bund, lay in a "workers' peace without annexations, without reparations." Repairs to areas hard hit by the fighting should be paid for by the warring nations; there should be immediate reduction in arms, and an end to secret diplomacy; colonies too backward to rule themselves should be internationalized, and trade with these colonies should be open to all on an equal basis.

The patriotism displayed at the outbreak of war by many leading Socialist parties, particularly the German and French, required a new set of principles for the Socialist world. The Bundists opposed coalitions with non-Socialists, particularly those with "antidemocratic forces." To make certain that Socialists worked for democracy and did not participate in "bourgeois coalitions," the Vilno Bund organization proposed that the Second International maintain a close watch on the political activities of its constituent parties.[7]

THE GERMAN OCCUPATION

The corruption-infested Russian army was forced to withdraw from Poland in mid-1915. In August the city of Warsaw was abandoned and anarchy threatened; there was no effective police force in the city or its environs. To avoid total lawlessness and collapse, the Rahde helped form a citizens' militia which took over police duties until the Germans arrived. It was a short-lived experience, and the Rahde itself soon disintegrated under the pressure of events and ideological disagreements.[8]

[7] "Memorandum der Wilner Judischen Sozialdemokratischen Organisation Bund" [to the 1917 International Socialist Conference in Stockholm]; original in Bund Archives.
[8] Shulman, *op. cit.*, p. 772.

The Germans, who had long experience with a powerful Social Democratic Party and trade union movement, allowed the Polish Socialists considerable freedom. Anti-Semitism was not state policy in Germany, and Czarist restrictions against the Jews were likewise eased. Cultural and political clubs were formed by Socialist and Jewish groups almost immediately after the Germans arrived. The Bund greeted this new freedom of action with a major organization drive, which resulted in the formation of more than twenty legal pro-Bund trade unions, as well as children's homes and schools, kitchens, tea rooms, consumer cooperatives, and bakeries. Most important, from the Bund's point of view, was the permission of the Germans to resume publication of *Lebns-fragn*, the party's official organ, which had been banned by the Czarist regime after the appearance of one issue in 1912.[9]

The editor of *Lebnsfragn*, Vladimir Medem, showed his gratitude by publishing an editorial that went counter to the official Bund position; he excused the German Social Democrats' support of the war and defended their parliamentary action in favor of war credits. The German party had to support the war, Medem wrote; it was, after all, a party with 4,000,000 votes. To have taken another stand would have meant, for a party of that size, support of the enemy—which in turn meant support for the Czar. "Only a small party can be neutral . . . " Failure by a major party to take sides, he wrote, would have serious consequences, "and these are often tragic." [10] There was a growing comradeship with the German party, which the occupying forces appeared to be encourag-

[9] Aaron Holtz, "Der Grosser Klub in Varshe un di Kommunistishe Bavegung in Amerika" (letter), *Jewish Daily Forward* (New York), February 18, 1954; David Meyer (secretary of the conference), "Barikht fun der Lubliner Konferents," (1917), Yiddish typescript in Bund Archives; *Lebnsfragn*, I, February 4, 1916.

[10] *Lebnsfragn*, I, February 4, 1916. There are other possible explanations for the editorial. German censors may have extracted the editorial as a price for permitting the Bund organ to resume publication. The pro-German sentiment in many other Socialist parties, particularly in the United States, from whom the Bund received

ing; leaders of the German party visited Poland, and the Bund, and were well received.[11]

This editorial was the only instance in which the Bund's antiwar position might be questioned. No other article of such a nature appeared in *Lebnsfragn*, or in any other Bund publication issued during the occupation.

All of the Socialist parties in Poland—except the PPS—took advantage of the easing of controls to propagandize for peace and against the inequitable distribution of gifts from abroad. The municipal elections were used as propaganda forums for socialism and peace; Socialists elected to city councils turned the office into a platform for spreading their views.[12]

There was little else they could do. Poland's economy was paralyzed; strikes were out of the question.

ECONOMIC PARALYSIS

The Polish economy was in a state of total collapse; manufacturing was at a standstill; inflation was rampant. The most important cause of the economic catastrophe was the German policy of denuding Poland of industrial plants by destroying them or removing them to the Reich. Germany wanted Poland to become farmland, to supply the food for the empire. It also hoped for a reservoir of manpower for its industries. To achieve this end, 600,000 men and women were deported to work in German industry.[13]

Mass unemployment offered the Germans a handy low-

---

financial assistance, cannot be ignored. It is also likely that the anti-Czarist feeling among the Bundists was translated into a pro-German sentiment, although aside from Medem's editorial there is no evidence for this hypothesis.

[11] *Lebnsfragn*, I, July 13, 1916.

[12] Minc, *op. cit.*, p. 16.

[13] Z. *dokumentow chwili*, (Warsaw, 1917–1918), p. 64, cited in Dziewanowski, *op. cit.*, pp. 62–63.

cost labor force. Those men not deported to Germany faced forced labor in remote areas, particularly near the Baltic where they "were treated like prisoners" while they worked at menial tasks under indescribably poor conditions. Men who volunteered to work for the occupying army near their homes were forced to go to Warsaw and were then transferred to Latvia or other faroff places. In these areas they helped build military railroads for the German army. Guards beat the men with whips and sticks; the barracks were cold and vermin-infested; food was meager and poor in quality. Within six months almost 10,000 forced laborers died of hunger and disease. The Bund appealed to the Socialist International to intervene, but no appeals or protests availed. Forced labor continued until the end of the war.[14]

All of Poland was starving, and the Jewish population was no exception.[15] Philanthropy primarily from America, supplied the food needed to keep the Polish-Jewish population alive. Much of this supply was distributed by non-Socialist groups, and the rest by the Bund. During the first three months of 1917, for example, the Bund distributed food valued at more than 90,000 rubles in the form of several hundred thousand meals plus tens of thousands of food packages. In this capacity the Bund was more than a political organization; it was in effect an organ of the community, serving a need that would otherwise have been ignored.[16]

The question of Polish independence became crucial in late

[14] Holtz, *loc. cit.*; "Memorandum der Wilner . . . Bund" [1917], p. 4.

[15] Anti-Semitic spokesmen were to charge some twenty years later that "Jews pocketed the greatest benefits during the war." See Jan Drohojowski, *Brief Outline of the Jewish Problem in Poland* (Brooklyn: Polish National Alliance, 1938), p. 16. The accusation was patently false. An examination of philanthropies by American Jewish organizations to Polish Jewry during the war period, and of unbiased reports on the conditions of the Jewish population, show conclusively that the Jews suffered equally with non-Jews during the period.

[16] Appeals for contributions to the relief fund appeared almost daily in the *Jewish Daily Forward* during the years 1916–1918. A random

THE QUESTION OF INDEPENDENCE

1916, when the Central Powers proposed the establishment of a subservient Polish state. The Bund opposed the establishment of a synthetic Poland whose prime function would be to further the military aims of an occupying power.

> The class-conscious Jewish proletariat has opposed and fought strongly against the so-called nationalistic politics of certain sections of the Polish . . . and Jewish bourgeoisie, seeing in it an attempt to weaken the class interests of the broad masses [in order] to use [the workers] for their own class interests.
> . . . We reject every attempt to settle the fate of a nation without the approval, or against the will of the people.[17]

But the Bund was at least sympathetic to genuine Polish independence. At the plenum of the St. Petersburg Soviet in June 1917, its representative, Henryk Erlich, who was later to become a leader of the Polish Bund, proposed the resolution calling for Polish independence. The Bund insisted, however, that the fate of Poland be decided in "free, open, and proportional elections" and not by an occupying power.[18]

The Bund supported Polish independence only on condition that assurances would first be given that the rights of all national minorities would be protected. There were at least four large ethnic or national minorities within the boundaries

examination of the *Forward* during that period will disclose the extent of the drive. The Bund's activity is detailed in *Barikht fun der Virtshafts Komitet fun Idishe Arbeiter in Varshe* (Warsaw, Algemajner Idishe Arbeiter Bund, 1917); mimeographed copy in Bund Archives.

[17] *Tsvai Konferentzen,* pp. 12–13.

[18] *Ibid.; Henryk Erlich un Victor Alter, Gedank Bukh* (Buenos Aires: Agrupacion Socialista Israelita "Bund," 1943), p. 11. Drohojowski, *op. cit.,* maintains that the Jews took "a passive or indifferent attitude" with regard to Polish independence. That this, like many of Drohojowski's charges, is baseless can be ascertained by the position of the Bund noted above, and the fact that there were many Jews in the PPS.

of occupied Poland—Ukrainians, Jews, Byelorussians, and Germans. Forty per cent of Galicia's inhabitants, for example, were Ukrainians. The Bund insisted that the minorities were entitled to equality and cultural autonomy in the event they were incorporated into any new Polish state.[19]

Unresolved differences on this issue prevented the Bund and the PPS from uniting on other minor issues. Polish independence was the keystone of the PPS platform, and the party was unwilling to grant any conditions. The Bund, on the contrary, was unwilling to fight for Polish independence without what it considered adequate protection for the minorities.[20]

ANTI-SEMITISM

Polish anti-Semitism was economic in origin, a result of the country's class structure. Since medieval times the Jews had been the commercial class of Poland (although most of them had been living at a subsistence level since the eighteenth century). They held this position because the Polish gentry refused to become involved in trade, and because the peasants could not do so since they were needed to tend the fields for the nobility. "While despising them, both the king and the nobles supported the Jews since they constituted an important source of revenue and performed necessary commercial tasks beneath the dignity and beyond the capacity of the gentry. The Jew served as an intermediary between the nobles and the gentry . . ."[21]

The Germans were the only other ethnic group in the Polish commercial class, and they resented the Jews as com-

[19] "Memorandum der Wilner . . . Bund" [1917]; *Lebnsfragn*, I, December 8, 1916.
[20] *Lebnsfragn*, I, May 5, 1916. The extent of this estrangement can be seen in the refusal of the Bund to join the PPS in a Lublin rally for Polish independence on May 3, 1916, because the PPS would not endorse the Bund's position on cultural autonomy.
[21] Buell, *op. cit.*, pp. 290–291.

petitors. Local anti-Semitic incidents were often traced to them.

Polish interest in trade began in the middle of the last century and with this came the first hints of anti-Semitism. In 1870 Jan Jelenski published a pamphlet, *Zydzi, Niemcy i My* ("Jews, Germans and Ourselves"), which called for "nationalization of commerce and industry" in order to "abolish the Jewish commercial monopoly created through the centuries." [22]

The first political movement hostile to the Jews came into existence in 1897, when the National Democratic Party (Endek) was formed. Its original doctrine, although anti-Semitic, welcomed as national brothers those Jews who considered themselves to be Poles. The Endek was not considered a significant factor in Polish anti-Semitism until 1912, in which year most of Warsaw's Jews supported a Socialist candidate to the Czarist Duma and helped defeat his National Democratic opponent. The Endek retaliated by declaring a boycott of Jewish shops, and terrorized Poles who defied the boycott. Although the boycott was a failure, it was the first actively anti-Jewish action undertaken by a political movement. [23]

Roman Dmowski, leader of the Endek, believed that Poland's salvation could be achieved only through closer cooperation with the Czar. He supported the Russians during the war, in contrast to Pilsudski's support of Austria. During the war Dmowski accused the Jews of being pro-German, as in fact they were—not illogically, in view of the anti-Semitic character of the Czarist regime. [24]

David Lloyd George has commented that "in Russia when failure was due to an incompetent and corrupt system the blame was attributed to other causes. The Jews always came in handy on occasions when corrupt or incompetent gentiles

[22] Quoted, *ibid.*, pp. 292–293.

[23] *Ibid.*, p. 294; Dr. Max Golfarb, "Di Poylishe-Idishe Betsiyungen un der Bund," *Zukunft*, XIX (1914), 306.

[24] Bernard Pares, *The Fall of the Russian Monarchy* (New York: Alfred A. Knopf, 1939), p. 180; Buell, *loc. cit.*, p. 294.

made a mess of national affairs." [25] Fraudulent charges of Jewish espionage and sabotage against the Czarist regime were frequent during the early days of the war. Many Jews feared these charges would lead to the instigation of pogroms by Czarist officials who wanted to escape blame for the military catastrophe, or by Endeks who wanted to make political capital out of the situation.

The Bund acted to forestall the pogroms. Its newly formed Polish Committee issued a handbill answering the charges and warning of possible consequences. The missive was distributed in factories throughout Russian Poland and to all foreign consulates in Warsaw.[26]

The German occupation did not end the anti-Semitic peril. The National Democrats simply shifted their allegiance from the Czar to the Kaiser, and accused the Jews of being anti-German instead of anti-Russian. Animosity between Germany and Austria over a Polish policy in 1918 gave the Endeks an opportunity to issue a proclamation blaming the Jews for Poland's plight:

> The coming Polish nation has many enemies; Austria doesn't want a strong Polish neighbor which can retake Galicia. Therefore the Austrian command used money to buy out influential people and create difficulties in the path of the now forming Polish army.
>
> In Germany a strong party wanted to make of Poland a mere province of the Reich. Only the German rulers look to the future and want a strong and true Polish ally. We must help them in this work.
>
> The worst enemies of the Polish nation are Jews who live in Poland. The Jews are enemies of all nations where they can't rook the public, take usurious interest on loans, or sell smuggled

[25] David Lloyd George, *War Memoirs of David Lloyd George,* 1914–1915 (Boston: Little, Brown and Co., 1933), p. 387.
[26] See, for example, Yanushkewitsh (Chief of General Staff) to Sukhomlinoff (Secretary of State for War), 27 April 1917, *ibid.*, p. 387: ". . . In some places they are already blowing up bridges and stores. This is all done for money; probably the Jews are doing it." Copy of handbill in Bund Archives; Shulman, *op. cit.*, pp. 772–773.

alcohol. They would want to create here what they have created in Russia—anarchy and revolution. They could then destroy bridges, as was done here in 1905. Under such conditions the Jew can get his price for potatoes and bread. . . . The *goy* can die of hunger so long as the Jew can get rich. It is in order to get rich that the Jew wants a revolution; in time of war it isn't hard to find an opportunity.[27]

The proclamation accused Pilsudski of being in fact a Jewish agent: were not two of his leading adherents Jews? It charged that the Jews' true aim was to set up a dictatorship of the proletariat by instigating student demonstrations and workers' strikes. These strikes would shut down all Polish-owned businesses—but, "an amazing thing, Jewish business [would not] be affected." A strike against the gas works would bring higher prices to Jewish coal and wood dealers. Thus the Jews, said the Endeks, gained from Polish misfortune.

The proclamation asserted that a small strike—the work of the Jews—had led to a skirmish with the German police: "A silly uprising, a few poorly armed Poles against 8,000,000 well-armed German soldiers," it chided the participants. And what did it achieve? It lasted only half an hour, angered the Germans, and resulted in the ouster of their Polish friends from positions of power. All this, said the proclamation, was the work of the Jews and their allies the Socialists. "Jews, Socialists, and other traitors must pay as Judas paid! Be careful, citizens, revolution is what the Jews want." [28]

Although anti-Semitism remained a problem, there were few overt acts against the Jews during the war years. The German occupiers at any rate did not instigate pogroms against the Jews. The economic dislocation affected Poles as well as Jews. Whatever political restrictions existed were imposed equally on all nationalities. Attempts to make the life

---

[27] "Proklamacja Antysemicka z Czasow Okupacji Niemieckiej, 1918," *Dziennik Poranny*, January 19, 1919.
[28] *Ibid.*

of the Jews more difficult were of Polish rather than German origin, and were less violent than such attempts had previously been. One that created a dilemma for the Bund leadership in Warsaw was the proposal by the Endek majority in the Warsaw City Council of a compulsory Sunday closing law. This would have meant a serious hardship for the city's Jewish population, which normally observed Saturday as the Sabbath. The Bund had ordinarily been opposed to the Orthodox community, and had been openly antagonistic to the Orthodox insistence on Saturday as the divinely ordained day of rest. To escape the onus of refusing to support the Jewish community on a major issue, and at the same time to remain true to its anti-religious Socialist principles, the Bund offered a substitute proposal that would have ordered each business in the city to close for one day a week, the day to be decided by the workers in the establishment. The Bund could thus support the Jewish community, reiterate its own position in favor of a reduced work week, and avoid directly supporting the Orthodox community.[29]

JEWISH SCHOOLS

The Bund did not limit its activities to politics, trade unionism, and philanthropy; during the war years it also assumed a cultural responsibility, which was, however, closely linked with its political principles. This was to promote the spread of Yiddish as a second language in independent Poland. To this end the Bund organized schools for children and cultural clubs for adult workers. The schools taught children their "mother tongue," Yiddish, and attempted to use the "most modern pedagogic methods." Finances for these schools came from American Jewish Socialists.[30]

The Bund had little choice but to organize schools for the teaching of Yiddish, since the only alternative was tacit sup-

[29] *Lebnsfragn*, I, November 3, 1916.
[30] *Ibid.*, March 3, 1916.

port for the religious schools (Kheders) which had heretofore dominated Polish-Jewish education. To the Bundists, these Kheders were anathema: they taught by rote, one Jewish Socialist educator charged, drumming into the heads of the children "religious nonsense that is of no interest to the child. . . . They fill his small brain with nonsense and rob him of his abilities. . . ." The same educator went on to describe conditions thus:

> And who doesn't know of the filthy, dark, and tiny crowded rooms where they learn?
> Teachers in the Kheders are people without learning, people who have failed at every other type of work, people who have become teachers only to keep from starving.
> Most of them are very old men. A third of them have not completed their education. They were formerly workers, merchants, sextons . . . anything but teachers.
> And they have a sturdy assistant for teaching these young children—ofttimes three or four years old—the cat-o'-nine-tails.[31]

SOCIALIST COALITION

A party that is a minority within a minority must realize that it can serve little purpose except as part of an alliance through which it can gain some modicum of power, or in which it can eventually hope to be part of the ruling power in the state. From its earliest days this rule of politics guided the Bund, which had always sought to be the representative of the Jewish population within the Socialist party of the state. Before the war it was thus, except for a short period, an integral part of the Russian Social Democratic Workers Party, and in Poland it had allied itself with either the Lewica or the SDKPiL, or with a combination of both.

The separation of Poland from Russia, and the semi-demo-

[31] *Ibid.*, May 12, 1916.

cratic rule during the German occupation, left the Bund with no alternative but to seek a coalition with one of the Socialist parties. In 1916 the Bund therefore appealed to all Socialist parties to form an electoral bloc for the first free election to the Warsaw city council. Only the Lewica agreed; the PPS was too much involved with Polish independence, and the SDKPiL was in the midst of factional strife.[32]

The Socialist election bloc—the alliance of the Bund and the Lewica—used the election to spread the political and national aims of the parties rather than to offer a program to meet the immediate needs of the municipality. The bloc was seen by the Bund as a first step in the direction of Socialist unity in Poland; it was considered the beginning of a mass Socialist movement. There was little chance of capturing control of the municipality. Local elections could not, under any conditions, bring about the millennium. They were minor skirmishes in the political struggle for democratic socialism.

There was only one concession to municipal issues. The Socialist bloc called for democratization of the city government, since it wanted the administration of the city to be in the hands of an elected council. Beyond that the platform was composed of slogans aimed at making the "broad masses more class-conscious." The Socialists used the campaign to fight the growing nationalism and anti-Semitism; and they agreed to include the Bund's requirement that Yiddish be recognized as the second language in official transactions.[33]

[32] *Ibid.*, April 28, 1916; June 23, 1916. The SDKPiL had been torn by internal strife since 1911. One of the two warring factions was led by the Warsaw Committee; the other was headed by a committee-in-exile in Berlin. The exile leadership included Rosa Luxmburg and Leo Jogiches; the Warsaw leadership included no such illustrious names. The Warsaw leaders accepted Lenin's elitist party theory, which the exiles rejected. Each side charged the other with dictatorial and dishonest tactics. The feud, which lasted for seven years, virtually paralyzed the SDKPiL except during rare periods. See M. K. Dziewanowski, *The Communist Party of Poland* (Cambridge, Mass.: Harvard University Press, 1959), pp. 50–53, 59–62.

[33] *Lebnsfragn*, I, June 16, 1916.

Attempts by the other Jewish parties to interest the Bund in an all-inclusive Jewish bloc were rebuffed. Since the Bund was after all a Socialist party, and a class-conscious one, it could not align itself with its "class enemies," Jewish or otherwise. The Jewish bloc had to be formed without the Bund; it had to be satisfied with the General Zionists, the Orthodox, and the so-called bourgeois parties. *Lebnsfragn* said that the bloc was organized to represent everybody and thus represented nobody; that in order to unite everybody it had to get along without a program.[34]

The other Jewish Socialist party, the Poale Zion, had no such scruples. It tacitly supported both blocs. Officially it announced that it endorsed the Socialist bloc, but the only Poale Zionist elected to the city council was a candidate of the Jewish bloc.[35]

The voting was based on the complicated electoral system of curias (districts), and was weighted against the Socialists.[36] In the Sixth Curia, a working-class district, the Socialist bloc polled only 10 per cent of the vote and elected only one of the city's ninety councilmen. It elected no councilmen in the other curias. The anti-Semitic bloc elected a majority.[37]

In other Polish cities also, the Bund formed election alliances with the Lewica. Some of these had limited success; in Łodz the local leader of the Bund, Israel Lichtenstein, was elected. Generally, however, the Socialists met with defeat.[38]

CONCLUSION

The war and the German occupation had forced the Bund organization within Poland to become a Polish Jewish Socialist party. The Bund in Poland had been forced by conditions to develop new tactics adapted to the new conditions.

---

[34] *Ibid.*, June 23, 1916.   [35] *Ibid.*, July 21, 1916.
[36] The curia system divided the city on economic and social lines, and strongly favored the upper classes.
[37] *Lebnsfragn*, I, July 21, 1916.   [38] *Ibid.*, January 26, 1917.

It was no longer, except in name, a part of the General Jewish Workers Bund of Poland, Lithuania, and Russia. The Polish Bund became increasingly independent of the rest of the Bund organizations; it could no longer depend on the Bund center in St. Petersburg for direction and guidance. The Polish Bund's interests, and those of Bundists in Russia, Lithuania, Latvia, the Ukraine, and Bessarabia, had become increasingly divergent. Although it was soon to break its formal ties with the Russian Bund, incidents in Russia were to affect it for years to come. Indeed, the Russian Revolution was to have on the Bund in Poland an effect far different from its effect on the Bund in other parts of the old Russian empire.

III

The Polish Bund and the Russian Revolution

THE Russian Revolution raised and shattered more hopes than perhaps any other historic event in recent times. Starting as a movement for the liberation of 150,000,000 people from autocratic rule, it degenerated into a dictatorship more rigid than the Czarism it overthrew. It was a revolution that destroyed the dreams of its makers and, eventually, the makers themselves.

The Polish Bund was a near participant in the revolution. Many of its leaders had been Russian-born; its parent organization had been an important element in the Russian Social Democratic movement, which was instrumental in organizing the revolutionary forces. Only the German occupation kept the Polish Bund from becoming directly involved in the revolution. Yet in the end the revolution was to devour the Bund's parent organization in Russia, and to threaten the existence of the Polish Bund itself. For almost five years the issues of the Russian revolution were to divide the Bund ideologically.

REJOICING IN MARCH

The news that the Czar had been overthrown was greeted with elation by the Polish Bundists. "It is not a dream!" *Lebnsfragn* proclaimed. "We greet our newly freed comrades and friends with supreme joy; and we wish them renewed strength and energy in the struggle for our great cause." [1]

[1] *Lebnsfragn*, II, March 23, 1917.

The enthusiasm of the Bund was matched by the rejoicing of the rest of the Jewish population of Russia. One Jewish leader exclaimed: "For the first time in two thousand years we shall celebrate our Passover, our feast of freedom, not as slaves but as free citizens." [2]

The Bund's hopes ran high. The Russian Bund resumed publication of the *Arbeiter Shtimme* after a twelve-year lapse. Between 1897 and 1905 this had been an illegal, underground revolutionary journal; now it was a legal newspaper. Celebrations were organized in small towns, villages, and cities of the Jewish sections of Russia. For the Bundists these celebrations had a double significance: they were marking both the revolution and the twentieth anniversary of the founding of their party.[3]

The democratic revolution meant an end to oppression, the Russian Bund wired its American friends. "The Russian workers move today in the world democracies as equal members. The time for freeing all the world's people draws nigh. The workers of the world must unite behind the new government to protect its newly won freedoms." [4]

The Russian Bund began the fight for its national program. It demanded the immediate granting of national cultural autonomy "in a revolutionary manner"; it demanded that all languages within the empire be given equal status, "in order that all people be given the right to express themselves on all laws, and in order that all people can communicate with the government." It also called for the immediate election—on the basis of full suffrage for all Jews—of a national Jewish congress from all parts of Russia.[5]

There were two centers of power in the new Russia: the

---

[2] *The Times* (London), April 11, 1917.

[3] *Fraje Vort* (Wilno), March 12, 1921; *Lebnsfragn*, II, May 11, 1917.

[4] Cablegram from Der Tsentraler Komitet fun Bund in Rusland to Di Amerikaner Khaverim, May 23, 1917, via the *Jewish Daily Forward;* copy in Bund Archives.

[5] *Lebnsfragn*, II, June 1, 1917; May 11, 1917.

government, and the soviets of workers' and soldiers' deputies. The soviets arose spontaneously almost immediately after the revolution. Their leadership was in the hands of the radical parties: both factions of the Social Democrats, the Social Revolutionaries, the Popular Socialists, and the Trudoviks. Alexander Kerensky, who headed the least radical of the Socialist parties—the Trudoviks—was the accepted leader of the soviets, and the most popular figure with the masses during the early days of the revolution. The government tended to be more conservative than the soviets, particularly during the first four months while Prince George Lvov was premier. Lvov represented the liberal bourgeois Constitutional Democratic (Kadet) party.[6]

The Russian Bund was the only Jewish party within the soviets. It used this position to propagate its aim: the organizing of all workers, regardless of race, nationality, or religion, in the furthering of the avowed aims of the revolution—democracy and peace.

One of the leaders of the Petrograd Soviet was Henryk Erlich, Polish-born leader of the Bund. He was chosen in June as emissary of the Soviet to an international Socialist conference in Stockholm.[7]

The splintering within the Russian Social Democratic movement increased after the Czar's demise. Three groups emerged, each with a separate program for the salvation of Russia: the right-wing, led by the old Marxist scholar Georgi Plekhanov, supported the liberal government and the continuation of the war; the center, led by Tchekiadze and Skobelev—who was in the cabinet—wanted to support the government as long as it continued "in its revolutionary path," and to strive for peace; the third wing, under Lenin, wanted

[6] See Raphael R. Abramovitch, *The Soviet Revolution, 1917–1939* (New York: International Universities Press, 1962), pp. 15–17, 19. Abramovitch, a leading member of the Russian Bund at that time, was a participant in the events.

[7] *Lebnsfragn*, II, September 28, 1917.

to overthrow the liberal-democratic government, set up an immediate dictatorship of the proletariat, and end the war immediately at any price. Although there had often been splits in the RSDRP during its twenty-year life, this new one was far more severe. The earlier disagreements had been on tactics; this one was a matter of principle.[8]

The Bund's position was somewhat to the left of center. Although the Bundists worked closely with the Mensheviks, who composed the center, they were opposed to coalition politics. At least a partial reason for the close cooperation between the Bund and the Mensheviks can be found in the latter's endorsement of the Bund's proposal for settling the nationality problem. More important, perhaps, was the fact that there was no other party with which the Bund could in conscience cooperate. The Bolsheviks made no secret of their desire to split the world Socialist movement, and in the Bundists' view this was an inexcusable heresy. Lenin's minions had sabotaged the Stockholm conference, which might have helped reunite the old International.[9]

The right wing and the center were likewise not immune from criticism by the Bund. Medem called the action of Plekhanov, Tsertelli, and Skobelev, in joining a coalition government, a betrayal of the working class. Coalitions tended to reduce the power of the workers, he said, because that power depended upon the workers' ability to defend their interests and to distinguish their friends from their enemies. Thus, he reasoned, it was necessary to have free play in the parliamentary struggle. Under present conditions, however, "a minister's hands are tied. When you support someone you must be loyal to him. You must defend him from his enemies, you must ignore his errors. This is the case with ministers in a government. They must be loyal to their government, defend it from its enemies, and ignore its errors. Socialist

[8] *Ibid.*, June 1, 1917.
[9] *Ibid.*, August 10, 1917; September 28, 1917.

ministers must defend their bourgeois fellows; that is the
minimum condition for collective responsibility." [10] Within
the Menshevik movement there were individuals, among them
Iulli (Lev) Martov, who supported Medem's position.[11]

Lenin opened his drive for power in June, when his party
led riots in St. Petersburg under the slogan, "All power to the
soviets." The Polish Bund leaders were shocked. "Against
whom did they fight?" *Lebnsfragn* asked. "Actually against
the workers' and soldiers' soviets which oppose the Bolsheviks
and do not desire all power in their own hands." The soviets,
according to *Lebnsfragn*'s editor, feared the results of such a
seizure of power. The Bolsheviks were, after all, only a
minority in the soviets. Would the Bolsheviks be pleased to
see all power in the hands of antagonistic soviets, in which
opposition parties held a majority? No, Medem replied, they
would change the cry from "Down with the government!"
to "Down with the soviets!" until Lenin became dictator of
Russia.[12]

The Bolshevik disorders led the tottering government to
take emergency repressive measures. The Polish Bund's leadership were critical of the attempt at suppressing the Bolsheviks, an attempt they feared would be dangerous for both
sides. "As with all dictatorships, so with Kerensky's repression
is the first order of the day. Today Kerensky arrests Lenin;
tomorrow Tsertelli will arrest Kerensky, and the next
day...." [13]

Medem warned that fighting among the Socialists was a
catastrophe, and declared that it should be brought to an end.
He proposed a unity of all Socialist factions against the lib-
eral-bourgeois parties. "The history of the Russian Social
Democracy has developed a very tragic, very harmful tradi-

[10] *Ibid.*, May 25, 1917.
[11] Vladimir Medem, "Der Goirl fun der Russishe Revolutsie,"
Uncer Sztyme, I (August 1918).
[12] *Lebnsfragn*, II, July 27, 1917.
[13] *Ibid.*, July 27, 1917; August 10, 1917.

tion; the tradition of splits and splintering. The basis for these splits was generally unimportant. This tradition is harmful in normal times; in critical times such as these, it is disastrous." [14]

The Bund's leaders believed that the revolution was in danger from two sides: externally, from the continuation of the war; internally, from the Bolshevik street riots. "The danger to the revolution will not end until the guns are silenced on the warfronts and the streets of St. Petersburg." Unless the chaos caused by the riots and the war ended, there was a danger that the people would become disillusioned with democracy. And the Bundists feared the majority of Russians might demand a return to the monarchy, if necessary, to restore order. [15]

From the outset, the Bundists considered peace the chief aim of the revolution. "The bourgeoisie of the Allied powers want to keep Russia in the war. . . . They want to fight till the last drop of someone else's blood. Peace must come!" the Bund organ insisted. "Peace must be won against all those who want to stay in the war. The great spring offensive has begun . . . the offensive for peace." [16]

Five months later the Bundists were still repeating their cry of March, "The people must demand peace." But now they felt constrained to explain why the democratic Russian republic, with Socialist support, had been unable to end the war. No single people could free the entire world; a people could only take the first step; the rest of the world must follow. "The call of the Russian workers has not yet heard the necessary echo—the echo must come, and with the echo will come the peace and the new world." [17]

Mikhail Goldman (Liber), the newly elected president of the Bund of Poland, Lithuania, and Russia, appealed for a report from the government on peace negotiations. Until

[14] *Ibid.*, April 20, 1917.
[15] *Ibid.*, July 27, 1917; April 20, 1917.
[16] *Ibid.*, April 6, 1917.
[17] *Ibid.*, March 23, 1917; August 3, 1917.

peace was effectuated, however, he urged his followers to support their country and the new regime—so long as it remained true to the ideals of the revolution. This appeal represented a major change in the Bund's position, from all-out opposition to the war in 1914 to grudging support for it in 1917.[18]

As late as the last week in September the Bundists were optimistic; even the counterrevolution attempted by Kornilov did not change their outlook. The workers' and soldiers' soviets would know what to do to prevent the counterrevolution from being victorious, said an editorial in Lebnsfragn.[19]

[18] *Ibid.*, May 18, 1917; June 1, 1917.

[19] *Ibid.*, September 21, 1917. The Kornilov coup had many of the aspects of a comic opera. Its consequences, however, were disastrous for the democratic forces of the revolution. After a series of Communist disorders in July and August, Kerensky conferred with General Lev Kornilov, commander-in-chief of the military forces of the provisional government, on the use of troops in the event of a Bolshevik uprising. Kornilov offered the use of the troops with the proviso that he be made absolute ruler. Kerensky refused. The right-wing parties supported Kornilov's demand and plotted for a seizure of power. They were convinced that a strong ruler was needed to save Russia from anarchy. Kerensky knew of the plot, but he procrastinated. In early September Prince Lvov handed Kerensky an ultimatum demanding that all state power be turned over to Kornilov. Kerensky again refused. Kornilov then attempted to march on Petrograd with the aim of seizing power. The soviets and the government armed the workers to stop Kornilov. But they weren't needed. Agitators from the soviets convinced the soldiers that they were fighting in a hopeless cause, and the coup collapsed of its own ineptitude. Kornilov and his aides were arrested. The coup did, however, strengthen the Bolsheviks in two ways. First, it raised the issue of counterrevolution and supported the Bolshevik contention that the non-Socialist parties had to be destroyed lest they destroy the revolution. Second, it permitted the Bolsheviks to form Red Guard military units, organized ostensibly to fight the coup, but intended instead to overthrow the democratic government, as they did two months later. See James Bunyan and H. H. Fisher, *The Bolshevik Revolution, 1917–1918: Documents and Materials* (Stanford, Calif.: Stanford University Press, 1934), pp. 20, 711; Abramovitch, *op. cit.*, pp. 60–65; E. H. Carr, *The Bolshevik Revolution, 1917–1923* (London: Macmillan, 1950), I, 92–93. For the Bolshevik version see Leon Trotsky, *History of the Russian Revolution* (New York: Simon and Schuster, 1937), II, 136–248.

The party remained officially the General Jewish Workers Bund of Poland, Lithuania, and Russia, and most of the leaders of the party still considered themselves only temporarily divided. The new central committee, named in May 1917, consisted of Goldman, Erlich, Medem, and Jeremiah Weinshtein. But Medem was in Poland, and his attempt to get to St. Petersburg failed. That the Bund had changed should have been apparent, but a perverse nostaligia and a sentimental attachment to the revolution kept alive the fiction that the split could be healed for another half year.[20]

THE BOLSHEVIKS TAKE POWER

Eight months after the revolution began, all the hopes of the Bund in Russia were shattered. The Bolsheviks seized power in November 1917, and before the end of 1921 the Bund had virtually ceased to exist in Russia. In March, the Bund and most Jews in Russia still thought a brighter day was dawning. Alexander Kerensky, the last democratic ruler of Russia, described the Jewish antipathy for the Bolsheviks:

. . . Many of the Bolshevik chiefs are Jews; unfortunately so for the Jewish people. But, on the other hand, 99 per cent of the Russian Jews are against the Bolsheviki, and during the whole of the revolution the Jewish intellectuals and the Jewish masses . . . were . . . faithful to the revolution. . . . And although numerous Jews are to be found among the Bolshevik leaders, they are renegades, most of whom had emigrated, had lost every contact with Russia, and were no longer representative of Russian Jewry.

The Jewish bankers, firms, workers' unions, the Bund—they were all for national defense and for cooperation with the moderate bourgeois elements in the upbuilding of the new state.[21]

[20] Victor Shulman, "Medem in Poyln," in *Vladimir Medem Tsum Tsvantsikstn Yortsayt* (New York: Amerikaner Representants fun Algemajner Idishn Arbeiter Bund in Poyln, 1943), p. 108; *Lebnsfragn*, II, September 14, 1917.

[21] "Are Bolsheviks Mainly Jewish," *Literary Digest*, LIX (December 14, 1918), 32.

The Bund's leaders did not agree with Kerensky's analysis. They were neither for national defense nor for cooperation with the moderate bourgeoisie. But most did oppose the Bolshevik seizure of power.

What had caused this "great calamity," this seizure of power by a minority faction? The revolution of November 7, said Erlich, was the result of a successful conspiracy and not of a victorious revolution of the workers and peasants. "Not in the spontaneous power, not in the mass character of the rebellion, but in the complete lack of power on the part of Kerensky, in the complete vacuum which existed lay the . . . power of the Bolsheviks." [22]

The Bund's leaders maintained that Kerensky and the democratic government had failed to make needed reforms. "If there was a real endeavor to repair the damage done by the Czarist regime, it would have been necessary to make deep-seated reforms prior to the calling of a constituent assembly." Kerensky had done the opposite. "The expense of the war should have been taken off the shoulders of the working class and the peasantry," *Lebnsfragn* declared. "The cost of government should have been borne by the wealthy."

"A genuine peace politics, the rejection and dissociation from all aggrandizement plans . . . these could have proved to the Russian people that Kerensky and his government did not serve the interests of imperialism." But, *Lebnsfragn* charged, the Kerensky government had failed to carry out the necessary program. It had also failed to fight the Russian bourgeoisie, "which refused to drop its counterrevolutionary plans . . . openly announced at the congresses of the Kadets, Octobrists, and other [conservative] parties, who openly came out against the revolution and organized against it." [23]

[22] *Vtoroii Vserosiiski Sezd Sovetov Ri, S.D.* (Petrograd: All-Russian Council of Soviets, 1917), pp. 27–30; Henryk Erlich, "Tsi iz der Sovetn Regirung an Arbeiter Regirung?" *Uncer Sztyme*, III (November 1918), 1.

[23] *Lebnsfragn*, II, November 16, 1916. The Octobrists believed in a constitutional monarchy.

Medem believed that the Mensheviks were unwilling to hold power, that they had surrendered to the Bolsheviks because they could not rule. The Mensheviks had misjudged conditions, the Bund's leader thought. They did not believe Russia's capitalism had developed sufficiently for a Socialist revolution; and the workers could not take the responsibility for developing Russia's capitalism. Medem agreed that logic was on their side. But formal logic, Medem pointed out, had a way of falling before the hard facts of history. The class struggle was at hand, brought on by economic and political facts of life: hunger, inflation, unemployment, and military collapse. "The class struggle was stronger than the oratorical skill of Kerensky and Tsertelli." [24]

The result, said Medem, was the November revolution, the Bolshevik seizure of power. "The workers cried, 'All we have to do is stretch out our hands and we are the rulers of the whole world—we, the proletarians: . . . so why don't we do it?' The unclass-conscious reached this conclusion naturally, and on this base the Bolshevik revolution was made."

Perhaps, Medem conceded, the Menshevik argument was logical and sensible. But it would have taken a more advanced people to understand such an argument. The Mensheviks faced a colossal, blind, spontaneous mass uprising. "There was an energy abroad which knew nothing of complex political deductions; an energy that could only have been captured by the simple slogans: 'Down with the lords!' 'Down with the bosses!' 'Let's become the rulers of the land ourselves!' The workers deserted the Mensheviks and went under Lenin's banner." [25]

A WORKERS' GOVERNMENT?

Was the Soviet government a workers' government? "No!" Erlich replied. "It has no right to call itself a workers' govern-

[24] Medem, *op. cit.*, pp. 1-3. Irakii Georgievich Tsertelli was a leading Georgian Menshevik.
[25] *Ibid.*, pp. 3-5.

ment. It has no right to speak in the name of the Russian working class."

Erlich, who had returned to his native Poland shortly after the Bolsheviks rose to power, was bitter in denouncing Lenin and his followers. He believed the Bolsheviks had fallen into the trap of seizing power before the time was ripe. "The Communism of the Bolshevik power has no relation whatsoever with proletarian socialism." [26]

The Bund's leaders agreed that the Bolsheviks knew what they were doing, that they realized that the Russian workers were not class-conscious enough to have made a social revolution. "On the contrary," said Benush Michalewicz, one of the intellectual leaders of the Polish Bund, "they concede that the workers are not yet ready for the revolution." The Bolsheviks weren't interested in a social revolution in the Bund sense; they wanted power. [27]

The fact that the masses were not yet politically developed enough to make the social revolution doomed it to failure, in Medem's view. The rationale was simple: most of the Bolsheviks' 240,000 members were "March Socialists," who joined the movement after the first revolution. They did not become Bolsheviks because they agreed with Lenin's theses; they joined the revolutionary movement because they wanted to be on the winning side; they became Bolsheviks because they expected the Bolsheviks to win. They thus became a determined minority, "full of energy and initiative," which could "carry along the broad masses in time of battle and stress." But this sort of minority could not get from the masses the support necessary for the building of a Socialist society.

Medem rejected the idea that socialism could be created by a minority. Scientific Socialists—and by this Medem meant Marxists—defined socialism as the rule of economic life by

[26] Erlich, *op. cit.*, pp. 16–17.
[27] B. Michalewicz, "Di Sotsiale Revolutsie un der Marxism," *Uncer Sztyme*, II, October 2, 1918, p. 13.

the workers themselves. "Socialism is the rule—the true, not the fictional rule—of the majority which must in the end take its fate into its own hands. A socialism based on the rule of the minority, however, is absurd." The Bolsheviks admitted that they were a minority; thus the socialism of the Bolsheviks "is a socialism of the minority." And, said Medem, minority socialism was "a self-contradictory term." [28]

An even more serious failing of the Bolsheviks, from Medem's point of view, was the use of force to stay in power. The Bolsheviks "stay in power only because their terror has destroyed and made powerless all of their opponents. Moreover, it is impossible to find anyone willing to take over from the Bolshevik mess. They hold power because of the apathy in the country."

The use of force to maintain power was a condition which Medem equated with "a time of deep reaction." Rule by force would lead to counterrevolution and a return to the past. "Now the reaction is decorated with the red Bolshevik flag. The time is drawing near when the reaction will be non-Marxian; the stage has been prepared." [29]

Medem charged that the terror was backed by the bayonets of the Red Army, composed of hired men who served only so long as they were paid; and this was militarism. Michalewicz pointed out that instead of destroying militarism, the arch enemy of socialism, "Socialist" Russia was "spending all its energies on building a strong standing army." This emphasis was planned and deliberate; a minority dictatorship required a strong military force. Michalewicz accused the Bolsheviks of building, for this reason, a large army of unemployed workers.[30]

Marx, Engels, and Bebel were no longer gospel to the Bundists; they had made "errors in their prophecies." But the Bund's leaders denied any connection between Lenin's Russia and Marx's Utopia. Soviet Bolshevik communism, Er-

[28] Medem, *op. cit.*, pp. 9–10.   [29] *Ibid.*, p. 18.
[30] Michalewicz, *loc. cit.*, pp. 14–15.

lich said, "has the same relationship to the socialism of Marx as the social ideals of a middle-class peasant mass, 'thoroughly saturated with the ideal of private ownership,' has with the ideals of a revolutionary proletariat." [31]

If Bolshevism was not a form of Marxian socialism, what was it? "Blanquism," a Bund leader replied. He said that the Bolsheviks believed political rule, "the iron dictatorship by physical power," was the primary, most powerful factor in society. He accused the Bolsheviks of considering brute political power superior to economic factors or to the class struggle; thus whoever held political power could also dictate economic orders and direct the economic system as he desired. This would follow closely the theories of Louis Blanqui, and would contradict the Marxian position that economic factors were the determinants of the political. [32]

COUNTERREVOLUTION

After the Bolsheviks had consolidated their position, many of the leaders of the Polish Bund faced a dilemma. They considered the Bolshevik revolution an immense disappointment for the working class. The revolution, said Erlich, had "engendered a period of struggle for freedom from the new yoke."

But how was the Bolshevik power to be fought? A counterrevolution was predicted. The counterrevolution would, Erlich said, get the aid of the Allied Powers; its aim would be to sink "in a sea of blood" the revolutionary gains; its cry would be the eradication of the Bolshevik danger. This counterrevolution, said Erlich, had to be defeated. He called on the workers of Poland to unite to defend Russia from it. The Bund leader wanted the "reactionary Bolshevik regime" liquidated by the Social Democrats of Russia. Liber told the last congress of the Mensheviks in Moscow in 1918 that Russia

[31] Erlich, *op. cit.*, p. 17; Medem, *op. cit.*, p. 16.
[32] Michalewicz, *loc. cit.*, p. 13.

had to be emancipated by the workers. The alternative was a return to capitalist reaction.

The non-Bolshevik working class movements, however, were divided and fighting among themselves. Their division, said Erlich, was all that stood in the way of the overthrow of the Bolshevik regime and rise of a democratic Socialist government in Russia.[33]

TIME . . . AND TIDE

The democratic Socialist revolution never came. The Bund in Russia splintered on the issue of support for the Lenin regime, and its remnants were finally absorbed into the Communist Party. The Russian Bundists who remained true to their Social-Democratic ideals were forced into exile or died in prisons during the decade that followed.

It was during this period that the Bund in Poland became a separate organization. Its relations with Russia became more and more tenuous. It adjusted to new conditions as they arose. The German occupation was nearing its end; the new independent Poland was going through its birth pangs. Time and the vicissitudes of history had forced new conditions upon the Bund.

[33] *Ibid.*, p. 19; Erlich, *op. cit.*, p. 18; *Svoboda Rosiia*, I, May 23, 1918.

IV

An Independent Bund in
an Independent Poland

WAR and revolution had changed the face of Poland. From a colony divded among three major powers it emerged as an independent nation, with all of the benefits and more than its share of the problems that are the corollaries of independence. Poland overthrew the yoke of foreign domination, and emerged as a nation; but it inherited a nationality problem of the first magnitude. The Poles were at best a bare majority of the population. There were millions of Ukrainians, Germans, Byelorussians, Lithuanians, and Jews within the boundaries of the new state; and each nationality had its own heritage, religion, language, and aspirations. These aspirations of the minority nationalities created problems that Poland was to fail to solve, problems that turned the hopes for a free democratic Poland of November 12, 1918—the day it became an independent nation—into a quasi-anarchic, authoritarian nightmare.

The Bund had also become a completely independent organization; its last tenuous ties with the old organization of Czarist days broken, it had to adjust to an independent Poland that was a nationalistic, schizophrenic Poland as well. The Bund could no longer be part of a conspiratorial movement with a secret press and a clandestine emigré leadership; it had to adjust itself to the problems of legality—although the status of the Bund varied from that to semi-legality. The Bund had to represent the interests of the Jewish working class within the state itself and among the various Socialist organizations that existed throughout the different national groups in Poland.

Conditions within Poland shaped the Bund into a new party, with at most a merely historical connection to the General Jewish Workers Bund of Poland, Lithuania, and Russia.

THE LUBLIN CONFERENCE

The connection between the Polish and Russian Bunds had been weakening since the start of the German occupation. Communication between the two organizations was difficult, and they faced different problems. The Committee of Bund Organizations in Poland had emerged as a virtually independent body long before Poland and Russia became separate nations. The fiction was maintained, however, that the Polish party was merely a large part of the general organization.[1]

By late 1917 it was apparent that the old relations were no longer tenable, and that Poland and Russia would no longer be under one rule. The Polish Bund Committee decided to call a conference to organize itself into a separate Polish party. This was not an easy task. Restrictions and economic collapse made it, in fact, almost impossible, but a conference in Lublin was called for December.[2]

Lublin was chosen as the site for the conference becase it was in the sector of Poland held by the Austrians, whose occupying force followed a more democratic policy than the German. The Bund's opposition to the establishment of a quasi-independent Poland under the protection of the Central Powers had resulted in the arrest and repression of Bund leaders. Those leaders had been outspoken in their opposition to the Polish protectorate scheme proposed by the Germans; as councilmen, they used the rostrums of the various city

[1] Novogrodsky, *Entsiklopedea Shel Galut*, II, 72.
[2] Meyer, "Barikht fun der Lubliner Konferents," p. 1.

governments to denounce the scheme, and were often jailed as a consequence.[3]

Aside from such political repression, economic conditions in German-occupied Poland were not conducive to a successful meeting. Hunger and epidemics had wiped out large portions of the population. The populace was described as apathetic and tired. No early end to the occupation was in sight. Conditions in the Austrian sector were better. A delegate described Lublin as "a live city, not starving, but with open stores laden with food and other products; not a city of people dressed in rags, not a city of funerals, but a live city with the movement of vital people. A different life than in Warsaw . . . and in the other cities in the German zone." [4]

Travel between the German and Austrian zones of occupation was difficult. Restrictions intended to halt smuggling of goods between the two zones were also effective against Bundists and others traveling for revolutionary purposes. To make the trip it was necessary to obtain permission from the German authorities. To obtain permission meant filing not only medical papers attesting to health and lack of contagious disease, but a statement of purpose as well. Because they feared repression, Bund delegates felt it unsafe to divulge the nature of their travel. They thus found it expedient to bribe German officials—via intermediaries—in order to reach Lublin. Moreover, because of the danger of arrest the delegates traveled separately. Despite the less restricted political atmosphere in Lublin, the Bund met secretly in a dining hall and at night.[5]

The conference at which the Polish Bund was born offered a foretaste of the internal strife that was to persist for years to come, a battle between the right, center, and left wings.

[3] Millman, "Barikht fun der Lubliner Konferents," p. 1.

[4] I. Fishman, Report on Lublin Conference (original Yiddish typescript in Bund Archives), pp. 1–2.

[5] Millman, *loc. cit.*, pp. 3, 5.

The Lublin conference opened within a month of the Bolsheviks' seizure of power in Russia. There was little reliable information about conditions in Russia. Reports of the mass murder of non-Bolshevik Socialists in St. Petersburg and Moscow had filtered out; there had also been rumors of the Bolshevik dispersal of the democratic government by force. On the other hand, there were reports that the Bolsheviks had stopped the war, begun instituting socialism, and proclaimed that all people were equal. Among the common people of Poland, many believed the latter reports. They were weary of war and economic dislocation, and these rumors offered hope in a period of despair. So many Poles were ready to bless the Bolsheviks, "who would make of Russia a veritable Eden" where all people would be equal. There were heated assertions that what Poland needed was a Bolshevik seizure of power and a feverish confidence that somehow the Bolsheviks would end the starvation, the epidemics, and the mass funerals that plagued Poland.[6]

Victor Shulman, spokesman for the right wing of the party, opposed the Bolshevik seizure of power. He assailed Lenin and his cohorts for their "adventurism" and their destruction of the newborn democracy, for establishing their own dictatorship and for holding power "by fearful terror over the people." Shulman told the delegates, "This is not our way! This is not the way of the Bund, the way of Social Democrats."[7]

Haym Vasser, one of the leaders of the left wing, took a diametrically opposite stand. The Bolshevik revolution was, he said, a key moment in world history, a turning point toward socialism. But not all of the left wing agreed with him. Some of the leaders of the faction joined Shulman in his anti-Bolshevik position.[8]

The left wing was primarily opposed to the "reformist" groups within world socialism who had supported the war;

[6] Fishman, *loc. cit.* pp. 1–2.   [7] *Ibid.*, pp. 3–4.   [8] *Ibid.*, p. 4.

the leftists were not Bolsheviks, they were revolutionary Socialists. The war, they said, was making the rich richer and
the poor poorer. "That portion of the international Socialist
movement was correct, which from the start had declared
'war on war.'" The left-wingers' animosity was particularly
strong toward the German Social Democratic Party, which
had voted for war credits and had appealed for "class peace"
during the war. The left was closely allied with the antiwar
group of democratic Socialists led by Karl Kautsky, and with
the Independent Socialist Party of Germany. The opposition
to the pro-war Socialists was so strong that the left wing of
the Bund opposed participating in the international Socialist
conference at Stockholm, organized by the soviets of Russia
under the leadership of Mensheviks and Bundists, should the
pro-war parties be invited.[9]

The Bund's position on war and revolution, as finally
adopted, was a clear statement of revolutionary democratic
socialism. The Bund wanted a social revolution, and it wanted
one immediately:

> The Russian Revolution and the role of the proletariat in it
> has thrown a pall over the ruling classes in the warring nations,
> who see in it a direct threat to the basic power of the existing
> capitalist system—and will thus be forced to liquidate the
> bloody war.
> The class-conscious working class cannot permit the great
> chasm which has been deepened in the capitalist world by the
> war to be without result for the Socialist ideal.[10]

The revolution the Bundists wanted was, however, not a
Bolshevik seizure of power. Instead, the conference urged
increased democracy and opposed all forms of dictatorship.
The Bundists called for a democratically elected constituent
assembly to decide Poland's internal form and its relations
with its neighboring states.[11]

On the issue of national minorities, the Bund remained

[9] *Tsvai Konferentsn*, pp. 10–11; Millman, *loc. cit.*, p. 4.
[10] *Tsvai Konferentsn*, p. 11.
[11] *Ibid.*, pp. 11–12; Meyer, *loc. cit.*, p. 3.

adamant in its insistence on full rights for all with national cultural autonomy for each. This was to be one of the clarion calls of the Bund during its twenty-six years as a political party in independent Poland.[12]

The Bund in Poland thus became an independent party of the Polish republic even before Poland itself was born.[13]

POLAND IS BORN

Within a day after the war ended, Poland, under Pilsudski, was declared an independent nation. The Bund's position was clear; it favored an independent Poland. The fate of the Jews was tied to the fate of Poland, the Bund's leaders maintained, but they insisted that the more than 3,000,000 Jews within the new state were entitled to cultural autonomy.[14]

The Bund's position separated it from the other Jewish parties and from the Polish Socialists. Shortly after the formation of the new Polish state, Pilsudski invited all political parties to consult with him. The other Jewish parties accepted, but the Bund would have nothing to do with the new nationalistic regime unless all minorities were granted national cultural autonomy.[15]

Within the boundaries of the new Polish state were approximately 2,500,000 of the 4,500,000 Jews who had lived in the old Russian empire, plus additional hundreds of thousands of Jews from Galicia, the area formerly ruled by Austria. With the first breath of independence the Jewish population was elated; but its hopes were soon dashed as the Polish reaction set in. Soon the cry of "Jews to Palestine" was heard, and in free Poland the pogroms of Czarist times became commonplace.[16]

[12] *Tsvai Konferentsn*, p. 13.
[13] V. Medem, "Farvos iz der Bund in Poyln Nit Farnandergefaln," *Tsukunft*, XXIV (1921), 159.
[14] Novogrodsky, *op. cit.*, pp. 72–74.
[15] Medem, *loc. cit.*, p. 161.
[16] *Ibid.*, pp. 159–160; Holtz, letter, *Jewish Daily Forward*, February 18, 1954.

POGROMS AGAIN

Jews have historically been scapegoats for corrupt, inefficient, unstable, or tottering regimes; inevitably they have offered an easy target for the animosity of the general population, and have thus been made to suffer in place of the corrupt or inefficient ruler. The new Polish regime was weak, its rule was in doubt, and its pretensions to geographic greatness were beyond realization. It was in a constant state of war. Its soldiers were almost all youths who had been raised in the anti-Semitic atmosphere of Czarist Russia; its officers were nationalists who opposed equality with the Poles for any other people within their exaggerated idea of what was Poland. Such economic causes of excesses against the Jews as have already been noted in Chapter II had little bearing on the wholesale slaughter of 1918 and 1919.

The first reports of anti-Semitic attacks reached the United States in early December 1918. Secretary of State Lansing, who had played an important role in the establishment of independent Poland, was disturbed by the reports. At the instance of Polish nationalist groups in the United States, he named a commission headed by Henry Morgenthau, Sr., to investigate. The report, which was severely criticized by even the most moderate Jewish groups because it minimized the extent of the pogroms, nevertheless gave some idea of the havoc wrought on the Jewish population, and described the pillage and slaughter by Polish troops in major cities.[17]

The Morgenthau Commission blamed the slaughter on the troops themselves, on poor organization, and on false rumors that the Jews were either Bolsheviks or on the side of the Ukrainians, with whom Poland was then at war. The excesses were attributed by the commission to uncontrolled troops, and were said not to be premeditated. The implication

---

[17] The report described attacks on Jews in Kielce, Lemberg (Lwów), Pinsk, Lida, Czenstahowa, and Kolbusowo. Almost 250 Jews died in these attacks.

that the government was not connected with the excesses is open to serious doubt, for the assaults by the troops were only the most violent of numerous anti-Semitic acts. Jews were also discharged from government jobs to make way for Poles, since the government considered the Jews an alien group. And the pro-government press backed the troops who had committed the atrocities.[18]

The Bund hoped for aid from the Socialist International in ending the pogroms. The 1919 International Socialist Conference in Berne, Switzerland, adopted a Socialist program against anti-Semitism which asked equality for Jews in their home countries, upheld their right to return if they had fled deprivation, and demanded protection against physical attacks or economic disabilities. The Socialist program urged liberty of migrations, self-determination for Jews in any region where they were a majority, and representation for Jews in the League of Nations. The international Socialist conference blamed the anti-Semitic wave on nationalistic chauvinism and declared it to be the chief task of the Polish Socialists to fight the pogroms. The new Poland, the resolution continued, must achieve a spirit of national tolerance lest Polish independence degenerate into persecution of Jews and other minority groups.[19]

Resolutions passed at pious international conferences rarely accomplish very much, and this one did little to end the excesses.

THE BEGINNING OF THE POLISH COMMUNIST PARTY

The Russian Bolshevik revolution caused division in all Socialist parties. Its effect in Eastern Europe, which was linked

---

[18] The full Morgenthau Report was published in *The New York Times,* January 19, 1920, p. 6. For an account of the Polish Jews resentment see Buell, *op. cit.,* p. 295.

[19] *Die Judenfrage,* Resolution of International Socialist Conference, Berne, Switzerland, 1919; original in Bund Archives, mimeographed with penciled corrections.

closely by geography and history to Russia, was particularly strong. The Polish Socialists, already split into three parties, had to be completely realigned. Within even the nationalist, reformist PPS groups were enamored of the revolution and of the prospect of "proletarian power" and socialism. The SDKPiL was closely allied with the Bolsheviks before the revolution, and the members of the Lewica were almost universally delighted by the Bolsheviks' seizure of power.[20]

Relations between the Bund and the SDKPiL had never been cordial. The Bund's insistence upon a solution to the Jewish problem outside the context of social revolution was a chief cause for the antipathy that developed between the two parties. The SDKPiL weekly, *Nasza Trybuna*, engaged in long polemics against the Bund, particularly with regard to its insistence that Yiddish be recognized as an official language. The Bund, *Nasza Trybuna* charged, was willing to call off the class struggle if it would help strengthen the position of the Yiddish "jargon."

The antipathy was not all on one side, either. The Bund considered the SDKPiL a party of dreamers deluded by their own imaginings. Michalewicz derided the SDKPiL's insistence that the Socialist revolution was near at hand. The Social Democrats, he warned, were ignoring the counterindications, particularly the signs that the Polish working class was generally under the influence of the chauvinist and reactionary parties. "The Social Democracy," he said, "mechanically carries over Russian conditions to Poland and the rest of Europe, and [its leaders] keep shouting, 'The social revolution is knocking on the door.' Its position is comical."

The corollary of such deluded thinking, said Michalewicz, was the inability of the SDKPiL to develop a Polish program. "As true guards they [SDKPiL leaders] stand watch over the Bolshevik tactics, praising and acclaiming everything, with no trace of critical study, with no attempt to establish a theoretical position of their own." [21]

[20] Minc, *Di Geshikhte fun a Falshe Iluzie*, pp. 24–26.
[21] *Lebnsfragn*, I, May 12, 1916; Michalewicz, *loc. cit.*, pp. 16–17.

The relations between the Bund and the Lewica had generally been friendly. During the occupation the two parties had formed a bloc for elections to the city council, and the Lewica was favorably inclined toward the Bund's position on national cultural autonomy.

The Russian Revolution changed all this. The Lewica's membership insisted on supporting the Bolsheviks who had succeeded in establishing a proletarian dictatorship in the neighboring state. The Lewica's leadership was prepared to unite with the SDKPiL under almost any circumstances to form a Bolshevik vanguard in Poland, a Communist Party with the aim of emulating the Russian experience. But before the SDKPiL would accede to this proposal, it insisted that the Lewica must sever its ties with the Bund. The Lewica did so, and denounced the Bund as a nationalist party.[22]

Thus the Communist Party of Poland (KPP), formed on December 16, 1918, by unification of the SDKPiL and the Lewica, began its life as an enemy of the Bund. In a few years the opposition would flare into open attack and occasional murder. The Communists would attack the Bundists as separatists and nationalists and, mockingly, as seasick Zionists, despite their opposition to Palestine as a Jewish homeland.[23]

The answer to the Jewish problem, the KPP maintained, was the same as the answer to the problems of all minority groups—the Socialist revolution. Rosa Luxemburg, who approved the program adopted at the founding congress of the Communist Party of Poland, insisted on this plank. The program of the KPP on the nationality problem contained this declaration:

In this epoch of the international social revolution, while the foundations of capitalism are being destroyed, the proletariat

[22] *Sztandar Socjalizmu,* I, December 19, 1918.
[23] Minc, *loc. cit.,* pp. 30–31, 53; Interview with S. I. Hertz, New York, June 19, 1963 (Hertz, historian of the Bund, was a member of the Bund during this period). It might be noted in passing that all of the leaders in the founding of the Communist Party of Poland were executed by Stalin as chauvinists and nationalists during the 1930's.

rejects all issues such as autonomy, political independence, or the demand for self-determination that had been developed at the political formation of the capitalist order. Struggling for the dictatorship of the proletariat and moving to place in opposition to all of its enemies the organized armed might of the revolution, the proletariat will fight all attempts to build a Polish bourgeois, counterrevolutionary army, and will reject any war for national boundaries. . . . No national boundaries exist for the international social revolution. Its territory is determined by the interests of the international working class, which rejects any national oppression and rejects any and every pretext for national conflict, either regarding existing borders or regarding national minorities within these borders.[24]

Despite its opposition to all proposals short of a Socialist revolution for solving the minority question, the KPP saw in the minorities a fertile field for propaganda. The Communist Party formed a separate section—as the Russian party had done—for propaganda and agitation among the Jewish working class. The section published Yiddish leaflets and journals, and sent speakers into Jewish areas to address the working population in Yiddish. The Jewish section was, however, controlled by the KPP central committee, whose direction was in the hands of a group chosen by the leadership of the party itself. Although the Jewish section could consult with Jewish activists within the party, it could not call any conferences.[25] The Communists were following to the letter the line of Lenin and Rosa Luxemburg, who insisted that the Jews were not a separate nationality, but merely people who used a separate language, and that it was only because Jews did not learn the language of the land that their "jargon" might be used for propaganda purposes. The KPP insisted that assimilation of the Jews among the workers of Poland—in one party, one trade union body, and one cultural organization—was the only means of preventing anti-Semitism.[26]

[24] *Sztandar Socjalizmu*, I, December 19, 1918; Minc, *op. cit.*, pp. 32–33.
[25] *Ibid.*, pp. 53–54.   [26] *Ibid.*, p. 54.

The hopes of the KPP for a Bolshevik takeover of Poland almost became a reality. In the spring of 1920, Poland's dream of empire led to an invasion of Russia which penetrated deeply into Byelorussia and the Ukraine. Military miscalculation resulted in a military rout, and in a counterinvasion of Poland by the Red Army that reached the banks of the Vistula River. The Polish Communists saw in the Russian invasion a way of effectuating the revolution. They assumed, erroneously, that the Polish masses would be ready to aid the Red Army. This miscalculation was based on the delusion then pervading the radical Marxist movements, that the revolution was near at hand.

Even before all-out war developed between Russia and Poland, the KPP had called for a Russian invasion. As early as February 1919, the Party declared: "Should the Polish revolution require the aid of the Russian proletariat, this help could not be considered an invasion, or the expression of an imperialistic tendency. . . . It would merely indicate that the international revolutionary solidarity is being effectuated." [27]

The war was settled in 1921 by negotiation. The invasion did not lead to a Communist Poland; it helped instead to solidify the reactionary, nationalist rule.

The organization of the Communist Party and its policy of rule or ruin was to play havoc with the Bund for the next twenty years. That it did not succeed in destroying the Bund, by first splitting and then absorbing it, was due to its own miscalculation concerning the loyalty of the Bundists to their party.

POLISH SOVIETS

For a short period immediately after the war there was a possibility that the government of Poland might be super-

[27] *Ibid.*, pp. 41–42. The Bund's reaction to the Russo-Polish war will be discussed later in this chapter, and in Chapter V. For a description of the war itself see Buell, *op. cit.*, pp. 74–81; for a highly critical study of the war, see F. W. von Oertzen, *So This Is Poland* (London: George Allen and Unwin, 1932), pp. 21–50.

seded by the soviets, which had been formed by workers of all political shadings. But the Polish soviets, unlike the Russian, never held actual power. They were little more than discussion groups.[28]

The soviets—more properly, the Councils of Workers' Delegates—were divided; some were Communist, most were closely allied with the PPS. A third group of councils was affiliated with the anti-Semitic Polish National Party of Workers.

The Bund took an active part in the establishment of the PPS soviets. Erlich was the first vice-chairman of the Warsaw Soviet, and acted as its chairman during most of its short life. The Bund tried to turn the soviets into revolutionary bodies, but with little success, since the Polish workers at that time were not interested in social revolution. The Polish workers, like their leaders in the PPS, were nationalists more than they were revolutionary Socialists.

In 1919 the Bund issued this statement to the soviets:

> The undeniable need of the moment is the life and death struggle for the most direct and speediest effectualization of socialism.
> The path which leads to this goal is the proletarian revolution, which will place all power in the hands of the proletariat. . . .
> The role of the [Polish] soviets must be the organization of the power of the working class; the protection . . . of the economic interests of the working class in the struggle against exploitation, the defense of the working masses against the assaults by the native counterrevolutionaries.
> One of the methods in this war must be an armed force which shall be under the direct control of the soviets.[29]

[28] Leon Ohler, "Di Linke Rikhtung in Bund in Poyln," in *Chmurner Bukh*, (New York: Ferlag Unser Tsait, 1958), pp. 30–31; see also Dziewanowski, *op. cit.*, pp. 70–74.
[29] A. Ratman (pseudonym of Gershon Ziebert), "Der Bund in Poyln," *Di Naye Velt*, VII, September 3, 1920, pp. 9, 19; Ohler, *loc. cit.*, p. 29.

The soviets ignored the Bund's call, and soon they were to face a new problem which was to end in their demise, namely the war with Russia. The Bund suggested to the Warsaw Soviet that the following resolution be adopted:

> The Warsaw Soviet of Workers Delegates condemns all wars which are undertaken by bourgeois governments, and therefore also the war being conducted by the present Polish regime —this war even more so because it must, under the logic of capitalism, become an imperialist war aimed at the robbing and suppression of other nations.
>
> The Warsaw Soviet of Workers Delegates affirms that regardless of the attitudes of the various segments of the Polish proletariat to the Bolsheviki, [the Polish working class] will oppose vigorously any attempt to destroy the Soviet Union.
>
> The Warsaw Soviet of Workers Delegates demands, in the name of the Warsaw proletariat, an end to the war politics which leads into the morass, that immediate peace negotiations be undertaken, and that the blood of the Polish working class stop flowing for the benefit of international capitalism.[30]

The PPS disagreed; it wanted to support the war. The parties split, and the soviets fell apart.[31]

Thus an independent Bund in an independent Poland began its life in the midst of strife with a nationalist, expansionist regime, with an antagonistic Communist party, and with the rest of the Socialist segment of Poland's political life.

[30] Quoted by Ohler, *ibid.*, p. 30.
[31] Ratman, *loc. cit.*, p. 19.

V

The Left in Control

THE fledgling Bund was beset from the start with almost insurmountable problems. The government was hostile to socialism and was anti-Semitic; the other Socialist parties—right and left—were antagonistic, and within the Bund itself there developed among the left, center, and right wings a struggle for control which was virtually to paralyze the party for the next four years.

THE FEUD BEGINS

Strong pro-Communist movements developed in the Jewish Socialist parties almost immediately after the Russian Bolsheviks had consolidated their power. The formation of the Communist Party in Poland strengthened the left-wing tendencies within the Bund, the Territorialists, a miniscule semi-Zionist Socialist group, and the Poale Zion. The Bund, with its long history of radical socialism, was the organization most seriously affected. A section of the Bund was drawn more and more into the Communist stream. The disagreement with the right-wing leadership on issues such as the imminence of the social revolution, violence, and the dictatorship of the proletariat, grew continually sharper.[1]

In the midst of the internal feuding and external repressions, the Bund's leadership in 1918 called a convention aimed at ending the dissension. The convention failed to achieve its

[1] Victor Shulman, "Medem in Poyln," in *Vladimir Medem: Tsum Tsvantsikstn Yortsayt* (New York: Amerikaner Representants fun Algemajner Idisher Arbeiter Bund in Poyln, 1943), p. 154; *Dos Fraje Vort* (Vilno), March 12, 1921.

aim; it resulted instead in open warfare between the two factions, and defiance of the right-wing majority by the left-wing minority. The centrist wing was dedicated to the apparently futile task of mediating the squabble.

The right-wing faction of the Bund was itself a revolutionary segment of the Socialist movement. It opposed the reformism of the German Social Democracy and the nationalism of the PPS, yet it was unwilling to support the destruction of democracy in the name of socialism. The resolution proposed by right-wingers and passed at the 1918 convention made its stand clear. The end of the war, the resolution said, meant the beginning of a social and economic battle that had "as its obligation the effectuation of socialism." To accomplish the social revolution would require solidarity "of the international proletariat," and this would make necessary the organization of a new and powerful Socialist International. The Bund did not preclude Communists from this proposed new international, but obviously such an organization would have to be centered on the Socialist movements throughout the world.

Poland, said the Bund resolution, was in a peculiar position. "In a land which for more than one hundred years found itself under a heavy yoke, in a land which has just been freed from military occupation, and in which, in great measure, there have been missing the most rudimentary prerequisites for a legal mass labor organization," the aim of the Socialist movement should be the creation and strengthening of such prerequisites. Chief among them would be democratic institutions, "which will be formed under working-class pressure." The working class would have to "seize the largest sector of political and social power" within these democratic organs of the state in order to carry to victory the fight for socialism.[2]

A heated debate preceded the adoption of the resolution.

[2] *Glos Bundu*, March 6, 1919.

The left-wing spokesmen opposed the use of parliamentary means for achieving power; they wanted the soviets to seize power by force and institute a proletarian dictatorship similar to that in the Soviet Union.

The resolution passed by the narrowest of margins, a vote of 32 to 31. The large minority acceded to the discipline of the majority, but when its spokesmen insisted on calling a new convention, the effectiveness of the resolution was weakened.

More important, perhaps, than the failure of the convention to accept the resolution as the final word on the issue was the refusal by the left-wing minority to vote for members of a new central committee, whose influence was thus lessened, making its position almost untenable at a time when elections were about to be held for the Sejm, the Polish parliament.[3]

The convention thus further alienated the two dominant wings of the party, and led to the creation of a third. The right wing insisted on democracy, parliamentarianism, "and other bourgeois niceties"; the left wing, bitterly assailing the right, insisted that the Bund should call openly for a revolution and a dictatorship of the proletariat; and the center tried to reconcile the parties in this quarrel.[4]

Within a matter of months it was apparent that the party had lost control of its members. A meeting of Bundists who were members of city councils rejected the stand of the party convention. The councilmen declared that "the only way out of the many-sided crises which affect our nation . . . is to be found in our maximal program—socialism—which requires the seizure of power by the working class." The chief duty of the Bund councilmen was therefore "to develop a revolutionary consciousness on the part of the masses." This would require expounding the maximal program and propagandizing for "our program for the transition period [the dictator-

[3] *Lebnsfragn,* IV, April 29, 1919.
[4] Ratman, Der Bund in Poyln," *Di Naye Velt,* VII, September 3, 1920, p. 9.

ship of the proletariat], which will have to be created by the working class on the day after the seizure of power." [5]

Internal squabbling impeded the work of the Bund until Noah Portnoy, its chairman, reported that there was serious doubt whether the party could continue to exist. "All of us— right or left—must agree that the conditions current in the party can no longer continue. Party differences of opinion may exist; there may be many opinions, but not many actions. An army cannot exist without discipline . . ." [6]

His appeal fell on deaf ears. The Warsaw, Lublin, and Chelm organizations, centers of left-wing strength, refused to participate in the 1919 elections to the Sejm. They kept the Bund from participating in its centers of strength, and thus caused it to suffer a serious defeat. Later that year these same organizations did participate in the municipal elections, electing a total of 130 councilmen. [7]

The refusal of the Warsaw organization to obey the instructions of the national organization—to participate in the elections to the Sejm—was the first open defiance of the central body by a local organization in the history of the Bund. Its result was a collapse of party discipline. The Bund, Portnoy reported to the next party convention, had virtually ceased to exist as a political organization. Near-anarchy reigned; individuals joined local organizations in ignoring orders from the national party, and soon these individuals defied even the local organizations by refusing to support Bund candidates in local elections. [8]

[5] Resolution of Conference of Bund City Councilmen, October 1919; quoted by Ohler, *loc. cit.*, p. 31.

[6] *Lebnsfragn*, IV, April 29, 1919.

[7] Ratman, *loc. cit.*

[8] *Lebnsfragn*, IV, April 29, 1919. A stenographic transcript of the convention proceedings was published in *Lebnsfragn*, the daily organ of the Bund. Names of speakers were deleted, however, because of police repressions. The transcript of the 1919 convention appeared in *Lebnsfragn* for April 26, 27, 28, 29, and 30 of that year. The Portnoy report dealt with conditions following the 1918 convention but preceding that of 1919.

To end the chaos in the party the central committee called a special convention in 1919. It was hoped that the convention would end the bickering, settle the Bund's position, and lead to a united Jewish Socialist party. Instead, the convention divided the party even further.

The left wing refused to retreat from its stand; it would not admit to having erred in refusing to obey orders to participate in the Sejm elections. A delegate from Radom insisted that the action had in fact saved the party, because the workers wanted the election to be boycotted. Moreover, the delegate continued, the Warsaw action did not violate the decision of the convention; the Sejm was not a democratic institution organized under pressure from the proletariat, and was therefore not covered by the resolution. Indeed, according to the left-wing delegate, the Warsaw organization had erred in participating in the city elections. Nor was the refusal to accept discipline so odious, another left-wing delegate opined, where the issue was revolution versus reformism. Had not the left-wing Socialists in Germany refused to obey decrees from the Social Democratic leadership, and had not Karl Kautsky supported them? Moreover, the same delegate said, the central committee was itself to blame for the breach of discipline; had it not refused to print the left-wing attacks on electoral activity? [9]

The basic position of the left wing was stated succinctly by one of its delegates:

> We have entered a revolutionary period not because of the discontent of the masses, or because we desire to carry out the revolution, but because of changes which the war has brought about in the capitalist world. The war . . . sped the crash of the capitalist world. On this we all agree.
>
> The issue that splits us is not whether or not to make a revolution. It is how the revolution is to be effectuated; democracy or dictatorship of the proletariat. At this time the dictatorship of the proletariat is the only possible way. De-

[9] *Lebnsfragn,* IV, April 27, 29, 1919.

mocracy represents the will of the capitalist class and gives it
the possibility to exploit the masses.

We are not bound to democracy. If democracy cannot meet
the needs of socialism, the Bund can reject it. Democracy now
gives the bourgeoisie . . . the material wherewithal to control
the government machinery. Because of economic domination
the bourgeoisie can control elections and obtain majorities. The
bourgeoisie turns democracy into a vehicle for its own use. The
proletariat must thus find other ways.

We believe in the dictatorship of the proletariat. We do not,
however, delude ourselves: the dictatorship will be the dictatorship of one party, a party of the enlightened working class
whose interest it will represent.

No revolution—not even a bourgeois revolution—has ever
succeeded without a period of dictatorship.

If the Soviet power—in Russia—became a dictatorship by a
small party, the guilt lies with the parties that boycotted the
Soviet: the Bund, the Mensheviks, and the Social Revolutionaries.

If we and the PPS did not place ourselves in the position of
the Mensheviks in Russia, we could avoid the situation now
obtaining there.[10]

The centrists, whose primary aim was to keep the Bund
from dividing into two hostile parties, took an anomalous
position in favor both of dictatorship of the proletariat and of
democracy. They rejected democratic forms in a period of
social revolution; but, they said, "until the social revolution
is actually under way we cannot reject the democratic organs
through which we can propagandize the masses." Not to use
democratic institutions would be a serious error. Should these
institutions, however, prove themselves unable to carry out
the social changes the Bund favored, as seemed likely, the
centrists wanted other, more drastic methods used.

It was not necessary, in the centrists' view, that revolutions
be made by a majority; revolutions had historically been
made by minorities. "We cannot refuse to support a revolu-

[10] *Ibid.*, April 29, 1919.

tion because it is the product of a minority, nor can we delay supporting it until a majority is ready to support it." The working class, on whom the Socialist revolution must depend for support, was not yet strong enough, however, to make that revolution. Therefore, the centrists argued, it was necessary to unite with the peasantry in the democratic organs in opposition to the reaction.

The centrists rejected the Communist position on one fundamental issue: the worst enemies of the revolution were not, as the Bolsheviks maintained, the non-Communist Socialists. "The worst enemy is the bourgeoisie." The centrists thus pleaded for a united working-class movement. Bolshevik politics, they charged, led to civil war within the ranks of the revolutionary working-class movement. To achieve unity, the centrists wanted to avoid further splintering.[11]

The Bund had to support the social revolution, which the centrists believed was drawing near. And, in view of the changed conditions which the social revolution's approach implied, they suggested a major ideological change by the Bund—abandonment of the demand for national cultural autonomy. "The social revolution which will shortly occur requires that we adapt our thinking to the new conditions. We must, therefore, now revise the position of our minimum program. . . . The nationality program has until now been based on conditions under the capitalist system . . . in which national cultural autonomy was the only possible demand. Now at the brink of the social revolution, we must reconsider our demand with a view to life in the period of transition." [12]

The optimism of the left and center, the view that a revolution was near, was not shared by the right-wingers. They doubted that the workers, who showed a reluctance to vote for even moderate Socialists, were ready to make a social revolution and accept a dictatorship of the proletariat.

Why, for example, asked Medem, the spokesman for the

[11] *Ibid.*, April 28, 1919.   [12] *Ibid.*

right wing, were the Polish soviets so weak? Why were they so powerless? Because conditions for their growth were not yet present in Poland. That the Russian soviets had become the basis for the anti-democratic Bolshevik takeover was beside the point; the fact was that they were the products of the democratic revolution in Russia. There had been no democratic revolution in Poland, however, especially in view of the rise to power of the Endeks. "You can't leap from rule by the Endeks into soviet rule," he said.[13]

The right-wingers, moreover, believed in democracy as a necessary concomitant of socialism. The question facing the world, they contended, was whether the proletarian majority or the bourgeois minority was to rule. "Then why fear democracy? Because the workers may vote for their class enemies? If this is so, then the workers are not entitled to the blessings of socialism, and the social revolution under any circumstances is impossible. To reject democracy and elections is to seek power for a conspiratorial minority. This would be dishonest; this should be rejected out of hand by the Bund." [14]

"Why not use the democratic institutions?" right-wing delegates asked. What was wrong with using the floor of the Sejm for Socialist propaganda? A Sejm speech would be "heard further than one in a soviet, with so few people in the soviets." Had not Karl Liebknecht's revolutionary speeches in the Reichstag had a greater effect than his talks to small gatherings? [15]

Nor was the right wing sure that an undemocratic seizure of power could lead to genuine socialism. The end result would more likely be a party dictatorship. Its spokesman said:

The soviet system is based on seizure of power by an autocracy —by a minority. It creates a self-anointed power. The soviet constitution gives power to the Communist Party alone to decide who shall have political rights. Opponents are denied

[13] *Ibid.*   [14] *Lebnsfragn*, IV, April 27, 1919.   [15] *Ibid.*

such rights. Instead of power deriving from the people, it derives from the party. The organs of government are not elected by the people but by the Communist Party. Party rule is not controlled from below—it is run from the top. In the end, the party becomes the boss and "the whole comedy of elections" is unnecessary. Power belongs to the Communist Party and not to the soviets; the soviet system is merely a cloak for rule by a one-party oligarchy. The time has come to call a halt to the political game of "hide and seek." [16]

History, the right wing contended, had made fools of the left-wingers, in Poland at least. Their dream of a world revolution at any moment was not borne out by occurrences within Poland. "The wheels of history turn slowly. . . . In Poland they have actually turned back from Moraczewski [a PPS leader who was head of the first Polish government] to Paderewski [the noted pianist, who headed the anti-Semitic, reactionary government in 1919]." [17]

The right wing may have had logic on its side, but it had no victorious revolution to emulate. It was able, with centrist support, to condemn the action at Warsaw and to warn against future breaches of discipline. But it made no effort to offer a resolution in defense of democracy, for it had too little support. The resolution finally adopted, by 52 votes to 15, with 6 right-wingers abstaining, backed soviet power and the dictatorship of the proletariat, with some minor reservations:

> The social revolution, already sweeping the defeated nations, will soon carry over to the victorious nations. The social revolution can be victorious only if it is international in scope. In Poland the capitalist reaction is leading to a revolutionary clash between the workers and the capitalists. The social revolution can achieve socialism—its ultimate goal—only when the workers themselves seize the entire state power in order to use it for the economic transformation of society. In this period of social revolution, the democratic institutions have

[16] *Ibid.*   [17] *Ibid.*

shown their inability to fulfill the revolutionary tasks which are required of the working class. Thus, the rule of the proletariat must take the form of soviets of workers of city and village. The soviet power is transitionary, but necessary for building a Socialist society. Parliamentary institutions must be used only for the spreading of revolutionary propaganda.[18]

The left and center factions were in complete control of the Bund; the old right-wing leaders were distinctly in the minority, although the new central committee was divided equally among the left, center, and right, each of which had two members. The turn to the left was now almost complete.[19]

THE LEFT SEIZES THE BUND

The 1919 convention instensified the struggle between the right and left wings of the party. New issues arose which split the Bund further; internal struggles clouded the external battles and sapped the strength of the once vital organization.

The most important of the new developments that had intensified the struggle was the birth of the Third (Communist) International (commonly known as the Comintern). Formed in January 1919, the Comintern acted as a magnet in attracting the new Communist parties and all the Socialist parties that had become disillusioned with the Second (Socialist) International. The struggle over the issue of international affiliation was to rage unabated within the Bund for ten years.[20]

The struggle began almost immediately after the 1919 convention. The left wing, believing that the Bolshevik seizure of power should serve as an example for the rest of the Socialist movements, wanted to affiliate with the Comintern almost

[18] *Lebnsfragn*, IV, April 30, 1919; Ratman, *loc. cit.*, p. 9.
[19] *Lebnsfragn*, IV, April 30, 1919.
[20] Ratman, *loc. cit.*, pp. 9–10; Leonard Shapiro, *The Communist Party of the Soviet Union* (New York: Random House, 1960), p. 196.

immediately. The centrists, critical though they were of the Bolsheviks, believed that the errors of the October Revolution would in time be corrected. They wanted the left-wing Socialist parties—including the Bund—and the Communists throughout the world to form a new revolutionary Socialist International. The right wing believed, even in the "honeymoon months" immediately following the revolution, that the Bolshevik seizure of power was a catastrophe for world socialism. Medem forecast that the Bolsheviks would kill each other off in a struggle for power. The right-wingers thus favored working with the other Social Democratic parties in an effort to reactivate the Second International.[21]

The right wing, which had previously avoided forming a definite faction, finally organized into a functioning body to prevent the threatened move toward affiliation with the Communist movement. Bernard Goldstein, a trade union leader, with Medem and Michalewicz, formed the group a short time before the Bund was to hold its 1920 convention. The right-wing leaders prepared a scathing denunciation of the Russian regime and a resolution favoring affiliation with the Second International. When it became apparent, however, that the left wing had considerably more support than they had anticipated, the right wing decided to support the centrist position with a slight modification: although they were willing to call for the organization of a new Left-Socialist International, with Communists, they wanted for the moment to remain unaffiliated.[22]

The 1920 convention was officially called for the mundane purpose of incorporating into the Bund the Jewish Socialist Party of Galicia, the part of Poland formerly under Austrian control. Although the merger was accomplished, it occupied an insignificant amount of the convention's time, compared with the question of affiliation with an international.

[21] Bernard Goldstein, *Tsvantski Yor in Varshever Bund* (New York: Ferlag Unser Tsayt, 1960), p. 24.
[22] *Ibid.*, pp. 24–25; Ratman, *loc. cit.*, p. 10.

The Galician party—which was right-wing in its orientation, having been affiliated for more than twenty years with the powerful Austrian Socialist Party—was admitted into the Polish Bund on the first day of the convention. The action was a mere formality. The central committees of the two parties had agreed on unification several months before.[23]

The convention voted to ignore Polish issues and to limit debate to the question of international affiliation and the merits of the internationals. The domestic issues were to be discussed by the party's central committee after the convention.[24]

The Central Committee refused to recommend any action to the convention, fearing that such a recommendation might result in open defiance by either side. It proposed instead that the convention study the issues and reach the decision least likely to destroy the Bund, and most likely to represent the view of the members of the Bund in all of Poland.[25]

The left-wing argument revolved chiefly on the issue of the program of the international. A revolutionary international, argued the spokesmen for the left, had to have a revolutionary program. Since the platform of the Comintern was revolutionary, it followed that the party of the revolutionary Jewish working class should affiliate with the Communist International.[26]

---

[23] The convention at which the unification was decided upon had been held, symbolically, in the Galician city of Cracow. The day before the convention each of the parties held separate gatherings in Cracow and unanimously ratified the move. Sixty of the 86 voting delegates at the convention were from the Bund, and 26 were from the Galician party. Goldstein, *op. cit.*, p. 24; *Lebnsfragn*, April 29, 1919; *Arbeiter Sztyme*, I, April 14, 1920.

[24] *Arbeiter Sztyme*, I, April 21, 1920.

[25] *Ibid.*, April 16, 1920.

[26] *Arbeiter Sztyme*, I, April 8, 1920. The left-wing position was poorly reported in the Bund press. Several issues of *Arbeiter Sztyme*, probably including one in which the left-wing position was more adequately reported, were seized by the Polish regime. See p. 99, below.

The centrists rejected this contention. True, they said, a platform must be revolutionary; but more important than a platform were the activities of an international. And the Comintern's activities were not conducive to Socialist revolution. The Comintern, the centrists charged, was instigating civil war "not against the class enemy but within the working-class parties." They wanted the Comintern to have more than a mere revolutionary platform; they wanted it to include within its ranks the working-class masses and to war against the capitalist system rather than against the Socialist movement.[27]

Erlich, who was now a spokesman for the centrists, attacked the Comintern as an enemy of the revolution. "The Communist International," he told the convention, "is not an international of the revolutionary working class; it is the Russian Bolsheviki!"

The Comintern, he charged, represented a Blanquist tendency that had developed within the left-wing Socialist movement throughout the world. This tendency was due to the growth of the working class after the war; the new workers, most of whom had previously been peasants and members of the lower middle class, had no Socialist background or training, and could thus be easily persuaded to accept anarchist or Blanquist theories.

"We are Social Democrats and not Blanquists," he declared. "We must therefore reject the theory of an 'activist minority.' The organizations of the working class—internationally as well as nationally—must be more than mere groups of conspirators, more than revolutionary general staffs; they must contain in all of their sections the working class itself." [28]

The convention debated the issue of international affiliation for two full days. The discussion was at times acrimonious, with both sides refusing to compromise on the issues. In the

[27] *Ibid.*   [28] *Ibid.*

end, the lure of a successful revolution could not be overcome, and the congress decided to affiliate with the Comintern
in Moscow. But the vote indicated that not all the Bundists
were fully prepared to break with their past; the left could
only carry the congress by a vote of 41 to 30, with 15 delegates abstaining.[29]

Although the final speaker at the convention could note
with some pride that despite sharp differences the Bund remained a united party at a time when the other Jewish
Socialist organizations had split into two hostile organizations, its strength had been sapped by the internal struggle,
and members of both left and right withdrew. From the
left, many members resigned to join the Polish Communist
Party.

From the right, the leading member of the party left
Poland in disgust.[30] Vladimir Medem had rejected all attempts
at compromise. He refused to join the other right-wingers in
supporting the centrists. When the convention backed the
left-wing position, Medem refused to accept any leading
position within the Bund and announced almost immediately
that he was leaving for America. His anger at the Bund's
action led him to veto a planned farewell meeting in his
honor.

Medem told a group of his followers that he doubted
whether the Bund would long remain a pro-Communist
organization, but for so long as it did he wanted nothing to
do with it. Upon his departure for America, where he died in
1923, the right wing was without a leader and the Bund had
lost one of its chief apologists.[31]

Significantly, the Polish Communists were less than

[29] Ratman, *loc. cit.*, p. 10; "Der Ekstra Tsuzamenfor fun Bund in
Poyln," *Der Wecker* (New York), June 28, 1930.
[30] *Arbeiter Sztyme*, I, April 21, 1920; Ratman, *loc. cit.*, p. 10; Goldstein, *op. cit.*, p. 27; Shulman, *loc. cit.*, pp. 154–155.
[31] *Arbeiter Sztyme*, I, April 30, 1920; Goldstein, *op. cit.*, pp. 26–27.

enthusiastic at the Bund's turn to the left. The KPP at its first conference, held within a week of the Bund's convention, called the vote a half-victory over the "anti-revolutionary party leadership." There could be no complete victory for the "revolutionary segment" of the Bund, the Communists said, until it had purged its leadership, abandoned the call for national cultural autonomy, and ceased to insist on a separate organization of Jewish Socialists. The Communists promised to continue their opposition to the Bund until these changes had been made.[32] The Bundists' refusal to oust their leaders or change their stance on cultural autonomy was to keep them out of the Comintern permanently.

REPRESSION FROM THE RIGHT

In 1920 war was raging between the Soviet Union and Poland. The origins of the conflict were to be found in the appetite of Poland's leaders for territory and in the civil war in the Soviet Union. Pilsudski saw the internal strife in the Soviet Union as his opportunity to seize the whole of the Ukraine, Byelorussia, and Lithuania in order to form a federal republic composed of the four nationalities under Polish domination. To carry out his plan, Pilsudski invaded the Ukraine and Byelorussia. Appeals by the Soviet government in late 1919 for a negotiated peace went unheeded. By May 1920, the Polish army had seized Kiev; but within two months, as the Soviet civil war ebbed, the Poles were in full retreat. By August, the Red Army was at the gates of Warsaw.[33]

---

[32] S. Zachariasz, *Di Kommunistishe Bavegung Tsvishn der Idisher Arbeiter Bafelkerung in Poyln* (Warsaw: Ferlag Idisz Bukh, 1954); pp. 124–125; another copy of the resolution, in Polish, is in the Bund Archives, and consists of a newspaper clipping without the name or date of the journal.

[33] This is at best a brief outline of an intricate conflict. See Josef Korbel, *Poland Between East and West* (Princeton University Press,

The morale of the Polish forces was near collapse. The working-class population in the cities, and much of the farm population, were not enthusiastic about supporting a government representing the most reactionary elements in the state.

To regain the support of the working-class population, the Polish military forced the Sejm to name a new government headed by Ignacy Daszynski of the PPS and Wincenty Witos of the Peasant Party. Called a workers' and peasants' government, it had as its real aim to encourage the support of the population for the defense of the capital. Its actions soon belied its title. The new "government of workers and peasants" ignored workers' and peasants' grievances, conscripted Jews and other minorities for work under extremely harsh conditions, permitted a continuation of the anti-Jewish excesses that had been the hallmark of the Endek regime, and conducted a reign of terror against non-PPS Socialist groups, particularly the Bund, the Poale Zion, and a small territorialist group, the Ferainigte.[34]

Although none of the Socialist parties favored the Soviet counterinvasion, none was enthusiastic about the Polish regime. The Bundists, despite their left-wing Socialist orientation, generally opposed the Soviet invasion. They favored a Socialist Poland, but insisted upon the country's independence. They did, however, demand an end to the hostilities and a negotiated peace.[35]

Opposing the war, which they insisted could be settled by negotiation, the Bundists became constantly more outspoken in their antipathy to the Daszynski-Witos government. In the fall of 1920 the Bund participated, with other left-wing

---

1963), pp. 16–59, particularly pp. 39–59; also S. Konovalov, *Russo-Polish Relations* (Princeton University Press, 1945), pp. 71–80.

[34] A. Nayer, "Brief fun Varshe," *Naye Velt*, IX, October 15, 1920, pp. 10–11, 30–31.

[35] A. Nayer, "Brief fun Varshe," *Naye Velt*, IX, October 8, 1920, p. 7; see also May Day proclamation of the Polish Bund in *Arbeiter Sztyme*, I, April 21, 1920.

groups, in a general strike against the militarization of the railroads and for peace with Soviet Russia. The general strike was aimed primarily at bringing down the government and thus forcing an end to hostilities.[36]

The Bund members of city councils denounced the war and called for immediate peace. The most significant of the attacks on the war was delivered by Erlich in the Warsaw City Council on July 8, 1920. "What are we fighting for?" he asked, and gave as the answer, "Land which does not belong to us." He charged that the war was aimed at making Poland an imperialistic power and at destroying whatever hope there was of socialism in Russia.[37]

After his speech had been delivered, before a hushed audience in a crowded chamber, there were cries of "Lynch him!" The five Bund councilmen present found it necessary to flee.[38]

Meanwhile, a report circulated by the Polish government asserted that the Bund had been given 10,000,000 rubles by the Soviet Communist Party in payment for aid during the war. This money had in fact been given to the Russian Bund, which had by this time become pro-Communist,[39] and from whom the Polish Bund had three years previously severed its ties. The pro-government Polish press used this report to raise the cry that the Polish Bund was in the enemy camp and should be declared illegal.[40]

As Bolshevik troops neared Warsaw, the hysterical opposi-

[36] *Folkscajtung*, II, February 17, 1922; Ratman, *op. cit.*, Part II, *Naye Velt*, IX, September 10, 1920, p. 20.

[37] *Robotnik Zydowski*, I, July–August 1920.

[38] A. Nayer, "Der Bund in Poyln," *Naye Velt*, X, October 25, 1921, p. 20.

[39] See Chapter VI.

[40] *Jewish Daily Forward* (New York), November 16, 1920; Emanuel Novogrodsky, "Der Lebnsveg fun Henryk Alter," *Henryk Erlich un Victor Alter* (New York: Ferlag Unser Tsayt, 1951). Novogrodsky places the figure at 5,000,000 rubles. The *Forward* report, written by David Meyer in Warsaw at the time, would appear to be more accurate.

tion to the Bund became intense. "The war against 'the internal enemy' grew stronger; repressions became worse; everywhere they [the regime] saw Bolsheviks." The repressions became so severe that cultural centers and trade unions were disbanded, along with the pro-Bund cooperatives, social clubs, schools, and youth groups.

Among those arrested during the period were Yudel Fink, editor of the *Arbeiter Sztyme*; the entire executive of the Yiddish school organizations in Lwów, Lublin, and Chelm; city councilmen in Warsaw, Piotrkow, Łodz, Lwów, and a score of smaller cities. The *Arbeiter Sztyme* was closed;[41] the Grosser Club in Warsaw was padlocked; in Lublin and Chelm, even the trade union headquarters and food stations were destroyed. The Central Committee of Jewish Unions in Warsaw reported that most of its active members—all of them Bundists—had been imprisoned and that its 30,000 members were leaderless. In effect, the party had been driven underground; it was forced to resume the illegal printing of proclamations and leaflets.[42]

The repressions cast a pall over the Bund. Its attitude toward the war had alienated it further from the PPS. The hope of the Bund's anti-Bolshevik wing for democratic political action within a free Poland had been set back; the increase of anti-Semitism had caused it new anguish and forced it to redirect its efforts from the social revolution to protecting the right of Jewish workers to keep the jobs they held.[43]

[41] After this event the Bund still published a daily paper, using a different name for each issue. Copies of *Arbeiter Tog*, one such issue, are available at the British Museum and in the Bund Archives.
[42] *Robotnik Zydowski*, I, July–August 1920; *Folkscajtung*, II, February 17, 1922; *Jewish Daily Forward*, November 16, 1920; Ratman, *loc. cit.*, p. 20; Nayer, *op. cit.*, October 8, 1920, p. 8; Goldstein, *op. cit.*, pp. 32–34.
[43] The PPS, which had fought anti-Semitism before 1920, now opposed giving the Jews minority status and rejected the Bund insistence that Yiddish be given status as a minority language. See *Jewish Daily Forward*, November 16, 1920; also *Folkscajtung*, II, February 17, 1922.

The Bund had thus turned, at least temporarily, sharply to the left. It had rejected its Social Democratic tradition and had aligned itself with the Bolsheviks, against whom it had fought for fifteen years. In a Poland hostile to Soviet Russia and the Jews, it was on the verge of becoming an ally of the Communists. Only the dogmatism of the Bolsheviks themselves, their insistence on total obedience or nothing, kept the Polish Bund from being absorbed into, and destroyed by, the Communist Party.

VI

The End of the Communist Romance

REPRESSIONS by the government during 1920 and 1921, a period of sharp reaction, had severely damaged the Bund organization throughout Poland. Many party groups and affiliated organizations were eradicated by the regime. The most urgent task facing the Bund was the rebuilding of its organization into a viable political body of Jewish Socialists. But, the internal disagreement became so intense that police repressions were ignored and intraparty warfare raged.[1]

The Bund was not alone in this predicament: two other Polish Jewish Socialist groups had split during that period, one of them disintegrating completely within a short time. The Poale Zion, had divided into pro-Communist and anti-Communist organizations within a year after the Bolshevik Revolution in Russia. The Territorialists likewise split on the issue of Bolshevism; one group went into the Communist Party of Poland, and the other eventually merged with the Bund.[2]

That the Polish Bund itelf did not split was due to the hidebound attitude of the Communists; the Bund's suicide was averted despite itself.

---

[1] Goldstein, *Tvantsik Yor in Varshever Bund* (New York: Ferlag Unser Tsait, 1960) p. 35; "Der Letster Tsusamenfor fun 'Bund'," *Der Wecker* (New York), II, March 18, 1922, p. 13.

[2] H. Goldfinger, M. Mirski, S. Zachariasz (eds.), *Unter der Fon fun KPP* (Warsaw: Ksiazka i Wiedza, 1959), p. 23; *Der Emes* (Moscow Jewish Communist daily), November 18, 1921.

DEATH OF THE RUSSIAN BUND

Where the Bolsheviks held the upper hand, the Bund was unable to exist. The first such group to be destroyed was the Ukrainian Bund. Separated from the rest of the Jewish Socialist movement by the civil wars, and isolated from the rest of the old organization, it was dissolved in 1919 and its members were absorbed into the Kommunistishe Farband, the Jewish section of the Ukrainian Communist Party.[3]

Next to be destroyed was the Russian Bund, which became involved in high-level machinations within the Communist Party of Russia. Originally it was to remain an autonomous group within the Russian Communist Party in much the same manner as the Georgian, Ukrainian, or Byelorussian Communist parties. This was the understanding at the 1920 Bund congress in Minsk at which the decision to enter the Communist Party was made. But the separate identity of the Bund was to be short-lived.

Raphael Abramovitch, leader of the Menshevik wing of the Bund, warned the congress that it would be signing the death warrant for the Bund as a separate organization once it became part of the Communist machine.

> . . . It is against the character and ideology of the Communist Party for there to be any possibility for the legal existence of a separate autonomous political organization of the Jewish proletariat, because the whole of the Bund's position on the nationality question, which the Bund developed over many years, is diametrically opposed to the view of the Communists. . . . As carriers of the banner of the Bund, your days are numbered. In the future you will appear under the banner of the Russian Communist Party. [You] will soon melt into the Russian Communist Party and will lose on the way all that is dear to every Bundist.[4]

---

[3] Vladimir Kossofsky, "Farvos un Vi Azoy der 'Bund' hot Zikh Tseshpoltn," *Zukunft*, XXVI (1921), 40–42.

[4] *Dos Fraje Vort*, April 9, 1921.

Before joining the Communist Party as a separate entity, the Russian Bund asked the Communists to name a separate commission so as to assure its continued existence. The commission was composed of three Bundists, three officials of the Jewish Section of the Communist Party (Yevsektsie), and an arbiter who was chosen by the Communist International. The Yevsektsie had long hated the Bund and had called for its liquidation. Within a matter of months the joint commission, with the Comintern representative supporting the Yevsektsie, decided that the Bund would have to be liquidated.[5]

The decision required the approval of both the Bund and the Communist Party to become effective. The final conference of the Russian Bund in February 1921, was cajoled by Jeremiah Weinshtein, leader of the pro-Bolshevik faction, who feared repressions, and who warned that the consequences of rejection would be far worse than acceptance. Despite Weinshtein's pleas a futile appeal was made to the Communist International for some concessions. In the end the Russian Bund decided to liquidate by a vote of 47 to 29.[6]

The remnants of the pro-Menshevik Bund which refused to enter the Communist Party, were destroyed by mass arrests, repression, and slaughter at the hands of the Russian Bolshevik police. In February 1921 the Moscow Bund Club, which was anti-Bolshevik, was raided twice; all its records were seized, its leaders arrested, its organization destroyed. That same month, mass arrests were made in Kiev, Kharkov, Rostov, Odessa, and Vitebsk. By the end of March there was no Bund organization of any sort left in Russia.[7]

The Vilno Bund organization, which considered itself more Russian than Polish, had split in 1920, the vast majority of its members going over to the Communist Bund. The demise of

[5] Emanuel Novogrodsky, "Der Bund in Kovner Litte," *Forois* (Mexico City), XVIII, April 1957, p. 16; *Dos Fraje Vort*, February 5, 1921.

[6] *Dos Fraje Vort*, April 9, 1921.

[7] *Ibid.*, April 23, 1921.

the Russian Bund left the Vilno majority without a base, and it soon vanished as a separate organization. The right-wing Social Democratic Bund was able, however, to maintain its separate existence until in 1924 it accepted the Polish control of Vilno and entered the Polish Bund.[8]

THE TWENTY-ONE POINTS

The Polish Bund was not the only Socialist Party seeking admission to the Third International; others in Norway, Italy, France, Holland, and the United States were also attempting to join. But the Comintern was not interested in having member parties that would not accept its monolithic rule; it desired, instead, their submission or eradication. It therefore decided at its 1920 congress to set up standards for admission designed to keep out Socialist parties and to force the splitting of the Socialist movements into separate Socialist and Communist parties. According to the official declaration of the Comintern, "The Communist International is being threatened with the danger of dilution by the fluctuating and half-and-half groups which have as yet not abandoned the ideology of the Second International." These groups composed of "reformist and social-pacifist wings" were not to be welcomed into the Communist International.[9]

The Comintern then issued twenty-one conditions for admission into its ranks, two of them obviously designed to prevent even the most radical of Socialist parties from entering. The two points which were to keep the Bund out of the Comintern were the seventh and the twenty-first. The seventh condition was as follows:

> Parties desirous of joining the Communist International must recognize the necessity of a complete and absolute rupture with reformism and the policy of the "centrists" and must

[8] *Unzer Gedank*, September 30, 1922.
[9] "Conditions of Admission to the Communist International," *Communist International*, IV (1924), 173–174.

advocate the rupture amongst the widest circles of the party membership without which condition a consistent Communist policy is impossible. The Communist International demands unconditionally and peremptorily that such rupture be brought about with the least possible delay. . . .[10]

The twenty-first condition was that "those members of the party who reject on principle the conditions and the theses of the Third International are to be excluded from the party." [11]

The nineteen other conditions were acceptable to most left-wing Socialists, but these two were not.[12] The seventh and twenty-first conditions meant that the party would have to split, and that leaders who disagreed with any decision of the Comintern, no matter how ridiculous it might appear in view of local national conditions, would be ousted. The ouster of leaders who might disagree with the Comintern would mean a condition in which the left-wing Socialist movement would alienate itself from the rest of the Socialists and would be in a position of ideological purity and political isolation. It was a policy which had only one intent: to rupture the world Socialist movement and create three separate parties, one right-wing Socialist, one left-wing

[10] *Ibid.*, p. 175.   [11] *Ibid.*, p. 178.

[12] The other conditions included support of the dictatorship of the proletariat, the ouster of "reformists" from positions of control, the creation of illegal underground organizations, agitation in the army, work among peasants, rejection of social-patriotism, fight against imperialism and colonialism, trade union work to be under party control with the destruction of the Amsterdam Trade Union International, limitation of parliamentary delegations to trusted Communists, strong discipline with control in the center, purge of petty-bourgeois support and defense of the USSR, changing of the name to Communist Party, publication by the party press of all Comintern decisions, convening of an extraordinary party congress to accept all twenty-one points, Comintern resolutions to be binding on the party, leading committees to accept Communist programmatic positions and be approved by the Comintern executive, and the party program to be changed from Social Democratic to Communist (*ibid.*, pp. 174–178).

Socialist, the other Communist. Moreover, control of the parties accepting the twenty-one conditions would be transferred from their national executives to the Russian leaders of the Comintern.

The promulgation of the twenty-one points resulted in long and acrimonious debate within the Bund, and caused its factional division to become even more complex. The left wing split into two opposing groups, one favoring the acceptance of nineteen conditions; the other of all twenty-one. The latter was intent upon joining the Communist movement regardless of conditions; it saw Communism as the wave of the future and wanted to be a part of it. The former was dedicated to the traditional policies of the Bund, and was unwilling to have it split into two hostile parties. There were other, minor problems dividing the two left-wing factions, but the two points on which they disagreed constituted the central issue.[13]

The pro-Comintern majority of the Central Committee of the Bund became a minority when two of its members announced that they could not accept the twenty-one points in toto; thereupon the Communists accused them of going over to the centrist faction. Moreover, the pro-Communists argued that since the Central Committee's complexion had been changed by the shift of the two members, the committee no longer reflected the true views of the membership. This, said the pro-Comintern group, was also noticeable in the party press, which was now biased against it.[14]

The Central Committee rejected the twenty-one points, and announced that it could accept only sixteen. Moreover, it expressed the hope that the next congress of the Comintern would change its position to make it possible for the Bund to

[13] *Memorandum fun der Delegatsie fun Idishn Kommunistishn Arbeiter Bund in Poyln (Combund) Tsum Oysfir Komitet fun III Kommunistishn International* (Warsaw: Land Eksekutiv fun Idishn Kommunistishn Arbeiter Bund in Poyln, 1922), p. 5.

[14] *Ibid., Der Wecker* (New York), II, March 18, 1922, p. 13.

join. But it refused under any condition to oust its centrist and moderate leaders or to allow the press to be controlled by an experienced Communist. It inisisted, to quote the Comintern Bulletin, "on the democratic right of the centrist majority to retain the leadership of the party." [15]

The Communists immediately stepped up their campaign to remove the Bund's leaders and replace them with others who would be willing to accept the conditions laid down by the Comintern. The Russian Bund, in one of its last actions before being absorbed into the Communist Party, dispatched a message to the members of the Polish Bund urging them to overturn the decision of the central committee and accept the conditions laid down by Moscow. The message read:

> To the Jewish workers of Poland! Having been informed that the Central Committee of the "Bund" in Poland has passed a resolution rejecting the twenty-one points for admission to the Communist International, the plenum of the Central Committee of the "Bund" of the Federated Soviet Republics appeals to the Jewish working masses of Poland, who are organized under the banner of the "Bund," with the following call:
> "Declare total war against this resolution! Pitilessly condemn the betrayal of this group of misleaders, and all as one unite under the banner of the Communist International!" [16]

Another message to the Bund's members, calling on them to oust their leaders and overturn the decision of the Central Committee, was dispatched by the Comintern Executive Committee. This missive was a duplicate of others sent to all left-wing Socialist parties who had rejected the twenty-one points; its object was, according to one of the leading pro-Communist Bundists, to deepen the strife then rending all Socialist Parties and to improve the position of the Communist factions before they instigated a formal split within

[15] "To All Members of the All-Jewish Workers' Union (The Bund) of Poland," *Bulletin of the Executive Committee of the Communist International*, II, September 20, 1921, pp. 43–44.
[16] *Dos Fraje Vort*, March 19, 1921.

the parties. The effect of the letter was to sharpen the internecine fight; it led to the formation of an organized Communist faction within the Bund, the "Combundishe Fraktsie." The faction adopted its own platform, which accepted the twenty-one conditions laid down by the Comintern and implied that it had no intention of becoming a separate organization, but would be a part of the Communist Party of Poland.[17]

The Comintern now opened an unrelenting attack on the Bund's leadership by dispatching a second message to the membership, going over the head of the Central Committee. It charged that the Bund leaders had adopted a "centrist, reformist, nay, counterrevolutionary character . . ." The Bund leaders had now assumed a stance, said the Comintern, which was anti-Communist in tone, and which the left wing was making no effort to counteract. The Bund organs had been used for the publication of "Martov's manifestoes" (Martov was then leader of the left-wing Menshevik movement) and for "Menshevik campaigns against Soviet Russia."

> We see before us an old workers' organization that is entrapped with strong social democratic and partly nationalist traditions, which has gone through the war and the revolution without any splits and [which] is being led by confused centrists. There is a "left wing" within the party, supported by a considerable part of the workers organized in the Bund which harbors strong and upright sympathy for Communism, but [which] is sadly lacking in clearheadedness and resoluteness.
>
> The prime task of these elements is to organize into a solid, conscious wing, to take an unreserved stand on the basis of the Third International and all the [decisions] of its congresses, and to take up a decided struggle against the centrists and nationalists for the conquest of the majority of the party. It will be the duty of these comrades not only to recognize the spiritual

---

[17] Minc, *op. cit.*, p. 82; Goldstein, *op. cit.*, pp. 38–39; *Memorandum . . . International*, p. 6.

leadership of the Comintern but also unhesitatingly to co-operate in closest union with the Communist Party of Poland. It will be the duty of the Communist Party of Poland to lend every assistance to the really revolutionary elements of the Bund. The former policy of systematic sabotage of the decisions . . . and the everlasting capitulations and compromises, of distrust and separatism as against the Communist Party must be totally abandoned for courageous, clear, and militant tactics.[18]

The second letter rent the Bund further; groups of pro-Comintern Bundists, particularly in Łodz, tried to persuade the majority of the members to accept the twenty-one conditions. The Combund Fraktsie worked closely with the Jewish Section of the Polish Communist Party. Internal strife grew more intense within the Bund; whole groups of Bundists were reported going into the Communist Party. The pro-Comintern group within the Bund was particularly active against members of the "so-called left-wing," trying to force them to "clarify their position with regard to the Comintern." [19]

The Bund still hoped for an easing of the twenty-one points so that it might be able to enter the Comintern as a body. The Bund sent three emissaries to negotiate with the Comintern. The first of these, Emanual Novogrodsky, a leader of the "nineteen-point left wing," went at the end of 1920, while the Polish-Russian war still raged. The meeting was to be held in Kovno, near the Russian-Polish frontier. To reach Kovno, Novogrodsky had to travel a circuitous route, leaving all of his personal effects behind in Grodno in order not to endanger the Bund. He met in Kovno with secret representatives of the Comintern, and it was arranged for him to travel to Moscow with a trainload of repatriated Red Army soldiers. The futile trip to Russia was made after

[18] *Bulletin of the Executive Committee of the Communist International,* II, p. 44.
[19] *Der Emes* (Moscow), November 18, 1921.

long delays, caused in most part by the Communists' reluctance to confer with him.

The two other emissaries, Victor Alter and Haym Vasser, were sent as consultative delegates to the Third Congress of the Comintern in Moscow in the spring of 1921. Alter, traveling under the pseudonym of Lorman, was arrested shortly after his arrival and after long delay was expelled from Russia for "trespass against the Soviet Republic." Vasser was never given the floor at the Comintern Congress, and the Comintern reported that the delegation "failed to get the desired results." [20]

A leader of the Combund faction of the Polish Bund, P. Minc, also traveled to Moscow at this time to receive instructions from the leaders of the Comintern. He went circuitously from Warsaw to Moscow and met in the Soviet capital with Weinshtein. The latter wanted the Polish Bund to overthrow its right-wing leaders and become a Communist party. He suggested that the Bund could remain a separate organization within the Comintern if it acted speedily. "If we had immediately supported the Bolsheviks we could have saved the Bund in Russia," he told Minc. "Go to Poland, split the Bund, get rid of your right wing and you'll be accepted in the Comintern. Don't repeat our errors by waiting until it is too late. Split the Bund." Weinshtein assured Minc that a Polish Combund would be admitted into the Comintern. Minc agreed, and money for the trip back to Poland was supplied by the Russian party. [21]

Minc's secret mission was discovered by the Bund when Stefan Krulikowski, a leader in the Polish Communist Party, inadvertently told a leader of the Bund right wing that Moscow had ordered Comrade Alexander (a pseudonym used by Minc) to return to Warsaw with the specific task of disrupting the party and forcing it to split. Called before the

[20] *Bulletin of the Executive Committee, loc. cit.*, p. 44; Novogrodsky, *loc. cit.*, p. 15.
[21] Minc, *op. cit.*, pp. 75–78.

Bund Central Committee, Minc admitted the charge and was ousted.[22]

The Comintern sent two other agents to Warsaw in an effort to split the Bund; they were Jacob Levine and Moshe Rafes. Both had been important Bundists before the revolution; Levine had worked for the underground Bund in Warsaw before the war, and Rafes had been the Bund representative in the Ukrainian Rahde. Rafes worked overtly among the Bundists; Levine denied that he had tried to wreck the Bund in Poland.[23]

CONDITIONS FOR VICTORY

The Communists should have been able to capture the Bund with a minimum of difficulty. Conditions were propitious for a Communist takeover of the Jewish Socialist movement in Eastern Europe, and the Comintern did succeed in most of the area. That the Communists failed in Poland can be blamed on their making certain conditions so onerous that few Bundists would accept them.

Major concessions had been made by the Bolsheviks to Jewish claims of cultural autonomy, concessions that ran completely counter to pre-revolutionary Bolshevik dogma. Moreover, the concessions came on the heels of growing anti-Semitism in Poland which brought with it political and economic disabilities.

Before the October Revolution, the Bolsheviks and the Polish Social Democrats had been opposed to any form of national cultural autonomy. Yet after the revolution the Bolsheviks granted—under the pressure of changed conditions—many concessions to what they had previously considered "Jewish separatism" in the USSR, organizing separate

[22] Goldstein, *op. cit.*, p. 37. Minc left the Communists in the 1930's and returned to the Bund. He died at Buenos Aires in 1959.

[23] Goldstein, *op. cit.*, p. 36; Yaakov Dar, "Ver iz Niderik Gefalln?", *Letste Nayes*, Tel Aviv, January 25–29, 1959.

Jewish sections in the Communist Party in the Ukraine and Byelorussia. Yiddish cultural organizations and schools were set up, and in a few local soviets Yiddish was permitted as the official language.

The Soviet actions affected the position of the Polish Communist Party, which had formerly opposed cultural autonomy for the Jews. The KPP changed its organizational structure and granted its Jewish sections considerably more autonomy, without relinquishing the Communist principle of strong central control.

Concessions by the Bolsheviks considerably influenced numbers of Bundists, but most of these were already in the pro-Communist camp. They saw in the Soviet concessions to the cultural autonomy of the Jews the removal of the last obstacle in the way of the Bund's affiliation with the Comintern, even on the hard terms laid down by the latter. But the effort was doomed to failure; the Bundists believed that despite the Soviet concessions, their existence as a separate organization was threatened. Moreover, they refused to change their stand rejecting the nationalism of the PPS and the pro-Moscow, left-wing ideology of the Communist Party of Poland.[24]

THE DANZIG CONVENTION

Dissension and internal strife had reached such a pitch that the Bund was close to disintegration. Its meetings almost invariably turned into verbal battles, replete with acrimonious accusations and charges of betrayal of principle and counter-revolutionary intrigue. The situation had become so malignant that the leadership of the Bund, intent on ending the strife, called a convention to decide whether to reject or accept the terms laid down by the Comintern.

Because of police repression it was impossible to hold the

[24] See Minc, *op. cit.*, pp. 54–55.

meeting in Poland. The police were not interested in the Bund's decision, but they were interested in preventing the Jewish Socialists from functioning. The convention was thus held in the Free City of Danzig on the border of Poland. Even in Danzig, which at that time had a democratic government, it was necessary to hold sessions in secret for fear of the Polish police agents stationed in the city.[25]

Three factions were represented at the congress; the left wing, which wanted to accept nineteen of the twenty-one points; the Combund, which called for unequivocal acceptance of the twenty-one conditions; and the center right, which considered the conditions totally unacceptable although it was willing, with reservations, to accept sixteen of them. The once dominant right wing was too weak to offer a program of its own, and supported the center-right faction. Forty-nine delegates were elected by secret ballot on a proportional basis. There were twenty-six left-wing delegates, seventeen from the center right, and six from the Combund Fraktsie. An attempt before the election to develop a fourth position acceptable to the other three met with failure.[26]

It was apparent from the outset that the left wing would be in control of the congress and that the Combund faction would leave the Bund. The presidium at the congress, composed of one centrist and two left-wing delegates, refused to allow Rafes, as official representative of the Comintern, to attend the sessions.[27]

The debate on affiliation with the Comintern raged throughout the convention. Each side presented its position, each side argued the issue in detail; and no one's position was altered by the opposing arguments.

The spokesman for the center right charged that the Com-

---

[25] Goldstein, *op. cit.*, p. 38; interview with I. S. Hertz, New York, December 28, 1963.
[26] *Folkscajtung*, 17 February 1922.
[27] "Der Letster Tsusamenfor fun 'Bund'," *Der Wecker* (New York), II, March 18, 1922, p. 13.

intern's stand was not designed to develop an international of revolutionary Socialists, or to further revolutionary socialism. Rather, the object of the twenty-one points was to "carry out the ideal of a powerful garrison centralism." Splitting tactics, he said, could only result in weakening the forces of the social revolution and strengthening the forces of capitalism and reaction. "The splitting of the West European Socialist parties was an outrage, especially since the splits occurred while the wave of revolution was on the descent." It was obvious to the center-right wing that the Comintern had no intention of compromising over the twenty-one points, and that therefore any suggestion that the Bund could still negotiate its entry into the Third International was ludicrous. The only way the affiliation could be achieved was by yielding; and in that way the party would eventually disappear. The demise of the Bund as a price for affiliation was unacceptable to the center-right faction: "The entry into the Comintern must not be purchased at the expense of the existence of the Jewish labor movement." [28]

The position of the left wing was basically unchanged; it still considered itself tied ideologically to the Comintern; but it rejected the condition of all twenty-one points or none.

The Combund faction insisted that "the twenty-one points are a unity and they must all be accepted without exception. The party must split and join the Comintern." Accepting the twenty-one points would not mean the liquidation of the Bund, the faction maintained, because there would still be room for independent Jewish Socialist action. The Combund faction wanted unity with the Polish Communist Party, but first it would be necessary to accept all of the twenty-one points. "The [non-Combund] left was consistent for three years; now it is frightened and retreating." Only full acceptance of the twenty-one points could assure that the Bund would be a genuinely revolutionary Marxist party.[29]

[28] *Ibid.*, p. 14.   [29] *Ibid.*

The congress, as expected, adopted the left-wing position. It proclaimed its close kinship with the Comintern, and then it decided to reject the twenty-one points.

> The twenty-one points are designed to assure the ability of parties to carry on the class struggle. These healthful directives are, however, not necessary here. Practically, the twenty-one points must be tailored to the concrete conditions of each party separately. The split called for by the twenty-one points would have made the Jewish proletariat unable to perform its tasks. At this time, when all available power is needed by the Jewish workers, a split would have a disastrous effect. It would liquidate and destroy the Bund.
>
> It is no secret that the Jewish working-class movement is accused of chauvinism, ghetto psychology, etc., whenever it calls for autonomy. This shows a lack of understanding of minimum Jewish needs. The problem is complicated by refusal to accept the idea that only in a healthy autonomy is there hope. There is a need for independent political existence for Jewish Socialists. The Bund calls for general unity of the working-class movements—with an autonomous Jewish movement within it. The Jewish working class chose to build an autonomous division—because only in autonomy can it settle its peculiar problems.[30]

The Bund thus repeated the stand it had taken eighteen months earlier at Cracow, with one significant change—it now knew that it was barred from joining the Comintern. The convention reiterated that the Bund was outside the Comintern only because it could not accept all twenty-one points, and not for reasons of principle. The Bundists reaffirmed their desire to be admitted, and their opposition to the Socialist International or any attempt to organize a "diluted" revolutionary Socialist international.

> There are two camps, the Second and the Third [Internationals]; any attempt to organize anything between the Second and the Third is a crime. The only revolutionary camp is the

[30] *Ibid.*, p. 13; *Folkscajtung*, January 6, 1922.

Third. Its platform is good and so, too, are its tactics. All that is wrong is its insistence that we split asunder. This means that we are officially outside, but we will still be tied, ideologically, to the Third International; its tactics will be our tactics.[31]

Seven of the eleven members of the new central committee were from the left faction, and four were from the center-right.[32] A new set of party rules aimed at ending the bickering and strife within the Bund, and incidentally at getting rid of the Combund faction, was adopted. Organized factions were prohibited, party control was vested in the central committee, and individuals were prohibited from negotiating with other parties. Although free discussion among Bundists and variance of opinion were still permitted, these were limited to discussions within the organization.[33]

THE COMBUND

The Combund faction took no part in the debate or discussions at the congress after its defeat on the issue of the twenty-one points. One of the six Combund faction delegates withdrew from the group immediately and joined the left-wing majority, leaving the Combund faction with only five of forty-nine. The Combund leaders decided, in view of their weak showing, to remain in the Bund for a short time and to engineer splits at the local level, particularly in Warsaw, Łodz, and Cracow, which were the main centers of its strength. The ouster of Minc made it obvious that a split had to be accomplished as speedily as possible lest the other leaders of the faction be forced out before the Bund could be disrupted further. But the plan met almost immediate obstacles when two more delegates of the Combund faction withdrew and joined the left-wing majority.[34]

[31] "Der IIIer Tsusamenfor fun Algemajner Idishn Arbeiter Bund in Poyln," *Arbeiter Luakh* (Warsaw), VI (1925), 243.

[32] *Der Emes* (Moscow), February 5, 1922.

[33] *Der Wecker*, II, March 18, 1922, p. 15.

[34] *Der Emes*, February 5, 1922; *Memorandum . . . International*, p. 7; Hertz interview.

The Combund tactic was to charge at meetings of Bund locals that the Danzig convention was not an authentic tribune of the membership, that it was based upon lies, and that another meeting should be called immediately to reverse its decisions. Failing to win their point, Combundists bolted from the meetings and formed their own organizations. A conference of such groups, now formally called Combund locals, was held in late January 1922, and set up the Jewish Communist Workers Bund (Combund) of Poland, which affiliated with the Comintern on the basis of the twenty-one conditions.[35]

The Socialist Bund was almost immediately involved in a struggle for control of the trade-union movement. The Combund journal attacked the Bund as a "rightist, centrist, and opportunist organization" with a revolutionary past but no revolutionary present or future, and called for its utter destruction. Within the trade unions the Combund joined forces with the Communist Party to disrupt and, where possible, seize control of organizations. Among those who went into the Combund on ideological grounds were active trade unionists, including the leaders of the textile, leather, and paper trades. The bickering and fighting drove many pro-Bund members from union activity; others were physically expelled from the labor movement. The leather workers' union, long one of the strongest pro-Bund organizations in the Polish labor movement, went over to Combund control almost immediately; the leaders of the clothing workers' union soon thereafter backed the Combund. The situation appeared to be disastrous for the Bund; the official Communist organ could boast: "Our party makes steady gains as the national Socialist parties, PPS, Bund, and Poale Zion, lose consistently."[36]

[35] *Memorandum . . . International*, p. 8; *Resolutsie fun Comintern Vegn Anshlus fun'm Combund in Comintern* (Warsaw: Land Eksekutiv fun Idisher Kommunistishn Arbeiter Bund, 1922), p. 15.
[36] *Folkscajtung*, February 24, 1922; *Der Emes*, February 5, 1922; *Der Gedank* (Warsaw), February 1922; *Unzer Gedank* (Vilno), I,

Where the Communists could not win control they tried to use force against the Bund, their objective being to capture or destroy. The use of physical terror between radical and union groups was new. Combundists used fists, knives, and guns in their effort to destroy the Bund unions; in these attacks they were joined by anti-Semites and police loyal to the reactionary government. "We have been forced to spend 90 per cent of our energies repelling the attacks by the Comintern," the Bund leader Henryk Erlich reported. The attacks made it almost impossible for the Bund to undertake any organizational work. Its protests to the Combund or the Communist party merely brought vituperative replies. The attacks were carried out regardless of the consequences or the type of organization or meeting that was to be disrupted. One meeting called to protest an anti-Semitic action by the government was broken up by Combund members after they had failed in their effort to seize control. The attacks became so serious that the plenum of the central committee of the trade union federation formally protested.[37]

The Combund had as its primary objective the destruction of the Bund by winning away as many members as possible. The Comintern had not intended the Combund to exist for a period longer than would be needed to attract the left-wing Bundists into the Communist movement. After this mimimal task had been accomplished, it was to be liquidated in the same manner as the Russian Combund. But early liquidation was not favored by those who helped form the Combund; many of them wanted to continue as a separate Jewish organization in opposition to the Social-Democratic Bund. This group, led by Minc, still believed in the need for an autono-

---

August 19, 1922; *Glos Komunistyczny*, I, September 1922, December 1922; Goldstein, *op. cit.*, pp. 35–36.

[37] *Folkscajtung*, January 27, 1922, February 24, 1924; *Der Emes*, February 4, 1922; *Arbeiter Luakh*, VI (1925), 238, 228; Goldstein, *op. cit.*, pp. 41–42; "A Blik in Varshe," *Der Wecker* (New York), II, February 25, 1922, p. 11.

mous Jewish organization within the Communist movement in Poland.[38]

It was apparent almost from the outset that the Combund was to be a short-lived organization. The Communists' desire to have it liquidated was the main cause of its short existence. Moreover, only a few Bundists were lured into the new organization, and most of those had favored the twenty-one points. Many even of those who favored the Comintern's conditions did not join; some became politically passive, some joined the Polish Communist Party, and others who believed that eventually they could prevail upon the Bund to accept the conditions remained within the old organization. In the end, less than 10 per cent of the Bund went into the new Combund.[39]

Within a month after its organization the leaders of the Combund realized that it had failed. At its first conference the organization set as its immediate goal "closer relations between the revolutionary Polish and revolutionary Jewish workers and the creation of a unified Communist Party in Poland." The Combund, it was decided, was to exist for one purpose only: to carry on special propaganda among the Jewish working-class movement, to seize the movement, and to war against the Bund in an effort to destroy whatever influence the Bundists might have over the Jewish workers. When it had accomplished that task, the Combund proposed to liquidate and enter the Polish Communist Party.[40]

The Polish party was less than enthusiastic about the Combund; it accepted the organization only after it had been ordered to do so by the Comintern. Once the Combund had been organized, it became a source of irritation to the KPP. The Combundists, many of whom had long experience in the revolutionary movement, were unwilling to take orders from the party leaders, whom they considered upstarts.[41]

Negotiations for the merger of the Combund and the Com-

---

[38] Minc, *op. cit.*, p. 82.   [39] *Ibid.*, p. 83.
[40] *Memorandum . . . International*, pp. 9–10.
[41] Minc, *op. cit.*, p. 82; *Der Emes*, February 5, 1922.

munist Party began almost as soon as the Combund was organized. The central question in the discussions was organizational; ideological questions were ignored. By February 1922, Moshe Rafes could report to Moscow that "the time is at hand when the Combund and the Polish Communist Party will merge into one party, and for the first time in the thirty-year history of the Jewish workers' movement the vanguard of the Jewish and Polish proletariat will flow as one centralized class party." But things did not go as smoothly as he predicted; almost immediately there were disagreements, and a joint commission had to be formed to iron them out. Finally, after months of negotation, only one issue remained unsolved: whether or not the Combund would be allowed to continue separate activities designed to attract more Jewish workers to the Communist cause. The party was adamant: it would not permit any independent groups within it, nor would it allow any action which it did not control. The Combund finally yielded, and by September 1922 it had been liquidated.[42]

The merger occurred at a moment of the Combund's lowest ebb. Union elections in Łodz and Cracow, in which the Combund had seemed certain to show great strength, proved it to be extremely weak. In the Warsaw Jewish cooperative, the Combund polled only 12 per cent of the vote, and in nationwide trade union elections it polled less than 10 per cent.[43] So the Polish Combund ended with a whimper.

CONCLUSION

Why, then, did the Bund not disintegrate? All the conditions for a total collapse were present: an opposition from the left within the party, an even more powerful opposition from

[42] *Der Emes*, February 5, 1922, February 11, 1922; *Memorandum . . . International*, p. 12; Minc, *op. cit.*, pp. 82–83; *Folkscajtung*, February 24, 1922.
[43] "Der Erfolg fun di Royte in Poyln," *Der Wecker* (New York), II, July 15, 1922.

the government on the right. The issue on which the Bund decided to remain outside the Communist International was not one of basic ideology: the Bund was ready to accept the discipline of the Comintern, it merely refused to accede to the twenty-one conditions as a matter of organizational method.

Rafes, the Bundist turned Communist, came close to explaining the phenomenon:

> Splits and differences, this has been the leitmotiv of the Russian and Polish movements during the past twenty-five years. "Unity at any price," that was the policy of the Bund. The Bund . . . lived through difficulties in these twenty-five years and remained whole. Even after the Bund had split in the Ukraine and Russia, Medem and Kossofsky declaimed that this was caused by disorganization of the Jewish working-class movement in the land of the Soviets, and that in Poland, where there is a mass Jewish movement, there would be no split.[44]

Rafes then condemned the insistence upon "unity within the Bund and separatism for the Jewish working-class movement," which he considered the hallmark of the Bund's "outspokenly nationalist ideology in recent times." But he misunderstood the real nature of the Bund's unity.

Even Medem, in his explanation of why the Polish Bund did not collapse during this period, misunderstood the basic underlying factor. Parties split, he wrote,

> . . . when differences make them, in fact, two distinct groups —differences not alone of theory but of the practical problems of actual politics. An example would be when one faction is friendly to an existing regime and the other fights and opposes the regime. Such was the case of the Bolsheviks and Mensheviks in Russia from 1917 on; such was the case in Russia's Bund. But this was not the case in Poland under any conditions; the conditions were totally different. The Russian Bund had to decide whether to back the Bolshevik regime or oppose it. This was the real issue, and it had to be met. But this was not the case with the Polish Bund. There was no government to sup-

[44] *Der Emes*, February 11, 1922.

port (except perhaps the short-lived PPS regime in 1918). There was never any question of supporting the government. There were never the slightest illusions. It would in fact have been impossible to have any illusions at the time of the Lemberg pogroms or the first shootings into Warsaw labor demonstrations. Perhaps Moraczewski [first PPS premier of Poland] was the Polish Kerensky. . . . But if in Russia Kerensky—knowingly or not—set the stage for the Bolshevik seizure of power, Moraczewski—knowingly or not—set the stage for capitalist-aristocratic reaction. . . . His heir was not Lenin, it was Paderewski.[45]

Although this explains why the Russian Bund fell an easy prey to the Communists, it fails to explain why the Polish Bund was not absorbed even though the Bundists were overwhelmingly in favor of a program linked to the Communists. Why, then, did the Polish Bundists refuse to accept the twenty-one points or to oust the right wing?

Medem gave the answer when he noted the strong adherence of the Bundists to the myth of the organization: "The Bund became a mass party in the worst Czarist days. It was cemented by the blood and tears of its martyrs. Blood and tears are thicker than the ink with which platforms are written." [46] It was the myth of the Bund, the indefinable "cause," that saved it. The Bund's rejection of the twenty-one points showed the Bund as it really was—an *ecclesia militanta*.

[45] Vladimir Medem, "Farvos iz der Bund in Poyln Nit Farnandergefaln," *Zukunft*, XXVI (1921), 160. Lemberg is the German name for Lwów.
[46] *Ibid.*, p. 161.

VII

Return to
Democratic Socialism

THERE was at times an Alice-in-Wonderland aura about the Bund. In the midst of political and ethnic oppression—its editors in prison, its trade-union headquarters padlocked, its cultural and educational institutions under interdict by the government—the Bund debated which of three internationals it should join. The escape from the real, immediate world, the dream of power in an international Socialist organization, the anticipation of having a forum for grandiose pronunciamentos and for learned discourses on the meaning of obscure passages from Marx—all of these were of distinct importance to the intellectuals who led the Bund but who were impotent in the political actualities of Poland.

In the 1920's there were erratic and violent upheavals throughout Poland, and no group suffered more than the labor and Socialist movement. Government power was generally in the hands of the chief antidemocratic forces in the country: the anti-Semitic, nationalist, clerical parties. When the power was in more friendly hands the reactionary parties turned to violence, or the rulers betrayed the trust of the democratic element and joined forces with the reactionaries. And there was no easier scapegoat for governmental or economic disaster than the Jews.

During the 1920's the basis was laid for the re-emergence of the Bund as a democratic Socialist party, which in the last days of Poland's independence was to become the voice of the Jewish community and a powerful force in the growing democratic Socialist movement in the nation. This period was the end of the Bund's search for alliance with the Communists, and the beginning of a serious, though very often futile, dialogue with PPS, the powerful Polish Socialist Party.

A TIME OF OPPRESSION

During the period immediately following its rejection of the Communist conditions for becoming part of the Third International, the Bund had to withstand attacks from two sides. From the right, as part of the labor movement in general, it was under assault by the nationalist, reactionary government; from the left, as a non-Bolshevik Socialist party, it was under constant attack by the Communists.

"The position of our party in the past three years has been particularly trying," Noah Portnoy, the chairman of the Bund, reported in 1924. "Not only did we have to withstand the attacks from the general, and Jewish, reaction and clerical-ism, but we also had to fight off the wild attacks by the Reds against the organizations of the Jewish proletariat generally, and our party in particular."[1]

The left-wing press was unable to operate effectively under the repressions of the government; issues containing articles unfriendly to the government were seized and editors were jailed, often for long terms. The Bund journal *Uncer Cajt* was one of the first to be confiscated; Jan Hempel, editor of the left-wing Polish magazine *Kultura Robotnicza*, was sen-tenced to two years in prison for publishing an excerpt from *The Communist Manifesto*. Almost every left-wing publica-tion was confiscated at one time or another during that period, and newspaper editors lived with the threat of imprisonment hanging over their heads.[2]

Schools organized by the Bund, and sympathetic cultural

---

[1] "Der IIIer Tsusamenfor fun Algemajner Idishn Bund fun Poyln," *Arbeiter Luakh*, VI (1925), 221.
[2] *Ibid.*, p. 229; *Unzer Gedank*, April 26, 1922; L. T., "Reaction in Poland," *The Nation*, CXVIII (May 11, 1924), 570.

organizations, were likewise liquidated by the government. The schools were among the few educational institutions in Poland that offered secular education to Jewish students. The government prohibited the Bund-sponsored schools from issuing diplomas, thus preventing Jewish students from continuing their education, and then closed down all Polish *gimnazja* (secondary schools) that offered to accept students from these Jewish folk schools. When the Jewish schools continued to operate even though their graduates could not continue elsewhere, the government found legal means to destroy them. The organization Uncer Kinder, that ran the schools, was closed on the pretext that it had close relations with "Communist organizations," though in fact was in no way connected with the Communist movement; its only political affiliation was with the right-wing element in the Bund.[3]

The repressions were described in 1924 by a Ukrainian Social Democratic member of the Polish Sejm:

> Wherever workers or peasants are trying to organize for their common struggle for the betterment of their hard life, immediately the police interfere, and under various pretexts and in various ways disband the workers' and peasants' Socialist groups, educational institutions, and trade unions.
>
> The Ukrainian Social Democratic Party is thirty years old, but neither under the Austrian authorities nor during the rule of the Czar's army has it been more viciously persecuted than at the present time.[4]

Although the labor movement generally was persecuted by the regime, its most particular target was the Jewish unions. Secret sessions of judicial bodies would decide which union to liquidate; police would then seize all its records, padock its offices, and arrest its officials. In Warsaw at least two-thirds of all trade unions were outlawed during this period, and Jewish unions found it extremely difficult to resume after the

---

[3] *Unzer Gedank*, September 2, 1922; April 14, 1923.
[4] Quoted in *The Nation*, CXVIII, 569.

police raids. Nine local unions affiliated with the Bund were completely disbanded in the three years between 1921 and 1924, and more were liquidated in other cities.[5]

In October 1923, the repressions reached their climax when an explosion ripped through the Citadel in Warsaw. The incident, of unknown origin, resulted in mass arrests of labor leaders, on the pretext that they had Communist affiliations. Three hundred and fifty union locals were closed down; Jewish unions in particular were raided and padlocked for long periods. More than 12,000 union members were arrested during the two weeks following the explosion.

The repressions took on a more deadly form in 1924. Throughout Poland, strikers and labor demonstrators were now shot down by police. In Tarnow and Borislav four strikers were slain; in Cracow during a general strike, the gendarmerie massacred eleven workers, and police killed two miners who asked for unemployment pay or advances on wages.[6]

Nor could the leftists count on cooperation in the face of a common enemy between the various parties; they were apparently more interested in fighting one another on issues of a theoretical nature than in protecting one another from assault. On May 1, 1922, an attack by nationalist hooligans on a Bund demonstration met with no resistance from either the Communists or the members of the PPS who were meeting near by. An agreement between the groups was ignored; the Communists propagandized against the Bund even during the attack.[7]

<hr>

[5] Henri Barbusse, "Jailing Workers in Poland," *The Nation*, CXX (March 11, 1925), 262; David Meyer, "Der Itztiger Tsushtand fun der Arbeiter Bavegung in Poyln,' *Der Wecker* (New York), III, August 16, 1924, p. 4.

[6] Barbusse, *loc. cit.*, p. 263; L. T., *The Nation*, CXVIII, 568.

[7] "Der Ershter Mai Pogrom oyf Idishe Arbeiter," *Der Wecker* (New York), II, June 3, 1922, pp. 12–13.

UNITY OF THE TRADE UNIONS

Harassed by continuing persecutions, the Polish trade-union movement was faced with the alternative of unity or destruction. The Polish trade union federation, Zwiazek Stowarzyszeń Zawodych w Polce, with 500,000 members, was under the aegis of the PPS; the Jewish unions, with 30,000 members in a limited number of trades, were closely allied with the Bund. There were also unions under Communist control. In 1922 a Jewish union federation, Wydzial Zydowski przy Komisji Centralnej, was formed by the Bund unions and a few others affiliated with the left-wing Poale Zion. The Communist unions refused to join in this federation, although they had almost all originally been Bund affiliates. Instead, they decided to give up their separate existence and become part of the Polish unions.

The PPS union organization wanted all of the unions except the Communist to be united into a single federation. The Bund insisted that the Communist unions were to be included in any united organization. After considerable negotiations, the PPS agreed, on condition that the executive committee of the new federation would be composed of a PPS majority, a Bund minority, and no Communists. The Bund refused, insisting that the Communists were entitled to proportional representation. Finally the PPS, realizing it could overwhelm the Communist minority at will, made a completely different arrangement in secret talks with the Communists; the PPS received the majority, the Communists the minority, and the Bund was left out of the executive completely. Under these conditions of fraternal distrust and betrayal, the United Polish Trade Union Federation was born.[8]

[8] Goldstein, *Tsvantsik Yor in Varshever Bund* (Ferlag Unser Tsait, 1960), p. 57; *Der Emes* (Moscow), June 7, 1923; David Meyer, "Der Itztiger Tsushtand fun der Arbeiter Bavegung in Poyln," *Der Wecker*

THE ELECTION OF 1922

Because of persecution and internal bickering, the labor and Socialist parties faced almost certain defeat in the national election of 1922. The Bund (which had boycotted the election of 1919) was participating in its first election since Poland had become independent. It nominated its leading members for the Sejm, and adopted a typical Socialist platform. Its program was an appeal for democracy and economic ameliora-tion. It called for an eight-hour day, improved working con-ditions, sickness and unemployment benefits, free press, free speech, amnesty for political prisoners, cultural autonomy for the minorities in Poland, civil rights and equality for the Jews, disarmament, and normal foreign relations with all nations, particularly with Poland's neighbor Soviet Russia.[9]

The Bund ran an extremely active campaign; it held meet-ings, distributed thousands of handbills, posted signs on the walls, and sent agitators from door to door in the Jewish areas. Its work was made more difficult by the combined forces of the police and the Communists. The police, in an attempt to prevent the Bund from holding meetings, advised owners of theaters and auditoriums not to rent to the organi-zation. When a hall was rented anyhow, police agents would try to stir up disorders as an excuse to disband the meeting; or they would keep close watch on the speeches, and at the first untoward remark about the government in power they would call a halt to the rally for "inciting against the government." All this made it difficult for the Bund to conduct an effective campaign; moreover, there was the added burden of raising

---

(New York), III, August 16, 1924, p. 12. The Union federations are listed in *The Activities of Trade Unions, 1922–1924* (Amsterdam: International Federation of Trade Unions, 1925), p. 13. The Yiddish name of the Jewish Federation was *Tsentral Komitet fun Idishe Pro-fesionale Feraynen.*

[9] *Unzer Gedank,* September 23, 1923.

funds to bribe police officials and their agents into allowing meetings to be held undisturbed.

The Communists could not be bought off; they were determined to destroy the Bund, since they considered it an impediment in the path to revolution. Thus its meetings were invariably invaded by Communists who created disturbances, giving the police yet another cause to disband them on the grounds of disturbing the peace. Bundist bill-posters, wagons carrying Bund placards, and house-to-house campaigners were set upon by their left-wing enemies. No such attacks were made against the PPS, after a first attempt in which the Communists were severely beaten, one of them fatally, by the Polish Socialists.[10]

The Communists attempted to impede the work of the Bund at polling places on election day by attacking propagandists near the precincts and watchers inside. The attackers were driven off, however, when in a rare show of fraternalism watchers and propagandists for the PPS defended the Bundists.[11]

The election results were a catastrophe for the divided left; the right-wing parties affiliated with the anti-Semitic Endeks won 163 of 444 seats in the Sejm, the centrist Peasants Party ("Piast") won 70, the liberal, anticlerical, agrarian Wyzwolenie 49, and the PPS only 41. The national minorities elected 67, of whom 22 were Jews—all of them conservative. The total Bund vote was just over 87,000; it failed to elect a single deputy.[12]

The Socialist movement suffered a serious defeat in the elections; its vote had fallen seriously in all areas, particularly in the cities. Yet a strong case can be made for the belief that a united Socialist ticket might have shown greater strength. In Łodz, an industrial center with a large Jewish population,

[10] Goldstein, *op. cit.*, pp. 51–55.
[11] *Ibid.*, p. 52.
[12] Simon Segal, *The New Poland and the Jews* (New York: Lee Furman, 1938), pp. 33–34.

the Bund polled 12,496, the PPS 19,123, and the left-wing Poale Zion 2,261, for a total Socialist vote of 34,240. Not a single Socialist was returned from the Łodz district, because no single Socialist party polled enough votes to be entitled to a deputy under the complicated election system then in effect. But if the parties had presented a joint ticket, they would have been represented in the Sejm by one Socialist from Łodz. The internal bickering was to aggravate the Socialist decline still further during the next year, when the municipal election showed a further trend to the right.[13]

ASSASSINATION

The election of 1922 was a defeat for both the right and the left. The Endeks, who had hoped to win a handsome majority, were in the minority; the left was in even worse shape; only the center parties of the peasants, together with the national minorities, could decide the future direction of Poland by throwing their support to either side. At the outset it appeared likely that they would support the democratic left, but a series of events led the center more and more to the right.

Gabriel Narutowicz, a close friend of Marshal Pilsudski, was elected president by the Parliament. He was the candidate of the left and was supported by part of the center and all of the national minorities. The Endeks immediately launched a campaign against this "President of the Jews"; they led riots, and boycotted the inaugural. Finally, on December 16, 1922, Narurowicz was shot to death by an artist crazed with nationalist fanaticism.[14]

The assassin, Eligiusz Niewiadomski, explained his act in a four-hour diatribe at his trial two weeks later:

> Jewry has inculcated into Socialism morbid poison and creative impotency.
> The era of Utopian socialism was followed half a century

[13] I. S. Hertz, *Di Geshikhte fun Bund in Łodz* (New York: Ferlag-Unser Tsait, 1958), pp. 300, 303.
[14] Segal, *op. cit.*, pp. 35–38.

later by so-called scientific socialism which will rightly be called the Jewish era. And history will so call our present era. The period of Marx, Kautsky, and other leaders. Jewry soon realized to what uses socialism could be put once it got it in its hands. The Jews gave to socialism their theories, distributors, agitators, material help, advertising, and the all-round swing [*sic*]. And not in vain. They have imbued that idea with all their radical characteristics and with the elements which have been the cause for social degeneration of the moral value of its nationalism.

The class struggle was invented by them in order to destroy the Aryan nations and thus avert racial animosities and struggles.[15]

The assassination frightened the centrists away from the moderate left and caused them to enter into an alliance with the right, with whose support they elected Stanislaw Wojciechowski, a right-centrist, president. With right-wing support, the centrists also named Wincenty Witos, leader of the Peasants' Party, premier. One of his first actions was to order the police to fire on the strikers in Cracow, causing the death of eleven workers, and bringing about his own demise. He was followed as premier by a right-winger, Wladislaw Grabski.[16]

RETURN OF THE VILNO BUND

Although the Bund in Poland was in serious straits, under attack from two sides and unable to work with other Socialist groups, it was an organization with a potential, no matter how insignificant it might have appeared. The Bund in the Lithuanian area, including districts incorporated into Poland, on the countrary had either disappeared completely or continued to exist as small isolated units dissociated from the rest of the

[15] Quoted in A. G. W., "Fomentations in Poland," *The Nation*, CXVI (February 28, 1923), 252. Niewiadomski was condemned and shot on January 21, 1923. See Robert Machray, *Poland: 1914–1931* (London: George Allen and Unwin, 1932), p. 438.

[16] Segal, *op. cit.*, p. 38.

Jewish and labor movements. This was the result of a long series of events related to the Russian Revolution, and of the peculiar circumstances under which hegemony was established over the area.

The most important city in this area was Vilno, whose population was basically Polish and Jewish, but whose neighboring area was populated primarily by Byelorussians. Vilno, which had been the center of Jewish intellectual life during the Czarist period and also the birthplace of the Bund, was known as the Jerusalem of Lithuania; its Jewish population, however, considered it a part of Russia rather than of either Poland or Lithuania. When the Polish Bund became independent of the Russian, the Vilno organization remained within the latter. When Vilno fell under Polish rule, the Vilno Bund was therefore in the anomalous position of political organization in an alien land. The Bundists there considered the Polish rule of the city to be a passing phase and expected the Russians to reclaim it. They also expected their group to be the cement for keeping the Polish and Russian Bund organizations united regardless of geographic divisions, and hoped that the Bund would again be the Jewish Socialist organization in Poland, Lithuania, and Russia. The Vilno group thus sent delegates to the 1920 conventions of both the Russian and the Polish Bunds.

The split of the Russian Bund into Communist and Social Democratic organizations thus affected the one at Vilno more than it did the Polish, and the Vilno Bund split into two warring factions—one left-wing and Bolshevik, the other right-wing and Social Democratic—long before the Combund walked out of the Polish organization. At a meeting in which heated debate raged for nine hours, the left-wing members seized control and those of the right wing stalked out, to organize their own newspaper and their own Social Democratic Bund.[17]

[17] Emanuel Novogrodsky, "Der Bund in Irushelayem De Litte," *Forois* (Mexico City), XVIII, October 1957, pp. 12–14.

Neither of the Vilno Bunds was prepared to give up its independent existence. After it became apparent that Poland's rule was permanent, each insisted on the need for an independent Bund. Leivik Hodes, editor of the left-wing Bund daily, even tried to persuade the other Bund organizations in Lithuania to continue their existence, but his appeals were futile.

Both Vilno groups were agreed in their refusal to join the Polish organization; the left-wingers considered it too far to the right, and the right-wingers accused it of being quasi-Communist. The Polish Bund was in no position to appeal to the Vilno organizations for members because of the bickering within its own ranks. But the refusal of the Social Democratic Vilno Bund to liquidate when the Russian organization surrendered to the Communist Party, and the changing conditions in Vilno as it became a Polish city, made it a foregone conclusion that in time the organizations would become part of the Polish Bund.[18]

The Social Democratic Bund, which was to become the more important of the two organizations in Vilno, maintained that the Polish Bund had ceased to be a Social Democratic organization when it accepted the ideology and tactics of the Comintern, regardless of whether or not it was an actual member of the Moscow International. The Bund had betrayed the old traditions and had become a Communist organization, a Vilno leader wrote. "The party has retained the old name but its principles are completely different. We, on the contrary, have remained Social Democrats, today as yesterday, opponents of Bolshevism on principle." What difference did it make whether nineteen or twenty-one points were accepted? "We cannot accept the basic principles of the Comintern." Tortured by the Soviet secret police, wiped out by the Communist governments in the Ukraine, Byelorussia, and Lithuania, "we refused to give up our

[18] Novogrodsky, *loc. cit.*, pp. 14–15.

social democracy." The chief issue in the Polish Bund had become, he said, how many of the Comintern's conditions to accept. "This we deny is a key issue. Were we overnight to accept the Communist ideology we would go into the Comintern itself." [19]

The Vilno right-wingers' attacks on the Polish Bund were sharp; they regarded it as a pariah among the world's Socialists.

> The Social Democrats of all nations hold conferences, meetings. The Communists hold their meetings and conferences. They seek ways and means, they prepare. The organized Jewish working class of Poland goes to no conferences, it doesn't seek, it doesn't prepare. As a matter of fact—it criticizes everything and everyone.[20]

The attack was in some ways unfair, but it did hit the Bund in a vulnerable spot—its isolation from the rest of the world Socialist movement. For four years the PPS had been considered too nationalistic by the rest of the Socialist Parties. But by 1923 it had returned to the Labor and Socialist International. In Vienna a group of more radical Socialist parties had formed their own international, which was dissolving by 1924; all of its members were re-entering the Labor and Socialist International. But not the Bund; it was affiliated with a group of small, quasi-Communist parties in the Paris-based Bureau of Revolutionary Socialist Parties. The Vilno Social Democratic Bund believed that the Polish Bund belonged in the LSI.[21]

The Vilno Social Democratic Bund had another reason for not wishing to enter the Polish organization: the fear that its

[19] A. Litvak (pseudonym of Haym-Yankel Helfand), "Varum Ikh Bin Kegn Poylishn Bund," *Der Wecker* (New York), II, August 2, 1922, p. 5. Litvak was leader of the Social Democratic Bund in Vilno.
[20] *Unzer Gedank*, March 17, 1923.
[21] A. Litvak, "Lederbour's Internatsional un der Poylisher Bund," *Der Wecker* (New York), II, August 18, 1923, pp. 11–12.

press would be either liquidated or put under the control of the national organization. The right-wing faction in Warsaw, a Vilno leader charged, was not permitted to spread its ideas within the Bund during the factional dispute of 1921. "Now we have our own printed word . . . which is read by Jewish working-class leaders and intellectuals of all factions and influences them." Should the Vilno Social Democrats unite with Warsaw, "we can get no guarantee of freedom of expression inside the Bund. We will have to close our newspaper or turn it over to the spirit of Warsaw." And this he refused to do.[22]

Negotiations aimed at the return of the Vilno Bund groups were carried on through a great part of 1923. Opposition to the entry existed among both the Polish Bund left-wingers—who considered the Social Democrats to be "opposed to us ideologically"—and the right-wing Vilno organization, which demanded the right to maintain a separate factional organization with its own press. In the end, however, the realization that Vilno was in fact a part of independent Poland, led both the right-wing and the left-wing Vilno Bunds to liquidate and enter the Polish Bund as a united local organization without factional divisions or factional publications.[23]

The rest of the Lithuanian Bund was unprepared for the changes that were made in the map of Russia after the fall of the Romanovs. Moreover, it was much more influenced by the October Revolution than were the Polish or the Vilno Bundists. The few who opposed the Bolshevik seizure of power dropped out of the Bund completely, while those imbued with the Bolshevik spirit were prepared to sacrifice the Bund for its sake. Thus when the Russian Bund went into the Communist Party, most of the Lithuanian organization did the same. When the Red Army withdrew from the Lithuanian part of Poland in 1921, many Bundists who agreed with the Bolsheviks went along to Russia. There was no Bund

[22] Litvak, "Varum Ikh Bin Kegn Poylishn Bund," *loc. cit.* p. 6.
[23] "Der IIIer Tsusamenfor . . . ," *loc. cit.*, pp. 225, 230, 239.

organization in Lithuania after the nation became independent.[24]

A combination of internal haggling and external persecution had delayed the Bund from calling its third convention for almost three years after the Danzig meeting; moreover, the complexion of the organization had changed. The left wing, which had been in control during 1920–1921, by 1924 was distinctly a minority. The dream of imminent revolution, and the reality of Soviet oppression, had dampened its members' revolutionary ardor.[25]

The debate still centered around which international body the Bund should join, or accept as its guiding light: the Labor and Socialist (Second) International, or the Vienna (Two-and-a-Half) International, which was somewhat to the left of the Second but still non-Communist, and which was soon to amalgamate with the second, or the Moscow-based Comintern.

At the 1924 convention of the Bund, the question of the Internationals had to be explored in a different context from that of 1921; the possibility of any easing of the twenty-one points had ceased to exist; other left-leaning Socialist parties had been excluded from the Comintern because they were unwilling to accept the dictates of Moscow; and the rigorous dictatorship of the Soviet Communist Party had stripped off the democratic façade that had previously attracted Socialists to it. There were still some Bundists who were unwilling or unable to accept the obvious, that the Comintern had become in fact little more than a mouthpiece for the Soviet Communist Party.

[24] Emanuel Novogrodsky, "Der Bund in Kovner Litte," *Forois* (Mexico City), XVIII, October 1957, pp. 15–16.
[25] "Di Tsvayer in Poylishn Bund," *Unser Tsait*, XVII, November–December, 1957, Ohler, pp. 36–37.

A minority of the Bund still insisted that the Third International was based on genuinely Socialist principles, which the Bund ought to accept, and that the only thing wrong with the Comintern was its internal monolithic control from above. But most of those who in 1921 accepted the Comintern's leadership—while rejecting the twenty-one conditions—now maintained that the Moscow international was wholly unacceptable, and that the organizational methods were wrong because the principles on which the Third International was based were wrong. "We maintain," one of their spokesmen told the convention, "that the Communists are a faction of the world Socialist movement, but a bad faction." [26]

The new majority, whose view reflected the centrist position of 1921, rejected the suggestion made by a delegate from the Vilno Social Democratic Bund that it enter one of the Socialist internationals, which were then reuniting. But the Bund majority insisted on making it clear that "we cannot belong to the Third International, that we are Socialists and not Communists."

> The difference between us and the Communists lies in the fact that they believe in the rule by the party and we believe in rule by the whole working class. We say the working-class government must be answerable to the whole class; the Communists, on the other hand, say that if the working class doesn't like the Communist Party government, the class must still accept the will of the government and not the reverse.
>
> The chief error of the Communist Party lies in its effort to turn the might of the working class into a dictatorship of the central committee of the party over the proletariat.[27]

Besides the question of dictatorship, the majority at the convention opposed the Communist view of revolution, which the Bundists considered to be anti-Marxian, and the monolithic internal structure within the party.

[26] "Der IIIer Tsusamenfor . . . ," p. 243.
[27] *Ibid.*, pp. 250, 244.

The second failing of Communism is found in its anti-Marxian view of the social revolution. To the Communist it [the social revolution] is not an organic process, but [is] instead the result of a mechanically prepared military conspiracy. . . . This is Bakhuninism and not Marxian.

[Moreover,] we cannot enter the Comintern because there we would not be permitted to disagree with our leaders. Even Trotsky was ousted because he dared think independently.[28]

The Bund majority had begun moving perceptibly closer to the world Socialist movement; its illusions about the Communists had begun to vanish. "Should we, against our will, be led to London [i.e., the Socialist International], it would be a tragedy for us but we would survive," a spokesman for the centrists said. "In the Third International, on the contrary, we would vanish." [29]

The left wing refused to concede that communism was becoming a synonym for "putschism or sectarianism," or that the Communists were carrying on "a civil war within the working-class movement." By the same reasoning, the left minority insisted, socialism could be called "coalition politics and civil peace with the bourgeoisie", for hadn't the German Social Democrats formed coalition governments with non-Socialist parties? The real difference between Social Democrats and Communists, said the leftists, was "the unremitting class war, the unyielding will to combat the present system on the part of the Communists. It is in this aspect that Communism shows itself to be in complete accord with revolutionary socialism and opposed to reformist socialism." [30]

The left-wing minority remained firm in the belief that the Third International "is still the center of the revolutionary working-class movement." But since the Third International remained closed to the Bund because of the twenty-one points, the left-wingers proposed that the left-wing Socialist parties

---

[28] *Ibid.*, pp. 244, 249. Trotsky had been dropped from the Executive Committee of the Communist International earlier in 1924.
[29] *Ibid.*, p. 252.   [30] *Ibid.*, p. 247.

in Italy, Norway, Sweden, France, and the Independent Socialists of Germany join with the Bund in creating a new
international, which would fight "with our consolidated
strength the harmful tendencies within the 'left' [Communist]
international which obstruct the consolidation of all genuinely
revolutionary parties." [31]

The vote on international affiliation favored the centrists,
30 to 24, with one vote for immediate affiliation with the
Labor and Socialist International. The Bund majority suggested that an attempt be made to reunite all of the internationals into one "mighty organ of world-wide working-class
solidarity." And then the majority added fuel to the fire by
forcing through a resolution condemning the terror in the
Soviet Union. The left wing had lost its last battle for a
Communist-oriented Bund.[32]

THE SEARCH FOR ALLIANCE

The Bund's strength had been sapped by the perennial
struggles within the party and without; it was losing ground.
"We have forgotten how to approach the masses because we
do not talk to the masses in their own language and about
their workaday lives," a delegate complained at the 1924 convention. A member of the Central Committee pleaded for
more practical work—"resolutions mean little"; but another
answered that "the theoretical and practical are equally important." [33]

The delegates from the provinces, too, were unhappy; control was in the hands of the organization in Warsaw, and they
were being ignored. "The sum total of our development is
not a happy one; our membership has decreased. The Central
Committee has ignored the provinces." And the youth section
of the Bund, upset by the gains scored by the Zionists—gains
they blamed on the anti-Semitic wave sweeping the country—

[31] *Ibid.*, pp. 246–248.   [32] *Ibid.*, pp. 228, 229, 254.
[33] *Ibid.*, pp. 233–234.

wanted more effort spent on the Jewish issue: "We should increase our anti-Zionist activity." The argument was rejected by the spokesman for the leadership: "We are above all revolutionary Socialists, and only secondarily Jewish Socialists."[34]

The spokesmen for the left wing insisted that the decline of the Bund was due to "coalition politics," and proposed that Bund members be prohibited from accepting election to the administrative bodies of city government—the magistracies. The left wanted membership in the city councils to be sought merely for propaganda purposes, the city councils to be used as no more than rostrums for the expression of Bund policy. The convention rejected this position. It voted to allow Bund members to enter magistracies, but only where there was a Socialist city council and then only with the permission of the Central Committee.[35]

The Bund was obviously powerless, however, and there seemed to be no way out of the morass. Between 1921 and 1924 the Bund had sponsored more than 1,100 rallies, its members had distributed 1,650,000 handbills, and yet it was in a period of sharp decline. It considered the organization of a united front of the Socialist and Communist parties in Poland, with the aim of fighting anti-Semitism, as its one hope of regaining lost ground. But the road toward such unity—in view of the national and ideological distinctions within the Marxist movements—was not an easy one, and defeat was more likely than success.[36]

In May 1923 the Bund executive proposed a conference of all Socialist and labor parties in Poland, to join in a fight against the anti-Semitism and nationalism that were rife throughout Poland, and that were causing difficulty for all the Socialist parties. But the Bund Central Committee rejected a PPS counterproposal for a single secretariat to be composed of all Socialist parties within Poland. The only party to reach an agreement with the Bund was the German

[34] *Ibid.*, pp. 230, 231, 234.   [35] *Ibid.*, pp. 257–258.
[36] *Ibid.*, pp. 227, 239–240.

Social Democratic Party in Poland, which also represented a national minority.[37]

But parties, like people, have a remarkable ability to delude themselves, and seeming advantage can be found even where it does not exist, if it is sought for hard enough. The PPS convention in February 1924, for example, failed to take a clear stand on the nationalities question; it failed to answer one of the central questions on which the Bund position was based—namely whether Jews were to be considered a minority nationality or a religious group. Some of the speeches indicated a growing belief that nationalism was dangerous, that minorities should not be treated as isolated organisms, and that they ought to have full rights and self-determination. But there were some speeches whose tone bordered on anti-Semitism and some Endek influence was noticed within the party. Despite the obvious lack of any progress within the PPS, the Bund daily proclaimed its elation—had not the tone of the speeches been an improvement over previous years? [38]

An agreement was finally reached in 1924 between the Bund and the PPS for coordinated action against fascism, nationalism, and anti-Semitism. But the agreement was short-lived; within a matter of months a PPS deputy had assailed the Yiddish school system in a speech before the Sejm, and the agreement was nullified.[39]

CONCLUSION

Slowly but surely, the Bund was returning to its original position as a Socialist party wedded to democracy and opposed to dictatorship within or outside the party. But it was arguing the issue in a context far removed from the needs of the Jewish working class of Poland, in a context of foggy unreality. It argued the issue of which international to join,

[37] *Ibid.*, pp. 226–228.
[38] *Uncer Folkscajtung*, IV, February 1, 1924.
[39] "Der IIIer Tsusamenfor . . . ," pp. 227, 239–240.

rather than how best to improve the condition of the Jewish working people in Poland. What did it matter to the Polish Jew whether the Bund was in the same international with Scheidemann and Hilferding, or with Thaelmann and Zinoviev? It mattered not in the least; all the Jewish worker wanted was some assurance of a job, of improved conditions, of political and social equality. The Bund, having spent all its efforts on debating points of dogma, was forced to ignore crucial issues, and so its position was seriously weakened.

It is to the Bund's credit that it sought alliance with the non-Jewish Socialist movement in its fight against anti-Semitism; but the Bundists' insistence that the unity be on their own conditions doomed their practical efforts to failure.

VIII

The Pilsudski Era,
1926-1935

WHEN a situation seems hopeless, when the alternatives appear to be between impossibly bad situations, any incident that offers the least improvement is seized upon. In a short time it may become evident that the hope was only a delusion, but for the moment it becomes a focus of enthusiasm.

The Poland of 1926 offered no genuine hope to the labor and Socialist movement, least of all among the Jews. Government power was in the hands of an anti-labor, anti-Semitic coalition of parties of the extreme and center right—a coalition that was openly hostile to everything in which the Bund believed. No new cabinet could be expected to be any less hostile; it would still require the backing of the only viable coalition in the Sejm—of right and center right—and that coalition could not be expected to yield its position. The two chief alternatives were between Witos and Grabski, the former a verbalizer of liberal ideas who had shown in Cracow his close attachment to the right, the latter an outspoken enemy of democracy and equality for the ethnic minorities.

But there was a third possibility—a government led by Pilsudski, a name revered in Socialist and anti-Czarist history. Such a government could be expected to evoke enthusiastic support from the Bund, and from the left in general.

HOPE AND DISILLUSION

Under the conditions prevailing in the Poland of 1926, the only hope which the Polish Socialists, minorities, and democrats could see was an overthrow by Pilsudski of the right-wing Witos-Grabski regime. This hope was based on two assumptions: first that Pilsudski could win the support of the Polish people, and second that because of his long association with the PPS, he would change the course of the government from authoritarian right to democratic left. The first assumption was based on logic and proved to be accurate. The second, in the light of Pilsudski's record, should have been suspect. That the hope persisted can be attributed to a self-delusion brought on by despair.

Josef Pilsudski was a nationalist whose self-proclaimed belief in socialism had always been a kind of window-dressing for his insistence on an independent Poland. His true hallmark was an unquenchable hatred of Russia and everything Russian. His record in the PPS was one of resolute opposition to anything at all that did not further his dream of a united and independent Poland. On this issue he had brought about a major split within the PPS, and finally had dissociated himself from the Socialist movement.

Pilsudski was born near Vilno in 1867, of mixed Polish-Lithuanian parentage. He was raised in an anti-Russian atmosphere. As a youth he became involved in a conspiracy against the Czar, for which he served five years (1887–1892) in Siberian exile. On his return from exile he became a founding member of the PPS, and editor of its illegal organ *Robotnik*. Another sojourn in prison ended with a daring escape. In 1904, during the Russo-Japanese War, he traveled to Tokyo in an effort to win Japan's support for a nationalist uprising in Poland. This effort was thwarted because of opposition within the Socialist movement and because Roman Dmowski, leader of the right-wing National Democrats, was able to convince the Japanese that such an uprising would be futile and of little value to the Japanese war effort.

Pilsudski's experience in Tokyo played a significant role in his later activities. It brought about an enmity between Dmowski and himself that would last throughout their lives, and that was in part responsible for the belief that Pilsudski was still of the left even after he had abandoned socialism. Moreover, his experience in Tokyo convinced him that Polish independence could only be achieved by an armed uprising; and this led him further and further from the Socialists.

From Tokyo, Pilsudski moved to Cracow in Austrian Poland. There he formed in 1905 a quasi-military organization, the League of Riflemen, whose goal was a war of liberation against Russia. The PPS at its 1906 congress rejected Pilsudski's militant nationalism. He thereupon led a schism in the organization, forming the PPS Revolutionary Faction (Frakcja) from among his followers.

The outbreak of World War I in 1914 found Pilsudski in Austrian Poland, attempting to form a guerrilla force for action in Russian Poland. His force did seize the town of Kielce, but the Austrians were unimpressed until he agreed to incorporate his military band into the Austrian army. By 1916 Pilsudski was completely alienated from the Polish Socialist movement and had withdrawn from even the Revolutionary Faction (which had by that time become the dominant group). He took with him many other onetime Socialist leaders.

In 1917 Pilsudski broke with the Central Powers and was imprisoned by the Germans at Magdeburg. He was freed in late 1918, and in November returned to Warsaw, where he became chief of the new State of Poland. After a short, stormy career in that post, he became chief of the military staff, and in 1919–1921 he led the war against the Bolsheviks.[1]

---

[1] Josef Korbel, *Poland Between East and West* (Princeton University Press, 1963), pp. 19–22; D. R. Gillie (editor and translator), *Joseph Pilsudski, The Memories of a Polish Revolutionary and Soldier* (London: Faber and Faber, 1931), pp. 31–35; W. F. Reddaway, *Marshal Pilsudski* (London: George Routledge and Sons, 1939), pp. 19–110; G. D. H. Cole, *A History of Socialist Thought: Communism and Social Democracy, 1914–1931* (London: Macmillan and Co., 1958), IV, 617–629, especially p. 622 on Pilsudski's final abandonment of the PPS in 1916; Victor Chernov, "Joseph Pilsudski: From Socialist to Autocrat," *Foreign Affairs*, XIV (October 1935), 146–155. Chernov was a Russian Social Revolutionist who had been a prison mate of Pilsudski under the Czar.

It should have been evident by 1921 that Pilsudski "knew no political philosophy . . . other than a romantic belief in his country's greatness." [2] But conditions conspired to prolong the Pilsudski myth among Poland's Socialists.

Pilsudski was an avowed opponent of the center-right governments that had ruled Poland after the assassination of Narutowicz in 1922. Although he was incensed at the growing corruption in Poland and at the increasing tendency to persecute Socialists, many of whom were his personal friends, the chief cause of concern to Pilsudski was the naming of his avowed enemies to the War Ministry. His animosity was especially strong toward Witos, who had appointed General Szeptycki, a particularly hated foe, minister of war. Witos again became prime minister in 1926, and Pilsudski was further incensed.[3]

Economic chaos was rife in Poland, and political dissension was strong among the working population. The right-wing government was determined to maintain its power by whatever means were available, and there were rumors that it planned to act in violation of the Constitution. In anticipation of an illegal seizure of power by the forces of the right, the leaders of the left and moderate parties in the Sejm approached Pilsudski with a proposal that he become premier. Pilsudski was believed to be the only man not of the right-center coalition who could win the support of a majority of the Sejm. The Marshal turned down the offer, explaining that he would refuse any power offered by the Sejm, which he considered corrupt.[4]

Instead, Pilsudski led a march on Warsaw by troops loyal to him in an effort to oust the Polish regime. The successful action, which occurred in mid-May 1926, evoked enthusiasm

[2] Korbel, *op. cit.*, p. 21.

[3] Casimir Smogorzewski, "Poland's Crisis and Its Background," *Living Age*, CCXXIX (June 26, 1926), 655.

[4] Aleksandr Werder (pseudonym of Emanuel Sherer). "Ostatnie Wypadki w Polsce," *Walka* (Cracow), III (June 1926), 106; *The New York Times*, November 26, 1931, p. 9.

from the working people, and from the Socialist and labor press. The vice-president of the PPS warned that a victory for the Witos government "would have meant a reaction against the working class and democracy." Besides, Pilsudski had a great following among the workers, from whom anything but support would have been impossible. "In such a situation we could not think, we had to go with Pilsudski. He was against the reaction."

All Socialist parties—the PPS, the Bund, the Poale Zion, the German Social Democracy in Poland—supported the uprising; even the Communists favored it. Within the Bund, enthusiasm reached fever pitch. Many Bundists offered to serve by fighting at the front for Pilsudski. The official organ of the Bund was outspoken in his support: "Jewish workers have too much at stake to stand aside during the uprising. You must raise your voice in protest; you must demand the overthrow of the anti-people's government of the Chjena-Piast (the right-center coalition). In its place must rise a government that will solve the urgent needs of the Polish workers." [5]

The PPS and Bund unions expressed their support of Pilsudski by calling a general strike that paralyzed all of Poland. The most important stoppage, called by the PPS railroad unions, prevented reinforcements from reaching the Witos regime.

Socialists later insisted that the support of the labor movement had made Pilsudski's victory possible. One Socialist wrote that the uprising would have been inconceivable without "the dissatisfaction among the masses who suffer from intense unemployment."

Labor had backed Pilsudski because of his old record as a

[5] Smogorzewski, *loc. cit.*, p. 659; Mieczyslaw Niedzialkowski (vice-president of the PPS), "Di Revolutsie in Poyln un di Poylishe Sotsialistn," *Der Wecker* (New York), IV, June 26, 1926, p. 7; D. M. (an unnamed leader of the Bund), "Der Bund un di Iberkerenishn in Poyln," *Der Wecker* (New York), IV, July 3, 1926, p. 11; *Uncer Folkscajtung*, May 14, 1926.

Socialist and an enemy of the Czar. Even though he was no longer a Socialist, the workers expected him to remain true to the basic precepts of the ideology. "In times of trouble people expect miracles"; and Pilsudski was regarded as the man who could perform them. But not all of the Bundists were certain that Pilsudski was the hope he appeared to be. At least some of them feared that too much was expected. They even doubted that he intended to take the steps toward economic reform and political freedom that they considered essential. The revolution was against the reaction; no one knew what it was for.[6]

> Pilsudski's march on Warsaw destroyed the sweet dreams of reaction. Although little was known of Pilsudski's plans for the future, the working class backed the revolution . . . because all were united on one point: an immense bitterness and enmity toward the reaction.[7]

What troubled the Bund from the beginning was that the seizure of power was a military one, and that a program was lacking. Despite the civilian population's enthusiasm for Pilsudski, the Bundists noted that in the overthrow of the government by the military there had been little civilian participation. "Even though the railroad strike kept troops from Posen from reaching Warsaw to support Witos, this does not alter the fact that it was a military uprising." [8] All the Socialists, particularly the Bundists, began to fear that the revolution would lead to a personal dictatorship. Even the PPS was soon showing less enthusiasm for Pilsudski, although many of the rank-and-file members maintained their attachment for a long time.[9]

Of even greater concern to the Bund was the lack of a pro-

[6] *Uncer Folkscajtung,* May 14, 1926; Niedzialkowski, *loc. cit.,* p. 7; Jacob Lestchinsky, "Di Revolutsionere Iberkerenish in Poyln," *Der Wecker* (New York), IV, June 12, 1926, p. 5; Werder, *op. cit.,* p. 107.
[7] "Nokh der Mai Iberkerenish," *Jugnt Vecker* (Warsaw), V, June 1926.
[8] Werder, *loc. cit.,* p. 107.   [9] D. M., *op. cit.,* p. 11.

gram on the part of Pilsudski and his new regime. When a foreign correspondent asked Pilsudski, shortly after the overthrow of the Witos government, what his future program was, he answered: "Don't ask me what I will do, because I don't know what I will do a week from now."

This position caused the Bund, and the whole Socialist movement, to question Pilsudski's intentions.

> What program has Pilsudski got? Only one thing is clear: he is far from any left-wing or working class position. His talk is limited to morality, nationalism, and animosity for the political. He has forgotten his Socialist background, [he is] only a romantic who doesn't understand the truth—the class struggle. The class struggle doesn't exist for him because he doesn't want it to exist. He ignores such issues as fair distribution of the tax load, working-class conditions, and agrarian reform. No bureaucracy can solve these problems; only a class-conscious program can solve them.[10]

The Bundists also opposed Pilsudski's antiparliamentarian policy. He not only was without a program to ameliorate the economic conditions of the working people, but he had also announced that he was opposed to political parties and parliamentary government. "All that emerges [from Pilsudski's programmatic statements] are generalizations about moral revolution, about a strong hand [by giving the president broad powers], and the like. Not a single Socialist party can accept Pilsudski's position with regard to parliamentary government, political parties, or the class struggle." [11]

In the period immediately following the May uprising, the PPS, German Social Democracy in Poland, and the Bund maintained a close liaison and total cooperation. Their policy was to wait and see what sort of rule Pilsudski as president, and his premier, Kazimierz Bartel, would propose.[12]

---

[10] Werder, *loc. cit.*, p. 107.
[11] *Jugnt Vecker, loc. cit.*, pp. 4–5.
[12] Niedzialkowski, *loc. cit.*, p. 6.

The PPS—and the other Socialist parties—saw three alternatives: (1) Pilsudski might try to establish a military dictatorship, and would then face conflict with the labor and Socialist organizations; (2) a new government based on democracy might be established; or (3) the forces of the right might instigate a civil war, and a Socialist or quasi-Socialist regime—including the liberal peasant parties—would then have to be formed. Of the three alternatives the Socialist preferred the second; to bring it about they proposed a three-point program:

1. Dissolution of the Sejm and Senate;
2. Immediate elections;
3. Organization of a government including the Socialist and peasant parties, on the basis of an as yet undeveloped program of economic, social, and political reforms, plus solution of the national minorities problem on a basis of equity and democracy.[13]

The program was a moderate one with reform rather than social revolution as its keystone. There could hardly have been a Socialist platform under the conditions of the uprising; the revolution was, from the Socialist point of view, a purely negative one, whose sole objective had been the ouster of the reactionary government. Moreover, it was made too quickly "to give it an economic or social meaning." [14]

Almost immediately after Pilsudski had seized power, the Bund Central Committee published in its daily organ *Uncer Folkscajtung* a statement supporting the new regime and proposing a program. The Pilsudski revolution, it said, was the first step in the direction of a long-overdue change in the social and economic situation of Poland. "Pilsudski's victorious uprising against the Witos government was a mighty blow against reaction. It opened new vistas, new perspectives for the struggle of the working masses." It had a democratic,

[13] *Ibid.*, pp. 5–6.   [14] *Ibid.*, p. 7.

"even a revolutionary character. It had no clear social program."

The creation of such a program is the duty of the working class and radical peasants, who must strive to give the occurrences of May 12–14 [the uprising] their political and social content and thus turn the uprising into a true revolution.

The working masses of Poland must therefore expend all their energies in order that only a government which is capable of creating a new Poland—a government of the working class and radical peasants—can be organized.

In order for this object to be accomplished it is necessary that all obstructions in the path of such a government be abolished.

The present reactionary Sejm and Senate should be dissolved, and the whole administrative apparatus should be cleansed of all reactionary elements.

The success of this struggle is, in the first instance, dependent on the determined and united stand of the working masses in Poland; it is therefore necessary to create an organizational unity of action among all proletarian and radical peasant parties. And if such unity is not possible, they should strive at least for united political action by these parties.

Only a workers' and peasants' government will be able to realize the most vital economic and political demands which all of the working class parties have made . . . Primary among these demands are:

Work or bread for the unemployed, land for the peasants;
Full freedom for the national minorities and political amnesty.

The Bundists soon learned they had expected too much from Pilsudski. The issue in which this statement appeared was confiscated by his government.[15]

The rest of the Socialists' illusions were soon shattered; Pilsudski permitted the old Sejm and Senate, dominated by the center right, to remain in power, and to elect the new president. The PPS was soon in the opposition; it refused to support Ignacy Moscicki, the successful candidate of the Pilsudski

[15] D. M., *loc. cit.*, p. 12.

regime. Nevertheless, Pilsudski's hold on the PPS members was still strong, and many former leaders resigned and went into his camp. Among them was A. Moraczewski, the first premier of Poland. The May uprising had been aimed against the regime based on the parties of the center right, the so-called bourgeois parties; yet the man who led that uprising now allied himself with these very forces. Pilsudski refused to call a new election. He allied himself with the Conservative Party, controlled by the large landholders and manufacturers.[16] It was now apparent that he had divorced himself completely from his Socialist past.

So the Bundists turned sharply against Pilsudski and his regime. "The new rulers have decided to attach themselves to the broad, fat shoulders of capital . . . The new regime have united with it and become supporters of the interests of capital. With the aid of the capitalists the May revolutionists remain in power." The Bundists now saw the choice before Poland narrowed to one of socialism or fascism.

Fascism, in the Bund spokesmen's reasoning, was the final defense of a capitalist system faced with a Socialist revolution or a growing Socialist power in Parliament. Pilsudski thus could not but fail in any attempt to destroy the reactionary movement so long as he did not accept socialism. Any attempt to stop reaction while maintaining capitalism would be doomed to failure; such an attempt would be based on "subjective desire, which is helpless against the objective fact of life, that fascism and capitalism are closely related." [17]

Socialists now wondered whether they had in fact chosen the lesser evil when they supported Pilsudski in May 1926. "Before May 12 Poland was on the verge of a Fascist dictator-

[16] *Jugnt Vecker, loc. cit.,* p. 4; Raymond Leslie Buell, "Political Conflicts in Poland," *Virginia Quarterly Review,* XV (April 1939), p. 236; I. Halpern, "Di Sotsiale Trayb Koikhes fun Sanacia Regime," *Uncer Cajt,* II, May 1928, p. 5; Chernov, *loc. cit.,* pp. 154–155.

[17] P. Krishtof, "Fun 'Goldenem Mitn' Tsum Shvartsn Rand," *Jugnt Vecker* (Warsaw), V, December 1926, p. 16; "Zay Hobn Zikh Tsusamengetrofn," *Jugnt Vecker,* V, July 1926, pp. 6–8.

ship; instead, it got the dictatorship of an individual." Erlich, an outstanding Bund leader, called the Pilsudski regime a new dictatorship "in the interests of the big landowners and capitalists." [18]
Another Bund leader expressed the disillusion two months after the uprising:

> When Pilsudski argued with right-wing parties it was expected that he would aid workers and intellectuals: it was expected that he would wipe out corruption; it was expected that there would be a moral revolution. The fate of Poland was left in Pilsudski's hands despite his lack of program. It turned out that the people had erred. In the end, all they got was a dictatorship.[19]

In only one area was a significant improvement brought about by the Pilsudski regime—anti-Semitism was on the wane. *The Nation*'s correspondent could report from Warsaw that "the present regime . . . shows signs of wanting to come to an understanding with the minorities. This is especially true in the case of the Jews. Compared to the persecution of the old Endek regime, the present condition of the Jews in Poland is greatly improved. The Marshal himself is probably one of the best friends of the Jews in Poland, and his administration . . . cannot be accused of lack of good will toward the Jews. . . ." [20]
The more friendly attitude of the regime toward the Jews led the Yiddish school organization to expect help from it; meetings were called in all cities to organize for aid to the schools, and the government was asked for its support. But there was opposition in the Sejm, particularly among the non-Socialist Zionists and the Orthodox Jews, who united with the anti-Semitic deputies to defeat the proposal. The Ministry

[18] Karol Grywicz, "Dyktatura," *Walka* (Cracow), III (July–August 1926), 139; Henryk Erlich, "Der Muser Hashakel," *Uncer Cajt*, III, 1929 (#3), p. 1.
[19] Grywicz, *loc. cit.*, p. 137.
[20] William Zukerman, "The Polish Election," *The Nation*, CXXVI (March 7, 1928), 304.

of Education likewise had no interest in aiding the Jewish schools, and the hopes died along with the dreams of a more democratic Poland.[21]

THE ELECTION OF 1928

Pilsudski's alliance with the conservative business groups led, within a year after his successful coup, to a complete break between himself and the PPS. The National Democrats and the Peasants' Party were likewise unwilling to support him, and he formed a "non-party government bloc" of his own.

The election, held in 1928 after a two-year delay, was fought between three blocs. The conservative Catholic bloc, based on the National Democrats and supported by the land-holders and wealthier peasants led by Witos, composed the right-wing opposition. The PPS, the Bund, and the agrarian radicals represented the left wing. And the "non-party bloc," headed by Pilsudski and Colonel Valerian Slawek, made up the third combination.

The rightist bloc was in a difficult position; the Catholic Church was unable to offer it any real support because of a warning from Pilsudski that he would withdraw the Church's privileges should it offer to support the Endeks. This left the bloc without any substantial base of support and with that "extreme Polish nationalism . . . is the only policy that the bloc has left now. . . ." [22]

The Bundists were reported to be unenthusiastic about the election campaign. Theirs was a defeatist attitude; no one expected a Socialist victory. Pilsudski was riding the crest of his general popularity, particularly among the Conservative Jews. The issues raised during the election were rarely based on principles; the Bund's campaign was based on the thesis that the "strongest party in the Jewish community deserves a

[21] "In Poyln," *Der Wecker* (New York), IV, July 31, 1926, p. 11.
[22] Zukerman, *loc. cit.*; Buell, *Poland: Key to Europe*, pp. 91–92.

seat in the Sejm." The Bund took as its chief slogan, "Without compromises defend the rights of Jewish workers," and campaigned as the defender of Jewish culture.[23]

The Bund and PPS worked together closely in the campaign. In four areas with sizable Jewish populations the Bund backed the PPS candidates; in the Białystok region a joint Socialist bloc was organized, and in other strongly Jewish areas the Bund ran its own candidates.

The Białystok bloc was headed by a Bund candidate because the Bund was the largest component of the alliance; in 1922 it had polled 5,645 of the total Socialist vote of 8,500. There had been doubt among PPS and Bund officials as to whether the Polish workers would support a Jewish candidate, and considerable pressure from the Warsaw headquarters of the PPS was necessary before the ticket could be approved by the local leadership. The fears of the local Socialists proved unfounded; the vote of the joint ticket was almost double the Bund–PPS total six years before, with significant gains in the predominantly Polish districts. This was the first united electoral action between the Bund and PPS—at the Sejm level— since Poland had become an independent nation, and although it failed by a few votes to elect a member to the Sejm, the possibilities of the alliance had been demonstrated.[24]

In the four districts where the Bund backed PPS candidates, there was considerable fear that the Jewish workers would refuse to support a non-Jewish ticket and would turn instead to the non-Socialist Jewish National Bloc. The Socialist vote actually increased sharply in these four districts, particularly in Jewish areas, and the Zionist and Jewish National Bloc vote showed a proportionate decrease.[25]

The total Bund vote increased from 87,000 to 100,000,

---

[23] E. Mus, "Der Bund un di Sejm Vahln," *Uncer Cajt* (Warsaw), II, March–April 1928, p. 2; M. Zylberfarb, "A Por Kritishe Bamerkungen Tsu der Vahl Kampanye fun Bund," *ibid.*, p. 15; *Do Ogołu Zydowskiej Inteligencji Pracujaci* [Election proclamation]: (Warsaw: Bund, 1928); copy in Bund Archives, New York.

[24] Mus, *loc. cit.*, pp. 9–10.   [25] *Ibid.*, pp. 11–13.

though not a single Bundist was elected to the Sejm since these votes were relatively scattered. The vote was, however, an indication of the Bund's considerable strength, as compared to the total vote of little more than 500,000 for candidates of the powerful Jewish parties. Moreover, the Bund total did not include Jewish votes for Socialist candidates where an alliance had been effected, or where there had been no Bund candidate because of the small size of the Jewish population.[26]

---

[26] *Ibid.*, p. 3. The vote by parties and blocs (including only those which elected members to the Sejm, since no statistics are available for other parties, including the Bund), was as follows:

Party or Bloc	Vote	Seats in Sejm
Non-Party Block for Cooperation with the Government	2,399,000	125
PPS	1,482,000	64
Wyzwolenie (Radical Peasants' Party)	835,000	41
National Workmen's Party	228,000	11
Ukrainian United Workmen's and Peasants' Party	180,000	4
Peasant Party, "Piast"	618,000	25
Workmen-Peasant Party	217,000	5
Peasants' Union	135,000	3
Jewish National Union	241,000	6
National Minorities Bloc	1,440,000	55
"Sel-Rob" (Radical Ukrainians)	143,000	3
Ruthenian Party	132,000	1
National Labor Bloc	147,000	4
Ukrainian Peasants' and Workmen's Bloc	270,000	9
Catholic National Party	926,000	38
Polish Catholic Bloc (Peasants and Christian Democrats)	771,000	34
Ukrainian Labor Party	45,000	1
Catholic Western Poland Union	193,000	3
Polish Silesian Catholic-Democratic Bloc	109,000	3
Economic Party	71,000	3
Workmen's Union (Łodz)	49,000	2
White Ruthenian Peasants' and Workmen's Bloc	35,000	2
Farmers' Union	19,000	1
Self-Help Party	18,000	1

Source: *Concise Statistical Year Book of Poland*, I, 1930 (Warsaw: Chief of the Bureau of Statistics, 1930), p. 137.

The gains scored in districts where alliances had been established raised serious doubts in the minds of some Bund leaders whether a separate Socialist party of the Jewish population was logical. One leading member wrote in the theoretical journal of the organization that since the Jewish workers comprised a scattered minority, their Socialist party was isolated from the basic Socialist movement in Poland. A separate Jewish party rather than an autonomous section of an all-Poland Socialist Party was thus not viable. "This condition has existed for too long in independent Poland." [27]

STRIVING FOR UNITY

The election of 1928 was a partial victory for Pilsudski, whose antiparty group had become the largest bloc in the Sejm, but it failed to obtain a majority. He turned to vituperative attack on the parliamentary organizations when it became apparent that he would be unable to control them. Soon the democratic and Socialist parties became his chief opponents. Ignacy Daszynski, leader of the PPS and marshal of the Sejm, became the symbol, during the trying next two years, of the fight to turn Poland into a democratic republic. [28]

The fact that the Socialists were divided into several parties further weakened opposition to the authoritatarian policies of Pilsudski. The Bund leadership, faced with the threat of dictatorship, began a concerted drive for unity with the Polish Socialist Party. "The Jewish working class organized in the Bund insists on the organizational unity of the working clalss, . . ." Erlich wrote. ". . . this is difficult to achieve. But we know no other way." The leaders rejected suggestions that the Bund might more logically unite with the Communists, despite the revolutoinary phraseology used by the latter in

[27] Mus, *loc. cit.*, pp. 4, 14.
[28] Buell, "Political Conflicts in Poland," *Virginia Quarterly Review*, XV (April 1939), 234, 236.

their attacks on the Pilsudski regime. The answer to the dictatorial threat, Erlich wrote, lay in complete unity of all working-class parties, or at least cooperation among them. "So long
as one part of the working class considers the second 'paid
agents for another nation' (the PPS view of the Communists),
or as 'lackeys of the bourgeoisie' (the Communist view of the
Socialists); so long as the working class parties remain at war
with each other, so long can reaction reign." [29]

The Bund leaders favored a federation of Socialist organizations, composed of the PPS, the Bund, the Ukrainian Social
Democrats (in Poland), and the German Social Democracy
(in Poland). They specifically excluded the Communists.
"The working class of each nationality needs it own organization but not its own party. In a land composed of several
nationalities there should be only one Socialist party, with as
many autonomous organizations within it as there are nationalities in the state."

The Bund was not a separate party by choice, but it did not
consider conditions in Poland ripe for unification of all the
Socialists. "The party of the Polish proletariat is not yet ready
to break the bounds of nationalism, to become a state party
rather than a national-Polish party; to become instead of a
Polish Socialist Party the Socialist Party of Poland."

The position of the Bund leadership was summed up by Erlich:

The working class of every nationality must have its own
organization, which will be attuned to the language and other
national characteristics of its specific culture; this is the
principle which the Bund has defended from the first minute
of its existence. The Bund has said: The general party of
the state, which must naturally be closely tied to conditions of
the national majority of the state, can win limited sections of the
working class of the other nationalities; but the job of getting
into the heart of the working class, shaking it up and bringing

[29] Editorial, *Uncer Cajt* (Warsaw), II, May 1928, pp. 1–4.

the proletariat into a compact mass under the banner of socialism—that is a job which can only be accomplished by an organization which has grown up within the given group of workers.[30]

There were, however, issues beyond nationality which tended to prevent the unification of the Socialist parties in Poland. "Our past teaches us to seek allies within the multi-national proletariat in Poland," one leading Bundist wrote. But he questioned whether such alliances could be formed easily, in view of the ideological antipathy which existed between the various parties. These ideological differences he divided into three tendencies: the Communist, the revolutionary Socialist represented by the Bund, and the reformist, represented by the PPS.

The difference between the reformist or right-wing Socialists and the revolutionary or left-wing Socialists was to be found in their stand on such issues as state and union.

What is the proof of revolutionary or opportunistic ideology or action? Is the desire for dictatorship the stamp of a revolutionary position . . . or are reformistic methods and the opportunistic actions characteristic of right-wing parties? Neither [is correct].

Is [the PPS leadership] an opponent of dictatorship and a fiery follower of democracy? Or are the Bolsheviks free of opportunism and reformism, in view of their flirtations with the Fascists and with the nationalists of Turkey, China, etc? It is not these issues which determined the revolutionary or reformist tendencies of a movement. The chief sign of reformism or revolution is, strange as it seems, internationalism—or better still, the relation to one's own state or nation to the question of statehood or the issue of nationalities. If the Socialist Party is ready to subordinate national interest to class interest, or to the interest of the Socialist movement . . . then it is a revolutionary party. If it does not have this outlook, if it looks on every

[30] Henryk Erlich, *Der Icker fun Bundism"* (Warsaw: Algemajner Jidiszer Arbeiter Bund, 1934), p. 5.

issue on the basis of the so-called national peril . . . then it is reformist.[31]

The distinction between the revolutionary socialism of the Bund and the Communist Party's socialism was even sharper, in the view of Erlich.

Just as we reject reformism, so also do we reject communism. We are against the anti-Marxist tactics of the Communists. We are totally opposed to the regime of "unfreedom," of the Prussian-type garrison state, of the dictatorship which the Communists have established even within their own party. We oppose their strivings to oppress the will of the working class establishing a dictatorship of the Politburo over the working class, and we condemn in the sharpest terms the disruptive tactics of the Communists, their politics of civil war within the ranks of the working class, which has caused serious distress to the labor movement of the world.[32]

This ideological difference was not enough, however, to keep the Bund a separate party; its leaders conceded that all other parties of the non-Communist Socialist left wing had merged with the Socialist parties of their countries. Even the Independent Socialists of Germany had rejoined the Social Democratic Party, which they considered totally reformist. But the Bund's position was different; it had to represent a distinct and persecuted constituency, the Jewish working class of Poland. "Had the Bund not been a party of the *Jewish* working class, which has unique interests and demands, the Bund would have had to merge, sooner or later, with the general Socialist movement of the state." [33]

To fail at this point to unite with the general Socialist party of Poland, the Bund's leaders insisted, or at least to coordinate their own activity with the PPS, would have meant isolation from the mainstream of Polish politics. "If we want to have

[31] H. Pizyc, "Mir un der P.P.S.," *Socialistisze Bleter*, I, June 1931, pp. 11–12.
[32] Erlich, *op. cit.*, p. 13.
[33] Pizyc, *loc. cit.*, p. 13; italics in original.

any political effect, it is necessary for us to coordinate our activity and struggle with the general movement, regardless of the fact that our political outlook is totally different than the other party's."

The question before the Bund thus appeared to be with whom to ally itself rather than whether to merge. Cooperation or unity with the Communists had by this time become impossible, since they were spewing vituperation at the Socialist parties, and particularly at the Bund, and their gangs had attacked insitutions organized by the Bund—such as the Medem Sanatorium for sick children from the homes of impoverished Jewish workingmen. The Communists had proclaimed to the world that they considered the Socialists— whom they labeled Social Fascists—the worst enemies of the working class. "The Communists are most revolutionary when they fight other proletarian parties. The experience of the past several years makes it unlikely that there can be any united front with the Communists. Their policy is the destruction of revolutionary Socialist parties by any means at their disposal." [34]

There was, however, an improvement in the outlook for unity with the PPS, which was losing much of its nationalist inclination and was becoming more of a Socialist and less of a Polish party—or so the Bund's leaders insisted. Historically the PPS was "a terrorist workers' and intellectuals' party whose goal was the independence of Poland." It had used "Socialist phrases from time to time in order to give itself a reason for existence and to add to the luster of the ideal of independence for Poland; it painted pretty pictures of a future Socialist Poland," though it had been, in the Bundists' view, merely a party dedicated to national independence for Poland.

But this was now changing, the Bund leadership believed. "Aren't we living witnesses to a new development in the

[34] *Ibid.*, pp. 13–14.

PPS? Don't we see the PPS cleansing itself?" Most of those who had joined the PPS only to fight for Polish independence had left the party shortly after the achievement of their goal in 1918. A few others had remained for a short time—until Pilsudski's coup and his renunciation of the Socialists—but there were practically none of them left in the party any longer. "The class orientation of the post-1926 PPS is alien to them. . . . And we see in the PPS the happy fact that the pre-war nationalist leadership is fleeing the party."

The Bund leaders conceded that the PPS was still basically not a revolutionary party, that its stand on the military budget (which it had favored) was based on national rather than class patriotism. "Certainly, the prewar traditions still play a part in the PPS. . . . But for the people who were only interested in an independent Poland there is now no place in the PPS—it is too class-oriented. Only the workers remain in the PPS, and they will sooner or later have to stand firm on the path to uncompromising, definite class struggle."

The PPS was drawing closer to the Bund in ideology, the Bund believed, because those who came in after independence wanted to join a Socialist party. The effect of these new elements was found by the Bundists to be a shift toward a Socialist orientation and an abandonment of the old state-oriented politics.[35]

There were two alternatives facing the Bund in its relations with the PPS: it could either attempt to speed the development of the Polish party into a genuinely Socialist organization that would sever its remaining ties with its nationalist past, or it could wait for the PPS to become "good and kosher." The majority of the Bund preferred to take the first attitude. "We must work energetically toward achieving this unity of action. The more energetically we work for this unity of action, the easier will we make it for the PPS to be-

[35] *Ibid.*, pp. 14–16.

come revolutionary, the sooner will the PPS come over to our point of view." [36]

Not all Bundists agreed with the majority; a strong left-wing minority doubted whether the PPS would change. The leader of the anti-PPS group was Joseph (Lestchinsky) Chmurner, who favored an even more radical program for the Bund, and who desired a close alliance with the Communists. He doubted that the PPS was genuinely anti-Pilsudski; it was, after all, Pilsudski who had divorced himself from it rather than the reverse. Moreover, he could cite the fact that the PPS deputies had failed to vote against the Pilsudski budget, and that they had supported Pilsudski actively on foreign policy issues. Chmurner asked: "Can it be shown, two years after the PPS became the opposition, that this forced opposition has been reflected, even in a tiny way, in the ideological position of the PPS? First the state and then the working class, this remains the basic policy of the PPS. Independence—and then socialism . . . this is now, as always, the leitmotiv of the PPS's orientation." [37]

IMPEDIMENTS TO UNITY

After decades of animosity, more was obviously required than a simple desire to unite two parties, even two Socialist parties, facing a hostile regime. The points of friction between the PPS and the Bund were too many to be erased in two or three years.

The first post-election disagreement between the two organizations occurred at the 1929 convention of the trade union federation. It was this convention that formalized the break between Pilsudski's followers and the pro-Socialist labor movement. Despite its stand against Pilsudski, according

[36] *Ibid.*, pp. 16–17.
[37] Joseph [Lestchinsky] Chmurner, "An Enderung?," *Uncer Cajt* (Warsaw), III, January 1929, pp. 5–7.

to a Bund spokesman, the trade union congress had failed to
become an open show of opposition.

The disagreement between the two parties was ideological
as well as tactical: the PPS leadership favored the concept of
economic democracy rather than socialism as the proper goal
for the labor movement; the Bund refused to retreat from its
insistence that only socialism could cure the ills of Poland's
working class.

Economic democracy, in the sense understood by the Social
Democratic parties during the period between 1925 and 1933,
meant essentially that the state, as the representative of all the
people, would regulate the economic life of the nation. Economic democracy was a system in many ways similar to the
New Deal in the United States; its object would be to improve conditions within the capitalist economy rather than to
overthrow the system and replace it with a new one. "Economic democracy is today an accepted and popular phrase in
Western Europe," Erlich wrote. "The right-wing reformists
of the labor movement consider this a . . . cure for all that is
wrong with the capitalist system; they see this as a means by
which socialism can develop peacefully in capitalism." [38]

Most Bundists rejected the contention that this so-called
economic democracy would lead gradually to socialism. Genuine democracy, they thought, could be achieved only after
the demise of the capitalist system and its replacement with a
Socialist society in which "the present class division of society
will be abolished." The same would also be true of economic
democracy; so long as the state remained the agent of the
class in power—as the Bund insisted it was—and so long as
that class was the capitalist class, for so long was "economic
democracy a snare and a delusion."

The Polish government, in particular, was not to be trusted
with carrying out "economic democracy," for the Bundists

[38] Henryk Erlich, "In Kampf Kegn Reformistishe Iluzies," *Uncer
Cajt* (Warsaw), III, March–April 1929, pp. 1–3.

insisted that the Pilsudski regime was "the executive committee for the cartels." Any "economic democracy" in Poland
would thus mean extending the control by the cartels. Before
"economic democracy" could even be considered, the Bundists believed, there would have to be (1) political democracy
within Poland, and (2) a more powerfully organized working
class movement capable of influencing actions by the state.[39]

Despite their displeasure with the labor federation's stand
on the economic issue, the Bundists were generally convinced
that unity with the PPS was still desirable, and that the PPS
was moving closer to their own position. There was no anticipation that the PPS would change its stand on internal and
foreign problems, or on the question of national minorities in
Poland. But the withdrawal of the pro-Pilsudski forces had
wrought changes in the PPS. The so-called left wing, whose
policy on many issues was almost identical with the Bund's,
was gaining strength and stature in the party. The split within
the Polish party had been going on for two years, and the
Bund leaders recognized that the tendency toward the left by
the PPS would be a slow process. "The split has undoubtedly
strengthened the left-wing, class-conscious elements in the
party in their opposition to the right, nationalist wing." [40]

Another major impediment to Socialist unity was meanwhile developing in Poland: the growing tendency toward
autocratic rule by Pilsudski, which forced the Socialists—
except for the Bund and a few minor Marxist sects—into a
bloc with non-Socialist parties in an effort to save democracy.
The struggle took the form of a continuing battle between the
parliamentary forces and Pilsudski's bloc. Jerzy Szapiro, correspondent in Warsaw for *The New York Times*, was able to
report early in 1930 that a climax was near. "Polish politics,"
he wrote, "has reached the stage where the conflict between

[39] *Ibid.*, p. 4.
[40] Henryk Erlich, "An Enderung?" *Uncer Cajt*, III, January 1929,
pp. 9–10.

parliament and Marshal Pilsudski's veiled dictatorship must find a solution." [41]

Pilsudski aimed his most effective assaults on his old party, the PPS, when his minister of labor, Colonel Alexander Prystor, ousted all duly elected officials of the Sick Fund Bureau, normally dominated by PPS followers, and replaced them with pro-Pilsudski administrators. He followed this with an unusually vituperative attack on the Sejm, and particularly on the Socialists, and with a demand that the democratic constitution based on a strong parliament give way to one which would be authoritarian in theory as well as in practice. By the end of August it was reported by Pilsudski's own daily, *Gazeta Polska*, that he, previously the dictator behind the scenes, would now assume the full responsibility of power. [42]

To meet the growing threat of dictatorship, the PPS, the Peasants' Party "Piast," the Wyzwolenie, and the Christian Democrats formed an alliance known as the Centrolew. Before the formation of the Centrolew, the Bund had invited the PPS to join it in forming an all-Socialist bloc which would include all of the Socialist parties in Poland. The PPS had countered with a proposal that the Bund join the Centrolew, in which it was offered seats. The Bund's Central Committee refused, charging that the "centrist politics of the PPS" had weakened fatally the Socialist movement in Poland in its struggle against fascism." When neither side would change its position, each decided to continue on its chosen path. The Bund then formed a bloc with the tiny Independent Socialist Party.

An election was pending, and Pilsudski feared that the new Centrolew alliance would endanger his position. He therefore ordered the arrest of fifteen leaders of opposition parties, including Herman Liebermann of the PPS. Jan Kwampinski, leader of the Agrarian Workers' Union, was arrested for a speech he had made under cloak of parliamentary immunity

[41] *The New York Times*, April 6, 1930, p. 3.
[42] *The New York Times*, April 6, 1930, Sec. III, p. 3; August 25, 1930, p. 10; *Gazeta Polska* (Warsaw), V, August 27, 1930.

months earlier; sixteen parliamentary deputies of the Ukrainian parties, four Byelorussian deputies, and one member of the Senate were also arrested. Others under arrest included Witos, the former premier, who had now decided that he favored a liberal democratic regime, and Thugutt, leader of the Wyzwolenie. Under an old Hapsburg law, they were charged with defaming the regime, because of an anti-Pilsudski resolution adopted at the meeting at which the electoral alliance was formed. One of the obvious reasons for the mass arrests was a Polish law which prohibited persons awaiting trial for criminal offenses from running for office.[43]

Those leaders of anti-Pilsudski parties who were not arrested found themselves penalized in other ways. Ignacy Daszynski, who in 1925 had written a biography of Pilsudski, called *The Great Man of Poland*, and whom Pilsudski had described as "my brother," was deprived of his passport.[44]

The treatment of the arrested politicians was brutal; they were held incommunicado in the military prison at Brześć (Brest-Litovsk), where their military guards maltreated them, and protests were futile. One issued by the Warsaw Chamber of Lawyers was seized by the censors, and the association was warned that it faced severe punishment if it tried to repeat the protest.[45]

Pilsudski won his majority at the election, but to do so he was obliged to cancel votes for the opposition and to suppress activities on its behalf.[46]

The Bund–Independent Socialist Bloc was a failure; it polled a vote of only 71,000 out of approximately 12,000,000 votes cast—a decline of almost 30 per cent from the Bund's vote of two years previous—and it won no seats. The PPS and the

---

[43] *The New York Times*, July 4, 1930, p. 6; September 1, 1930, p. 5; September 11, 1930, p. 9; October 5, 1930, p. 9; also Henryk Erlich, "Politishe Perspektivn," *Uncer Cajt*, VI, February 1932, p. 5.

[44] Chernov, *loc. cit.*, p. 146.

[45] *The New York Times*, September 14, 1930, p. 30.

[46] *Ibid.*, November 23, 1930, Sec. III, p. 4.

other Socialist parties also lost strength in the election. Most of the workers voted for the Sanacja, Pilsudski's regime.[47]

Both the Bund and the PPS were shaken by Pilsudski's victory, and began a slow move that would bring them closer to unity, although actual unification was to elude them until the end.

The Bund, in particular, rejected any coalition with non-Socialist parties. "Fascism," Erlich wrote, "is the most gruesome face of dying capitalism." Thus, he maintained, it was impossible to fight fascism without at the same time fighting capitalism as well. Moreover, the Bundists had begun to lose faith in the electoral process: "The elections of November 16 [1930] show irrefutably what has been shown in Italy and Hungary and other nations, that the hope of defeating fascism at the polls is a laughable illusion." [48]

The election, the Bund organ maintained, proved that unity with non-Socialist parties would drive away workers, that the workers wanted Socialist parties only. Some of the parties

[47] *Barikht fun Tsentral Komitet*, report of Central Committee to the 5th Convention of the Bund (Warsaw: Algemajner Jidiszer Arbeiter Bund in Poyln, 1935); copy in Bund Archives, New York, p. 24. The results of the election follow (only parties which elected at least one member to the Sejm are included):

Party or Bloc	Votes	Seats
Non-Party Bloc of Cooperation with the Government (Sanacja)	5,293,000	249
National Party	1,443,000	63
Socialist and Peasant Bloc (Centrolew)	1,966,000	79
Ukrainian and White-Ruthenian Bloc	726,000	21
German Bloc	310,000	5
Jewish National Bloc	185,000	4
Jewish National Rights Bloc	247,000	2
General Jewish National Economic Bloc	150,000	1
Catholic People's Bloc	430,000	14
Workmen's and Peasants' Union	232,000	4
Peasants' Self-Help Party (Left-Wing)	23,000	1
Socialists' Bloc	52,000	1

Source: *Concise Statistical Year Book of Poland*, II, 1931 (Warsaw: Chief of the Bureau of Statistics, 1931), p. 134.

[48] Erlich, *Politishe Perspektsivn, loc. cit.*, pp. 5, 2.

with whom the PPS allied itself were, the Bund daily said, "nationalist and reactionary," and this had led the workers to vote for the Pilsudski ticket; but they were not voting for fascism. "They were apathetic and disappointed. They could not become enthusiastic about the democracy proclaimed by parties that ignored the righs of workers." [49]

The Bundists still hoped for a united Socialist party in Poland, but they no longer expected that party to use only the legal means of parliamentary democracy to achieve its ends. Said Erlich:

> The best means of defense is attack . . . It cannot be used in every instance. Two years ago, when the bankruptcy of the May regime was not so obvious, when the mass of the people had as yet not overcome its May illusions, it would have been difficult to follow this advice. But today the situation has changed. Today the politics of waiting, avoiding, standing aside, and not allowing ourselves to be provoked is grist for the mill of the dictator, because it sows apathy and disinterest, which are valuable assets for the reaction, for the dictatorship.
>
> It is necessary to carry the fight against the Pilsudski regime outside the walls of the Sejm, into the open. It is necessary to get the support of the people, principally the workers, for action against the Pilsudski regime.[50]

THE FEUD CONTINUES

During the early 1930's, the hope for a united Socialist party in Poland faded as the oppression grew worse. At a meeting of the executive of the Socialist International an attempt was made to reconcile the two parties, in the hope of saving the movement in Poland from total destruction. Victor Alter, leader of the Jewish trade unions and second only to Erlich in the Bund hierarchy, declared: "Only a fight for

---

[49] *Najer Folkscajtung*, August 6, 1931.
[50] Henryk Erlich, "Der Muser Hashakel," *Uncer Cajt*, V, May 1931.

revolutionary proletarian democracy can lead to a unity of the Socialist groups." Mieczyslaw Niedzialkowski, who represented the PPS, answered that the Bund could more easily afford to spout revolutionary phrases, for it had never had responsibility for the fate of Poland, whereas the PPS had had that responsibility thrust upon it.[51]

New irritants developed also, most of them picayune. In the summer of 1932, during a period of sharp repression by the Pilsudski dictatorship, a group of Bundists led by Alter, and of Polish Socialists—members of the PPS—decided to transform a small monthly, *Nasza Walka*, into a Socialist daily, which was to be produced by the publishers of the Bund daily *Najer Folkscajtung*. The newspaper, although not directly responsible to the Bund, was closely tied by outlook and ideology to the Jewish Socialists. The object of the new daily, to be called *Pismo Codzienne*, was to present the Bund's views to the Polish Socialists in the hope of winning over the PPS to the same position. The new newspaper aroused consternation among the leaders of Pilsudski's government, who feared that it might swing the PPS into more revolutionary activity. To force the new daily to cease publication, the government decided to close down the printing plant that produced it, thus serving at the same time to warn other print shops against accepting the job if the publishers decided to continue operations. A building inspector sent to the plant of the *Najer Folkscajtung* accordingly declared the structure unsafe. This resulted in a seventeen-day shutdown of the *Najer Folkscajtung*, and the end—after two weeks—of the Polish daily.[52]

The Pilsudski regime was not alone in its antipathy toward the Polish daily. The PPS was also irritated, since the *Pismo Codzienne* had been sharply critical of the PPS on many issues. Its successor, the weekly *Nowe Pismo*, continued to be

[51] *Najer Folkscajtung*, March 12, 1931; August 6, 1931.
[52] *Najer Folkscajtung*, December 8, 1932; *Barikht fun Tsentral Comitet*, pp. 6, 12.

a thorn in the PPS's side, and brought sharp protests from the organization. Neidzialkowski charged that the attacks on its leadership raised serious doubts as to the honesty of the Bund's stated wish for a permanent union with the PPS.

This accusation led to a long polemic by Erlich in the *Najer Folkscajtung.* He denied that the Bund was obligated to be totally uncritical of the PPS if the two groups were to cooperate. "According to Niedzialkowski," Erlich wrote, "one Socialist Party either may not speak of another, or must speak of it only with praise. Honest, constructive criticism he considers unfriendly." Erlich doubted that it was necessary to treat other Socialist parties as untouchables. "We are over-joyed to report their successes and achievements; however, precisely because we feel ourselves closely tied to them, we feel free—and obligated—to speak openly and without diplomatic niceties about all of their actions which we consider false and damaging to our politics."[53]

Some united action by the PPS and the Bund was taken during the early 1930's, particularly in the local elections. In Cracow and Tarnow, two of Poland's leading industrial centers, the two groups ran a joint slate and scored remarkable successes; they elected 17 out of 40 city councilmen in Tarnow and 13 in Cracow. But the feuding continued to hurt both parties seriously.[54]

The membership of the Bund declined by more than 7 per cent from 7,590 in 1929 to 7,000 in 1935. Most of the decline evidently occurred in smaller towns, since 6,715 Bund members were reported from the twelve largest cities in Poland in 1935. Significantly, the number of Bund locals had increased during the six-year period from 200 to 213; but in 300 of the small towns only individual Bundists were left.[55]

Nine years after the Pilsudski uprising, and seven years after a joint Bund–PPS slate had shown that unity would add to the

[53] *Najer Folkscajtung,* August 13, 1933; *Freie Wort* (London), December 29, 1933, p. 6.
[54] *Ibid.,* p. 6.   [55] *Barikht,* pp. 6–7.

strength of each of the parties, the two were still squabbling
and unable to unite against a common enemy.

The Central Committee reported in 1935: "The reformist
behavior of the Polish Socialist Party (PPS), her opposition
to the Bund, make it impossible to unite with the party of the
Polish proletariat, against the nationalist and Zionist tendencies . . . as had been the case years ago in Russia." [56]

TROUBLE WITH THE COMMUNISTS

The Communists continued their warfare against the Bund
during the late 1920's and early 1930's; they intensified the
vituperation and even employed murder to further the political warfare. No falsification, no irresponsible attack was be-
yound their scruples; name-calling descended to levels un-
heard of before.

The Bundists were accused of being in league with the government in the latter's oppression of the Polish and Jewish
workers, and of being Social Fascists, paid lackeys of the
capitalist class.

The official Communist organ, *Czerwony Sztandar*, in a
typical editorial accused the Bund of representing "the black-
est betrayal of the interests of the working class." An attempt
by the Bund to assure for Jewish workers the right to their
jobs, a right which was under constant and serious pressure
from the nationalists, was condemned by the Communists as
an attempt to break the unity of the Polish and Jewish workers. "In the period of feverish preparation for a war against
the Soviet Union, the Bund assists—organizationally and politically—in preparing that war." Bund union leaders, said the
editorial, "act as strikebreakers," and a suggestion by Bund
members of the Warsaw Council, that *matzoth* be included
in the food packets distributed to the unemployed during the

[56] *Ibid.*, p. 3.

paschal season, was condemned as pro-clerical. Finally, the Communist journal accused the Bund of supporting attempts to prevent the national minorities from achieving autonomy.[57]

A young Bundist, Abraham Neuerman, who was a member of the anti-Communist minority of the Bakers' Union executive committee, was shot to death by Communist gunmen in broad daylight on a busy Warsaw street. He had been on his way to a meeting at which Communist control of the union might have been in jeopardy. More than fifty other Bundists were wounded by Communist gunmen and knife-wielders; among them were the secretary of the ladies' garment workers' union, the secretary of the leather workers' union, and officials of the metal workers', knitters', and transport unions. Communist gangs regularly attacked not only evening classes for adults that were run by the Bund, but also children's schools and the Medem Sanatorium.[58]

The Communist attacks were a planned part of an organized campaign of terror against the Jewish labor movement which they could not control. They were similar, the Bundists warned, to the anti-Socialist terror unleashed by the Italian Fascists before they seized power. But the Bundists remained unwilling to acknowledge that this was part of the Communist method. The attacks may have been the work of provocateurs. It was certain only that with these attacks on labor leaders "the Communists are helping the Fascist reaction." [59]

The police refused to protect the Bundists against the Communist assaults; either the perpetrators were released almost immediately, or else no effort was made to find them. An

---

[57] *Czerwony Sztandar,* #3, April, 1931 (clipping in Bund Archives).
[58] "Degeneratsye fun a Partei," *Uncer Cajt,* V, March–April 1932, p. 2; *Tsu Alle Idishe Arbeiter in Poyln* (Warsaw: Algemajner Jidisze Arbeiter Bund, November 10, 1931); leaflet in Bund Archives, New York.
[59] "Degeneratsye fun a Partei," *loc. cit.,* p. 3.

official report by the police named the assailant of the secretary of the ladies' garment union, but he was never arrested or questioned. This was in contrast to the fate of young Communists who distributed leaflets or did other agitational work; they were almost invariably arrested and convicted.[60]

Attempts at joint action against the repressions invariably resulted in failure, after long and acrimonious negotiations. In March 1933, the Communists asked the Bund for a united front against fascism. The Bund executive accepted, with two conditions: first, that the Communists stop their anti-Bund campaign, and second, that the negotiations be held in secret in order to avoid any possible trouble. The Communists agreed, and negotiations began; but almost immediately the attacks were renewed. They culminated in a shooting foray against food staff workers, most of whom belonged to the Bund, in which one man was killed and another severely wounded. The Bund's request for an explanation brought forth another leaflet filled with accusations against the Jewish Socialists. This ended the negotiations.

A second attempt at talks was begun in June 1934. Initiated by the Communists, it was limited this time to an attempt to save Ernst Thaelmann, the German Communist leader who was under death sentence for setting the Reichstag fire. The Bund suggested that the negotiations begin after the Communists had pledged to end the anti-Socialist campaign, and that the proposed action include all Socialist parties and deal with the threat of fascism in Poland as well. But no sooner had negotiations begun than the Communists resumed their attacks on the Bund. Once more the talks ended.

In 1933 two other attempts at united action between the Bund and the Communists against the Fascist threat ended when the Communists announced—without explanation—that they could not work with the Bund, the betrayer of the working class" and "enemy of the Soviet Union." [61]

[60] *Ibid.*, pp. 2–4.   [61] *Barikht*, pp. 42–44.

The leaders of the world's Socialist parties were convinced that the Communists were using the united-front tactic in an effort to win over members of the Social Democratic parties by discrediting their leaders. Such an effort was in keeping with Communist policy, since the Comintern in 1928 had adopted a program aimed at destroying the non-Communist influence on the working class. This meant the destruction of the Socialist parties. The Comintern's reasoning was that So- cialist—or Social Democratic—parties were the chief obstacle to the revolution. Not only did they lead the workers away from the only "true revolutionary party," but also they were precursors of fascism. The Socialists were labeled "Social Fascists" by the Comintern; and the destruction of the demo- cratic Socialist parties became the primary aim of the Communists.

Since the Communists considered the left-wing Socialist parties—such as the Bund—the most dangerous segment of the Social Democratic movement, these left-wing parties be- came their particular targets. The left-wing Socialists were accused of using revolutionary phraseology while deluding the proletariat into defending the parliamentary-democratic, "bourgeois" state structure.

A shift in the Communist position did occur for a short time during the early part of 1933, immediately after Hitler rose to power in Germany. At that time the Comintern pro- posed a united action with the Socialists to fight the world- wide threat of fascism. The unpleasant experiences of 1928– 1932 made the Socialists skeptical of cooperation with the Communists. By the end of 1933 the Communists had proved the Socialist fears to be well founded; they had reversed their stand and resumed their war against democratic Socialists.[62]

The Communist effort at a united front with the Bund was

[62] Kermit E. McKenzie, *The Comintern and World Revolution, 1928–1943* (New York: Columbia University Press, 1964), pp. 131– 135.

made during this period of hostility. It was thus a foregone conclusion that the negotiations would fail. The Communists' self-proclaimed intentions precluded a genuine effort at joint action; and the Bund had reason to suspect that the Communists were merely using another tactic aimed at the destruction of the left-wing Socialist movement.

The Bund leaders had, in the meantime, moved into open opposition to the Communist philosophy and the Soviet Union. The Communists were no longer to be considered revolutionists; nor was there much hope left that the Soviet Union would evolve into a free Socialist society. Erlich wrote of the situation: "The tragedy of communism, as an international movement, lies in its emptiness and lack of value. The entire philosophy of communism is limited to two things: (1) apologia for the Soviet Union; (2) hatred of all non-Communist workers' movements. The Communists have no other positive principles." [63] The dictatorial rule in Soviet Russia was antithetical to the Bundists' view of what Socialism should be. "There is no socialism in the Soviet Union," wrote Mauritzi Ozher, director of the *Najer Folkscajtung.* "There rules the terror . . ." [64]

According to the Bund's theoreticians, the economy of the Soviet Union was based on false premises which ignored the needs of the people. Industrialization was being accomplished by means of force and terror, and this had led to further pauperization of the people. The Five-Year Plan instituted by Stalin was not the true road to socialism, but was merely an attempt to turn the USSR into an industrial giant. The problem of instituting socialism in the Soviet Union was seen to be political as well as economic; it could not be achieved without an end to the dictatorial rule. "The way of the Five-Year

[63] Erlich, "Politishe Perspektivn," *loc. cit.,* p. 4.
[64] Mauritzi Ozher, "Unser Tog Ordnung: Sotsialism," *Socialistisze Bleter,* I, June 1931, pp. 24–25.

Plan is not the way to socialism, [it is] rather the false path to dictatorship." [65]

The Bundists believed that socialism could not be achieved by simply abolishing private property or developing heavy industry; these were no more than the necessary prerequisites of socialism. Heavy industrialization could occur under capitalism. Socialism required collective control of industry for the benefit of the whole of society. What the Five-Year Plan hoped to achieve was, instead, "a terrorist dictatorship of industry against the interests of the masses." Industry might be a necessary part of the Socialist society, but "only when we have an answer to what it is costing the working class and what it is giving in return will we be able to determine the value that the Five-Year Plan has to the working class." If the Five-Year Plan was actually a step toward socialism, a Bund leader maintained, it would raise considerable question as to the value of socialism; for capitalism had achieved industrialization at far less cost in human suffering than had the Five-Year Plan. [66]

In 1935, when the Soviet Union feared imminent invasion by the Germans, the Communists developed a new tactic, called the popular front. Essentially, it meant that the Communists would organize united actions by all anti-Fascist elements, in support of an anti-Nazi foreign policy. The popular front was supposed to be a united struggle against fascism; actually it was another in the long series of Communist tactics aimed at furthering Soviet foreign policy. [67]

The Bund leadership rejected the whole concept of the

[65] A——n, "A Por Bamerkungen tsum Artikl fun Altern, 'Di Internationaler Diskusie vegn Ratn Farband,'" *Uncer Cajt*, V, April 1931, p. 3; M. Kligsberg, "Sotsialism un 5-Yor Plan," *Socialistisze Bleter*, I, June 1931, p. 49.

[66] *Ibid.*, pp. 46–52.

[67] For a Communist exposition of the popular front, see *International Press Correspondence* (London), XIV (October 12, 1935), 1329.

popular front as against the best interests of the workers. An internal bulletin of the Bund declared:

> Just as the previous theory of united front from below (the tactic of warfare against the Socialists) was harmful to the working class, so, too, is the new tactic of popular front. To limit the struggle against fascism to the general-democratic issues such as defense of democracy, defense of the republic [would be a delusion]. Democracy alone is not enough.
>
> The Fascists made use of democracy to propagate their . . . ideas. Hitler came to power legally under the democratic Weimar Constitution.
>
> Under such conditions (where democracy can help a Fascist seizure of power) the working-class struggle is not for general democracy, but [it] favors the sharpest repressions against the Fascist organizations. . . .[68]

No further contact existed between the Bund and the Polish Communists; ironically, the Stalin regime ordered the Polish Communist Party dissolved in 1938 as a Trotskyite organization. The KPP's leaders, who had fled to the Soviet Union from persecution at home, were executed in Stalin's jails.[69]

JEWISH COMMUNAL POLITICS

Besides being Socialist in ideology, the Bund was a Jewish party, closely tied to the persecuted Jewish community and its problems. Historically there had been tendencies within the Bund that kept it apart from the rest of the Jewish com-

---

[68] *Tezn un Referat an der Teme "Folks Front oder Proletarishe Klasn Front* (Warsaw: Bund, 1936); mimeographed bulletin distributed by the Bund Central Committee to local party officials; copy in Bund Archives, New York.

[69] *World Views and News* [Organ of the Communist International] I, April 16, 1939, p. 382; *Pravda* (Moscow), April 4, 1956; Goldfinger, Mirski, Zachariasz (eds.), *Unter der Fon fun KPP*, pp. 36, 49; Clifford R. Barnett, *Poland: Its People, Its Society, Its Culture* (New York: Grove Press, Inc., 1958), p. 24.

munity: its antipathy toward Zionism, its opposition to clericalism, its rejection of Hebrew and preference for Yiddish
as the language of the people, and the insistence that it was a
Socialist party first and a Jewish party second.

One result of the powerlessness of the Bund was its devotion to abstract ideological discussions. A critic within the
organization described the situation thus:

> If the powerful labor movements of other nationalities are
> too closely rooted in the homeland, the Jewish labor move-
> ment suffers too much . . . from being abstract.
>
> The Jewish worker worries too little about himself and too
> much about others. Look at the Jewish labor press of the past
> few years. Note how much space is devoted the foreign news,
> alien news with which we have no direct contact, and which
> we cannot influence, and how little is devoted to Jewish news
> in general and the Jewish worker's life in particular. At Jew-
> ish labor rallies, called for specific purposes, discussion veers
> to all sorts of foreign issues and away from the point at issue.
> Jewish workers live much more each day with the problems
> of Germany, Russia, England, and America than with the im-
> mediate issues, which we must solve.[70]

This was, however, a natural result of the conditions of the
Jewish labor movement in Poland. Unable to affect the life
of the nation, isolated from the mainstream of Polish life,
persecuted economically and politically, the members of the
Jewish labor movement found escape through discussing
broad issues which did not directly affect them but which
allowed them to give vent to their proclivity for intellectual
debate. It was, to quote one Socialist observer, a natural outcome of the Jewish alienation from Polish life.[71]

Between 1919 and 1931, the Bund attempted to become an
active force in the Jewish community by participating in the
Jewish *Kehillath*, the local community councils that were a

[70] S. Hertz, "Aynike Shtrikhn Vegn der Idisher Arbeiter Bavegung,"
Socialistisze Bleter, I (June 1931), pp. 41–43.
[71] See *ibid.*, p. 40.

carryover from the late Middle Ages. They had certain definite though limited powers: the control of purely religious functions, the ownership of real estate, and the levying and collecting of taxes for the upkeep of such communal institutions as Hebrew schools and hospitals. The *Kehillath* were invariably in the hands of the religious leaders of the community, although members were elected by free ballot.[72]

In 1919 the Bund decided to contest these elections. The intention was to bore from within, in order to remake the community councils from purely religious into genuinely communal institutions. The Bundists were particularly interested in the development of more secular institutions of learning—in Yiddish—and in the protection of the workers' interests in various insurance and charitable establishments under their control. The reasoning of the Bundists was that since they had to pay the communal taxes anyway, and since they had the right to vote, there was nothing to be lost by participating in the councils. Moreover, they believed it would be possible to direct the expenditure of the funds in a manner more to their liking if they participated in the *Kehillath*.

The *Kehillath* had attracted little attention, and few Jews had actually taken part in the elections. It had thus been a simple matter for the religious groups to maintain control, and to prevent the Bund from using them as anything more than a tribune, and a minor one at that. The Pilsudski government reduced the secular functions of the *Kehillath* and intensified the relation of the councils to the clerical faction of the Jews. By 1929 the *Kehillath* were opposing any aid to Yiddish schools, and the Bund decided to refuse to participate in future elections.[73]

Shmuel Mordecai (Arthur) Zygelboym, one of the

[72] *Barikht, op. cit.*, pp. 22–23; Segal, *op. cit.*, pp. 178–179.

[73] Shmuel Mordecai (Arthur) Zygelboym, "In Kamf far Veltlakhe Kehillas," *Uncer Cajt*, III, April 1929, p. 63; *Barikht, loc. cit.*, pp. 22–23.

younger leaders of the Bund, who was to be its representative in the Polish Parliament-in-Exile during part of the war, led the move to withdraw from the community councils. There were three reasons for the proposal: (1) The law made it unlikely the *Kehillath* could be changed from religious to communal institutions, (2) they were by tradition religious, and (3) the public accepted them as religious rather than secular institutions, so that few people voted in the elections of delegates. "Is it worth the energy which participation in the *Kehillath* requires of us?" Zygelboym asked. The Bund agreed with him, and in 1931 withdrew from them completely.[74]

The Bund still considered itself a Jewish organization, interested in Jewish affairs and in the development of a specifically Jewish culture. It rejected assimilation into the Polish society as Poles of the Mosaic faith; it wanted the Jews to be recognized as one of the nationalities within Poland, with specific rights to cultural autonomy. The Bund recognized that there would be some assimilation of Jews into the general Polish culture—this was only natural—but it opposed forced or conscious assimilation. Its ultimate goal was the achievement of national culture autonomy for the Jews, as well as for all national minorities in Poland; but meanwhile it wanted immediate action toward making Yiddish an official language, and the recognition of schools operated in the Yiddish language.[75]

The Bund was not alone in trying to represent the Jewish Socialists; there were at least two other parties that described themselves as Socialist and that offered their own solutions to the Jewish problem. Both called themselves Poale Zionists; both favored development of a Jewish Socialist state in Palestine and fostered emigration from Poland to what they considered the homeland. While Jews remained in Poland, how-

---

[74] Zygelboym, *loc. cit.*, pp. 64–65.
[75] Erlich, *Der Icker fun Bundism*, p. 8.

ever, they believed it necessary to further the aims of the
Socialists in their alien land. The "Right" Poale Zion was
closely tied to the non-Socialist Zionist organizations; and the
"Left" Poale Zion had little to do with the other Zionist
groups. The "Right" Poale Zion was hostile toward the
Bund; the "Left Poale Zion had at times acted in concert
with it.[76]

The Bund was historically hostile toward Zionism, which it
considered a delusion and a snare. Medem believed Socialism
and Zionism to be anathema to one another. "We are asked
why we are opposed to Zionism," he wrote. "The answer is
simple: because we are Socialists. And not merely socialisti-
cally inclined or Socialists in belief only. But active Socialists.
And between the Zionist activity and the Socialist there is a
basic, deep chasm . . . and across that chasm there is no
bridge." [77]

The Bund insisted that the Jews were citizens of Poland and
not of Palestine, that they were Europeans and not a Middle
Eastern people, that their ties were with the countries in
which they lived and not with the land where some of their
ancestors had once lived. Palestine could not solve the Jewish
problem; it was futile to run away. The only answer to the
Jewish problem, Erlich said, was to be found in a complete
social revolution.[78]

Medem summed up the Bund's position:

> [The Zionists] speak of a national home in Palestine. But our
> entire organization, our entire work is based on precisely the
> opposite view, the view that our home is here: here in Poland,
> in Russia, in Lithuania, in the Ukraine, in America. Here we

[76] See *Labor Zionist Handbook* (New York: Poale Zion–Ziere Zion,
n.d.), pp. 8–12. The "Right" Poale Zion is now the dominant Mapai
Party in Israel; the "Left" Poale Zionists have divided into the Mapam
and Achdut Haavoda parties there.

[77] V. Medem, "Farvos Ikh Bin Kegn Tsionism," *Naye Velt* (New
York), X, July 2, 1920, p. 12.

[78] Erlich, *Der Icker fun Bundism*, p. 10.

live, here we struggle, here we build, here we hope. We are not here as strangers, we are here at home. It is on this basis that our entire being stands or falls. . . . Upset this basis and our entire work becomes senseless, illogical, without reason.

If my home is "there," I would be wasting every drop of sweat I expended here in an alien land. . . . Thus it is not without reason that the Zionists are angry and accuse us of wanting to turn Jewish blood into "lubricants for alien revolutions." The great revolutions of Europe are alien to them, their home is in Asia.

A national home in Palestine would not eliminate the Jewish exile. It is a denial of the exile and a spiritual disturbance of it. Should the national home in Palestine really set aside, wipe out, and destroy the Jewish exile, it would really create what it set out to do for the Jewish people. But this has long been abandoned as a daydream. The ingathering of the millions of Jews into Palestine is not even a matter for discussion. At best, with the most strenuous of efforts, under the most favorable conditions, on the basis of the most fantastic success, a tenth of the world's Jews could—after decades—be settled in Palestine. The Jewish exile would exist as before. All that would change would be that the belief of Jewry in its future—the hope of the Jews in exile—the struggle for a better life would be snuffed out.[79]

By the 1930's, Arab opposition and British attempts at placating the Moslems made it appear even more unlikely that the Zionists could accomplish their task. Under those conditions, Erlich saw Palestine becoming merely another land in the Diaspora, with at most 300,000 to 500,000 Jews.[80]

When in 1928 the Arabs attacked the Jewish settlers in Palestine, the Zionists called for massive protest rallies. The Bund, refusing to participate, called its own rallies to hear "the truth about Palestine." The Zionists, the Bund charged, were as much to blame for the slaughter as the Arabs and the British were; they had intruded on a land for the sake of

[79] Medem, *loc. cit.*, p. 12.   [80] Erlich, *op. cit.*, pp. 7–8.

taking it away from its inhabitants. But the Zionists gained sympathy and adherents during the period of attack when the Bund repeated "with all our energy we stand against the nationalist wave at the moment of its greatest growth." [81]

The Zionists spoke derisively of *Efendi Bundisti* (Arabic for "Sir Bundist"), and the animosity between the two groups became more intense. [82]

IN THE SOCIALIST INTERNATIONAL

The Bund had affiliated in 1923 with a small group of insignificant Socialist and quasi-Communist parties, known as the Bureau of Revolutionary Socialist Parties, with headquarters in Paris. The Bureau had been described by one Socialist observer as consisting "of tiny groups of yesterday's or tomorrow's Communists, without following, without influence." The Bund's leaders had believed for some time before 1929 that membership in it was useless, and that the Bureau itself served no purpose. [83]

The first step tward affiliation with the Labor and Socialist International was taken at the Bund's 1929 convention in Warsaw, held at a time when friendship with the PPS was at its height, and only two months after the 1928 election, in which the two parties had worked together in close harmony. It was also a time of great hope in the future of the organization; its membership had been stabilized at 7,000 after a decline to 4,500 five years earlier; the number of local Bund organizations had increased by almost 100 per cent since 1924; there were 187 Bundists serving on city councils, and thirteen in magistracies. [84]

[81] *Barikht, op. cit.*, p. 19.

[82] *Ibid.*, p. 20.

[83] "Der Poylisher Bund," *Der Wecker* (New York), IX, June 14, 1930, p. 3; John Price, *The International Labour Movement* (London: Oxford University Press, 1945), p. 31.

[84] A. Dunai, "Der Ferter Conferents fun Bund," *Der Wecker* (New York), VIII, March 23, 1929, pp. 7–8.

It had also become apparent, after ten years, that there was no hope of unity with the Communists. Since the withdrawal from the PPS of the nationalist pro-Pilsudski leadership, there had been a trend toward more fraternal relations with the Bund. The PPS had become more of a Socialist and less of a nationalist party, and the Bund had become less radical in its approach to socialism. One of the primary reasons for the Bund's refusal to consider entering the Socialist International had been the fact that the PPS was an affiliate. This was no longer a major deterrent.[85]

As if to emphasize the end of the strife between the two groups, the PPS sent the editor of its daily paper, *Robotnik*, as its fraternal delegate to the Bund convention. He helped ease the way into the Socialist International by calling for close cooperation between the two organizations and by backing the Bund's chief demand, a guarantee of the right of Jewish workers to their jobs.[86]

Not all of the Bund leaders were in favor of going into the Labor and Socialist International; some still considered the world organization anathema. The anti-LSI Bundists still expected the Communist International to change its stance and emerge as an organization with which they could affiliate. There was no point, they argued, in affiliating with the Socialist International, since it was lost in the "morass of reformism." This would continue so long as the PPS, the German Social Democratic Party, and other parties who did not believe in a cataclysmic end to capitalism were members. The Bund could never ally itself with the PPS or any of the other "reformist" parties.[87]

The majority of Bundists, however, wanted the party to end its illusions about Communism and the Comintern and enter the Socialist world organization. The majority doubted that the Communists would change, or that the Comintern

---

[85] *Ibid.*, p. 7; "Der Poylisher Bund," *loc. cit.*, pp. 3–4.
[86] *Ibid.*, p. 8.   [87] *Ibid.*, p. 7.

would end its rigid internal dictatorship or alter its totalitarian ideology or distruptive tactics. Under such conditions it was useless to discuss waiting for the opportunity to enter the Comintern. Even if the opportunity were to be offered, the Bund could not enter an organization with which it was in disagreement on basic issues of ideology.[88]

Alter proposed that the Bund enter the Labor and Socialist International, and that it attempt to get the other members of the Paris-based Bureau of Revolutionary Socialist Parties to take similar action. A long and heated debate followed. One delegate reported: "For three and a half days there was carried on within the party [at the convention] an ideological fight. Each of us fought stubbornly for the truth as he saw it, for each of us was convinced that his truth bespoke the best interests of the party." [89] In the end the Alter resolution was adopted, with an amendment that it would have to be ratified at a special convention the next year.[90]

The special convention was held in the Socialist-controlled city of Łodz. Although it was called to settle only one issue —affiliation with the LSI—it was also a demonstration of growing cordiality between the Bund and the PPS. Israel Lichtenstein, a Bund member of the City Council, expressed the spirit of the convention when he commented: "The Jewish workers of Łodz do not stand alone in the struggle. They stand shoulder to shoulder with the Polish and German working class." [91]

Zygmunt Zaremba, a member of the Sejm elected on a joint PPS–Bund slate, appealed for permanent unity between the two parties.

The Jewish and Polish workers have not only points of contact but also points of alienation. The enemy which divides

[88] *Ibid.*, p. 7.   [89] *Ibid.*, p. 6.   [90] *Ibid.*, pp. 8–9.
[91] "Der Ekstra Konferents fun Bund," *Der Wecker* (New York), IX, June 28, 1930, p. 7. Łodz had a sizable German population.

the workers of the various nationalities still wields a powerful influence over us. . . . If the Polish and Jewish workers
draw closer, despite this, it is because there is on the one side
the Bund and on the other side the PPS . . . both of which
are building a bridge of unity between the proletariat of the
two nationalities. If there are differences between us we should
not become angry; let us instead try to understand each other
and seek ways to end our differences. And, because there is
developing a better understanding of each other's viewpoints,
we are becoming—year by year—closer to each other.[92]

The spirit of the convention was possible, in part, because
the results were a foregone conclusion. Almost 60 per cent
of the Bund's membership had voted in favor of affiliation
with the Labor and Socialist International, and the delegates
were divided 60 to 43. Despite the air of fraternity that appeared to pervade the gathering, the opponents of reaffilia-
tion were embittered and refused to accept minority representation on the presidium.[93]

The resolution on affiliation, prepared by the Central Committee, made clear that there could be no compromise with
the Communist International. The resolution said that the
Comintern "is ideologically bankrupt and plays a deleterious
role in the labor movement; the International Socialist Bureau has failed, after seven years, to become a center for
revolutionary Socialist parties, and the Socialist International
has grown because of a growing desire among the non-
Communist Socialist parties for unity. The [Labor and] Socialist International now includes all of the divisions in the
Socialist movement except the Communists and [the Inter-
national] allows each to exist within its ranks." [94]

The opponents of the LSI proposed an alternative resolution, assailing the world body but suggesting no alternative
organization for the Bund to join. Moreover, a spokesman

[92] *Ibid.*, pp. 7–8.   [93] *Ibid.*, p. 7; *Barikht*, p. 8.
[94] "Der Ekstra . . . ," *loc. cit.*, p. 11.

for the minority group asked the convention to declare itself incompetent to decide the issue; in his opinion, it could only advise. He pleaded loyalty to the Bund, denied that the minority was asking special privileges, and insisted that it merely wanted the right to express its own opinions within the Bund. "How can you ask almost half of the party to belong to an international which we consider to be the most outrageous negation of the whole ideal of internationalism?" [95]

Erlich, speaking for the majority, denied that entering the Labor and Socialist International meant ideological capitulation: "We remain as much opposed to reformism as to Communism." [96]

The minority then attempted a parliamentary maneuver to prevent the convention from acting. Forty-two of the forty-three minority delegates walked out of the convention on the erroneous assumption that 60 per cent of the delegates had to be present for the convention to be able to conduct business. They announced they would refuse to accept the decisions of the convention on the ground that it was an illegal body.[97]

After the convention voted fifty nine to one for a return to the Socialist International (one majority delegate was absent, one left-winger voted in the negative, and forty-two left-wingers had walked out), the minority delegates came back, though they promised to continue the fight against affiliation. "We decided to attend the final session [after the vote] to make clear that our party remains organizationally unified as it had been prior to the convention." [98]

Having returned to the Labor and Socialist International, the Bundist spokesmen left no doubt that they would be a maverick group fighting to make of the International a revolutionary organization. Erlich explained the position:

[95] *Ibid.*, pp. 8–10.   [96] *Ibid.*, pp. 10–11.   [97] *Ibid.*, pp. 10–11.
[98] *Ibid.*, p. 11.

The convention had to answer a question: "How to end the paradox of our party's internationalist world view and its practical isolation?"

In the ranks of the [International Socialist] organization it is necessary for the Jewish working class to make a place for its party . . . the Bund. We make no effort to create any illusions about the Socialist International . . . we see all of its errors.[99]

DEMOCRATIC AND REVOLUTIONARY

Unity had historically been the keystone of the Bund's organization; but unity, in Bund terminology, did not entail a monolithic internal control. There was almost unlimited freedom of expression within the ranks, but discipline of action was enforced once a decision had been reached. Minority opinion was invariably represented on the Bund Central Committee and on the editorial board of the official newspaper; after Chmurner led the action against affiliation with the LSI, he was asked to sit on the board of the *Najer Folkscajtung* and to continue on the party central committee.[100]

Despite sharp ideological and tactical differences within the Bund, the myth that kept the organization together was considerably more potent than those differences. As a representative of the minority point of view described the phenomenon, "Both the majority and the minority, in moments of sharpest ideological or . . . organizational disagreement, had never lost their feeling of comradely unity." [101]

The defeat of the minority—the so-called left wing of the Bund—at the Łodz convention led to the organization of two factional publications: *Socialistisze Bleter*, a Social Demo-

[99] *Najer Folkscajtung*, June 6, 1930.
[100] Ohler, *loc. cit.*, pp. 13–15; *Najer Folkscajtung*, November 26, 1937.
[101] Ohler, *loc. cit.*, p. 14.

cratic journal representing the majority point of view, and *Kegn Shtrom*, the organ of the minority.[102] The arguments published by the so-called right-wing majority were no less Socialist than those of the minority.

A 1931 article by Chmurner, defending the Communists' splitting tactics of the 1921 period, was answered by Emanuel Sherer, a spokesman for the majority:

> The influence of reformism on the working-class movement was far weaker before the war than it is today. This was due to the unity of the Socialist movement in almost all important nations and in the International. Proletarian unity and not splitting is today, again, the most correct and most effective way to fight reformism. The Communists' politics of splitting . . . is a blow against revolutionary socialism. [Splitting of the working class movement] is therefore . . . criminal.[103]

Not all Bund leaders acquiesed to the factional organizations within the Bund; Alter was strongly opposed.

> Once there are organized factions within a party there must be discipline within factions. . . . Factions represent differing points of view—they thus turn parties from organizations of struggle to organizations of internal strife. Thus the discipline of the faction must become greater than the discipline of the party. The only discipline which I accept is the discipline of the party.[104]

What most of the Bund leaders wanted was a unity of all Socialist groups, from the most moderate to the most revolutionary, under a single banner. But they also hoped for the development of a Socialist movement that would be somewhere between the two extremes ideologically. The moderate

[102] *Ibid.*, p. 41.

[103] Emanuel Sherer, "Primo-Secundo-Terzio," *Socialistisze Bleter*, I, June 1931, p. 31.

[104] Victor Alter, "Farvos Ikh Hob Nisht Gevolt Shraybn," *Socialistisze Bleter*, I, June 1931, p. 71.

socialism of the German Social Democracy and the PPS was rejected because it failed to move swiftly enough. But the Communist position was even a greater anathema: "The regime without freedom, the garrison state which the Communist Party would install is strange to us." Almost all the Bundist leaders rejected the Communist attempt to "crush the will of the working class by setting up a dictatorship of the Politburo." [105]

The Bund was wedded to democracy, though regarding it —within the context of capitalism—as a form of rule by the owning classes. "Bourgeois democracy," an official Bund document said, "is one of the forms of class rule by the ruling classes. However, within the framework of the capitalist system, democracy creates the most fruitful arena for the class struggle. Therefore, the proletarian movement must . . . defend democratic freedoms from all attacks by the reaction and fascism." [106]

Some left-wing leaders of the organization spoke of a higher form of democracy, which they never defined, or intimated that they favored a dictatorship by the whole proletariat against the capitalist system; but once again this was never explained or defined, except to say that it was not the same as the Soviet dictatorship. "It doesn't follow that the Bund has pledged parliamentarianism eternal love and fidelity," one Bund theoretician wrote. He insisted, however, that representative democracy was the most "practical and fruitful [system] for the political needs of the working class." [107]

What the Bund leaders did make clear, however, was that they did not consider it possible for capitalism, faced with its own demise, to surrender power gracefully. They expected autocratic or totalitarian rule by the capitalist power elite to

[105] Erlich, *Der Icker fun Bundism*, p. 13.

[106] *Materialn tsum Diskusie farn V. Tsusamenfor* (Warsaw: Algemajner Jidiszer Arbeiter Bund, 1934), p. 10; copy in Bund Archives, New York.

[107] Ziberfarb, *op. cit.*, p. 16; *Najer Folkscajtung*, November 26, 1937.

develop as soon as the Socialists threatened to take power legitimately.

> Even having won a majority of the population to its side, the working class cannot expect that the bourgeoisie will willingly turn over the power. Neither arguments, nor justice, nor the number of people who speak out for socialism, but only the might and the fighting spirit of the workers will determine the outcome of the decisive battle.
>
> The bourgeoisie will not stand idly by while their class privileges are being diminished. We must expect a strong opposition by the reaction, which will defend its generations-long positions of power and will use any methods available against any attempt by the new order to reduce them. Under such conditions it is necessary for the Socialist powers to set up their own state apparatus—to defend the new order. . . .[108]

The role of the Pilsudski regime, the Bund leaders said, was to save the capitalist system. The only difference between the Sanacja and the National Democrats was in name, and—they said—the Endeks were "an eventual reserve army" for the Pilsudski regime.[109]

The Bund was in favor of reforming capitalism, of winning ameliorative measures that might tend to ease the burden of the impoverished working class in Poland, before the Socialist revolution could come. Erlich wrote: "We are not Communists, and we do not believe in the ridiculous theory that the worse it becomes the better it is and the better it becomes the worse it is." Neither did the Bundists believe that they could achieve equality for the Jews except as the conditions of all the people in Poland improved. But the Bund rejected a proposal to give up its position as a Jewish Socialist party and to enter the Polish party without specific quarantees. This, said the leaders of the party, would be silly, and would ignore psychological and political differences; it would be a

[108] *Materialn, tsum Diskusie farn V. Tsusamenfor,* pp. 13–15.
[109] *Ibid.,* pp. 23–32.

purely mechanical solution to a deep-rooted sociopsycholog-ical problem.[110]

CONCLUSION

For the Bund, the Pilsudski revolution was another hope that failed. From the dream of Poland as a democratic state in which it could play a major role, the Bund awoke to find itself again a persecuted minority within an autocratic state. The dreams of freedom that had led the Bund to hail the over-throw of the Witos-Grabski regime had ended in a nightmare of repression; and the conditions were to become still worse under the rule of Pilsudski's lieutenants in the years immedi-ately ahead.

By 1934 the world situation had raised new problems which the Bund was obliged to face; in Poland an anti-Semitic wave was in the making, and escape seemed almost totally foreclosed.

There had been, between 1926 and 1930 in the early years of the Pilsudski era, some hope of unity with the PPS; the end of the isolation of the Bund from the Polish Socialist move-ment seemed near at hand. But even this hope faded when the Bund, in its intransigence, refused to join with other demo-cratic parties to fight the autocratic regime. It insisted upon Socialist unity on its own terms or none at all.

But two significant changes had occurred within the Bund: its majority had lost all of their illusions about Communism, and in 1931 the Bund had entered the Labor and Socialist International. The pro-Communist minority had grown per-ceptibly smaller, and its disappearance was only a matter of time. Unfortunately, during this period the Bund was declining in strength. Its total vote had dropped from

[110] *Ibid.*, p. 3; Erlich, "An Enderung," *loc. cit.*, pp. 8–9; H. S. Kazhdan, "Es Vilt Zikh un Es Shtekht Zikh," *Socialistisze Bleter*, I, June 1931, p. 24.

100,000 to less than 50,000 between 1928 and 1934, and representation on municipal councils declined from 187 to 90 in the same six-year period.[111]

[111] Barikht, pp. 27–28.

IX

Prelude to Catastrophe

IN the face of insurmountable obstacles, with no hope for escape or alleviation of suffering, only a myth as strong as that which pervaded the Bund could permit it to survive and continue to struggle. This myth, with its faith in an ideal, led the Bund into battle against the growing animus toward the political and ethnic minority it represented. Only the almost total destruction of the ethnic group itself led to the demise of the Bund as a potent force among the Jews of Poland.

Three major events, one in neighboring Germany, the second in neighboring Russia, and the third within Poland itself, handed the Bund the leadership of Polish Jewry. Because the Bund was an *ecclesia militanta*, it was able to defy the threats from within and without, and to lead the Jewish people during a period of despair.

The events that so drastically changed the political situation in Poland were the rise of Hitler to power in Germany, the brutal trials of old Bolsheviks in Russia—leading to their extermination by Stalin—and the death of Pilsudski, which opened the way for anti-Semitic authoritarianism in the regime he had founded.

THE RISE OF HITLER

The German Social Democracy had been historically the pride of the world Socialist movement, and for many years the strongest party in the country. The National Socialists had been historically a weak group of fanatics, led by a former Austrian paperhanger and wartime army corporal whose writings and speeches most literate Germans considered vulgar nonsense. Few observers expected the Nazis, as they were known, to be taken seriously by as advanced a Western people as the Germans. Yet in the national election of 1931 the Nazis emerged as a major force, which was able to assume power and thus to end the democratic Weimar Republic, which had been the pride of the Social Democrats.

Faced with the threat of a Nazi seizure of power, the German Social Democrats supported the aging hero of the last war, Marshal Paul von Hindenburg, for the presidency. By supporting a militarist and Junker, the Socialists of Germany hoped to avoid splitting the anti-Nazi vote.

A minority of Bundists, led by Mauritzi Ozher, believed the German Socialists had acted correctly—that under existing conditions the Germans could only choose the lesser of two evils. Conditions in Germany, he wrote, could not be looked at in a vacuum in which the issue was between one bourgeois candidate and another. The issue was in fact whether Hitler would become president of Germany and fascism would triumph. Socialists, he said, could not agree with the Communist position "that it makes no difference to the German proletariat whether Hitler or Hindenburg is president, or that there will be little difference if the Bruening system [Chancellor Bruening was a moderate democrat] is supplanted by a Fascist regime." Ozher insisted that it did matter who was president of Germany, and that Hindenburg was to be preferred over Hitler. "It is obvious that the German Social Democracy had to do all that was possible to keep Hitler from being elected president." [1]

The German Socialists' action shocked most of the Bundists, who historically had opposed coalitions with non-Socialist parties, and particularly with forces not committed to democracy. The majority of the Bund's leaders warned that Hindenburg would in the end ally himself with Hitler. [2] At

[1] M. Ozher, "Di Daytshe S.D. un di Presidentn Vahln," *Uncer Cajt*, V, July 1931, pp. 21–22.
[2] *Ibid.*, p. 21.

the July 1931 meeting of the Socialist International, the Bund, the small Independent Labor Party of Great Britain, the Bataille Socialist faction of the French party, and the tiny Independent Socialist Party of Poland joined in assailing the German Social Democratic party. Alter urged Rudolf Hilferding, a leader of the SPD, to introduce into the Reichstag a proposal to manage fiscal policy along Keynesian lines, in an effort to save the economy and balk Hitler.[3] The suggestion was rejected. Otto Wels, who also represented the SPD, derided the Bund and its allies. He charged that because they were so small they had never had to carry the burden of government and had little to do except argue over minor points of dogma. "The Bund," he said, "has, all told, been a member of the International for five months, and it is already trying to tell the SPD what to do." [4]

The Bund's leaders were proved by events to have been correct in their assessment of the situation in Germany. With the support of the Social Democrats, Hindenburg did win the 1931 election, but within two years he called on Hitler to become chancellor of Germany; and the most powerful Socialist and labor movement in the world collapsed, its leaders going into exile or into concentration camps. Hitler's accession to power in Germany raised serious questions of policy throughout the Socialist world; it threatened the insistence on democracy as a condition for socialism, and brought disenchantment with the policy of joining in coalitions with moderate democratic parties; yet it did not lead to an acceptance of the Communist doctrine of monolithic party dictatorship following a cataclysmic demise of the capitalistic system.

[3] *Jewish Daily Forward* (New York), May 15, 1949. SPD is an abbreviation for *Sozialdemokratische Partei Deutschlands,* the German Social Democratic Party. The author of the article was Raphael Abramovitch, delegate of the Mensheviks at the meeting. See also *Najer Folkscajtung,* August 6, 1931.

[4] *Freie Wort* (London), December 29, 1931; *Najer Folkscajtung,* August 6, 1931.

By 1933 the Bund's position had won support in the American, Belgian, French, and Estonian Socialist parties. Despite this growth, the so-called revolutionary wing could muster only eighteen of 309 votes at the International congress.[5]

Erlich, as spokesman for the growing minority in the International, led the fight for a change in position on the part of the world's Socialists, for a rejection of the old belief that democracy was a natural complement of socialism. Yet he refused to support the Communist view that a dictatorship was a necessary prelude to socialism; and he insisted that the Communists were as much to blame for Hitler as the Socialists.

The responsibility for the situation in Germany, he insisted, had to be shared by the SPD and the Communists. The Communist leaders, he went on, had "invented the formula of the 'positive role' of Hitlerism"—the proposition that since Hitler represented fascism, and since fascism was the last stage of capitalism, his victory would bring with it the final collapse of capitalism. Moreover, Hitler had accomplished "in a short space of time what the Communists long had tried to do without success, namely the destruction of the Social Demo-

[5] Heinrich Erlich, *The Struggle for Revolutionary Socialism* (New York: The Bund Club, 1934), pp. 3–4. Erlich's given name was spelled "Heinrich" on the title page, (although he spelled it "Henryk"), apparently by the choice of the translators, Haim Kantorowich and Anna Bercowitz.

The votes of only four national parties were divided on the chief issue at the 1933 conference. The others voted as blocs, the majority right wing getting all the votes. The parties that allowed division were France, with 21 right-wing and 5 left-wing delegates; Estonia, with 2 of the right wing and one of the left; Italy, with 14 of the right wing and 2 of the left; and the United States, with 4 right-wing and 7 left-wing votes. The Bund cast all of its three votes with the left wing. The bloc voting of the other parties kept the left-wing vote down to 18. Votes of some left-wingers, such as Belgium's Paul Henri Spaak, were thus listed in favor of the right wing. For a tabulation of the vote see Price, *op. cit.*, p. 250.

cratic Party." [6] But great though the Communist guilt might be, it was not the only cause of Hitler's rise to power; the Social Democrats had also failed.

> We of course know how great a responsibility for Hitler rests upon the Communists. Their adventurist policy, and especially their belief that they can serve the proletariat by splitting its ranks, have suffered ignominious defeat in Germany. But no less is the defeat of the reformist policy, the policy of hanging on to formal democracy and legality. This must be made clear, not only that we may correctly judge the past, but also that we may learn how to act in the future. [7]

The German Socialists' policy of coalition with non-Socialist parties, said Erlich, had strengthened the very forces it had been meant to defeat. The SPD, by creating the illusion of democracy, had caused paralysis in the ranks of the working class and made action against Hitler impossible. Thus, when it should have acted to stop the threat of Hitler, "the party [SPD] was powerless to do anything." [8]

Wels conceded that the SPD had made errors, particularly in its insistence that Hitler be given the full freedom guaranteed by the Weimar Constitution. But, he insisted, the German Social Democratic Party could have done very little to stop Hitler. Resistance would have been futile; the workers had lost their zeal for militancy. In 1920, he said, when the militarists had tried to seize power, his order for a general strike had met with enthusiastic support; it was as though he had applied a torch to a powder magazine. By 1932 the same call would have "had the effect of throwing a torch into a barrel of wet straw." [9]

Erlich rejoined that Wels' statement ignored the basic problem facing the world Socialist body: What should now be the policy of Socialists? The outlook was not favorable; the

[6] Erlich, *op. cit.*, p. 27.   [7] *Ibid.*, pp. 17–18.   [8] *Ibid.*, p. 16.
[9] *Ibid.*, p. 18.

so-called reformists still controlled most of the Socialist parties, and the leadership of the Communists was even worse. In the Communist parties, he said, "Inertia and stagnation rule supreme . . . There is no hope in the Communist International. No longer can anything be expected from it." Thus the struggle for what Erlich called revolutionary socialism would have to be carried on within the Labor and Socialist International.[10]

A successful struggle against the Fascist threat throughout Europe, Erlich maintained, would necessitate a complete reversal of the Socialist position. Capitalism, he argued, was in decline, and with that condition came the downgrading of democracy. Capitalism, faced with its own defeat because of the inner contradictions of the system, tended to become fascistic. The question was "whether the working class can attain power and begin realizing the Socialist ideal through purely democratic means." [11]

The Erlich faction proposed, without success, that the International adopt a statement containing many of the doctrines espoused by Lenin:

> The experience of the last year has demonstrated that the prolonged economic crises, the frenzied attempts of the bourgeoisie to maintain its privileges in spite of all and to maintain by all means its position from the menace of socialism, place before the labor and peasant parties the necessity of fighting to realize socialism as the immediate objective of their struggle.
>
> The only choice before the classes is that between complete destruction under fascism and the immediate struggle for socialism.
>
> . . . It is not the task of the Socialist parties to attempt to straighten out the capitalist world or even to collaborate in such attempts. It declares, on the contrary, that by whatever means they are going to achieve power they must not secure the exercise of power within the structure of the capitalist regime, but must utilize power in order to destroy the bour-

[10] *Ibid.*, pp. 51–53.   [11] *Ibid.*, p. 25.

geois state and install the dictatorship of the revolutionary party during the period of Socialist construction.

During the period of struggle for the conquest of power, as well as later during the exercise of power, the Socialist parties must remain faithful to the principle of proletarian democracy, which is the only guarantee for the development of the dictatorship by the revolutionary classes into a dictatorship of the workers and peasants. Dictatorship must be exercised under the permanent control of organizations free to negotiate, to choose their representatives, and to determine themselves their line of action.

It is evident that the working class will defend energetically its democratic achievements against all reactionary attempts, but the struggle against fascism cannot have as its goal the maintenance or re-establishment of bourgeois democracy, which is based on economic inequality, but that of constructing a real Socialist democracy.[12]

The excursion into Leninism was to be short-lived; it was at most a reflex action in response to a major defeat, and in many ways it was more a cry of anguish over the failure of the democratic Socialists than it was an appeal for a new revolutionary stance.

Hitler's rise to power brought about a second ideological break for the Bundists—and this time a more lasting change from their old position. The Bund's leaders saw in the rise of Hitler a threat to Poland; and they showed their loyalty to the Polish state. In May 1933, Erlich warned Poland that Hitler posed an immediate threat to its existence. Hitler planned, Erlich warned, to do away with the Polish Corridor, Poland's one connection with the sea; to re-annex Poland's portion of Upper Silesia; to seize Danzig; and to turn Poland into a hinterland for Germany, a veritable colony of the Third Reich.[13]

---

[12] *Ibid.*, pp. 56–61.
[13] *Henryk Erlich un Victor Alter* (New York: Ferlag Unser Tsait, 1951), pp. 256–257.

THE MOSCOW TRIALS

A shot fired in Leningrad late in 1934 ended any affinity the Bundists had ever had with Soviet communism. The shot killed S. Kirov, a member of the ruling Politburo of the Soviet Communist Party and leader of the Leningrad party organization. Indirectly, it was to result in the deaths of thousands of Communists, some opposed to Stalin's method of rule, others innocent even of that charge. The murder, perpetrated by a young student, led to a series of trials at which the men chiefly responsible for the October Revolution, and for the successful defense of the Soviet state during the civil war, were executed as Czarist agents.[14]

The effect on the Bund was shattering. Many of those executed had been acquaintances of Erlich, Alter, and the other leaders of the Jewish Socialist movement in the years before 1917. They had disagreed on issues of principle, and on tactics, but they had once been comrades in arms against the Czarist regime. Zinoviev had been one of the most serious adversaries of the Bund in the early days, but his devotion to the revolution had never been doubted. Now he was facing trial—and probable execution—as a "White Guard Czarist agent." The leaders of the Bund believed that this and other trials had as their aim the solidification of Stalin's power, and that they were not related to the murder of Kirov. "That which has occurred since December 1," Erlich wrote in 1934, "and that which is still going on in the Soviet Union in relation to the murder [of Kirov]—no Socialist conscience can excuse." [15]

---

[14] See *Pravda* (Moscow), December 5 and December 27, 1934, for the official version of the murder. See also Shapiro, *The Communist Party of the Soviet Union*, pp. 400–417, for an expert account of the murder and the trials which followed.

[15] H. Erlich, "Terror in Ratn Farband" (December 1934), as reprinted in *Henryk Erlich un Victor Alter*, p. 265.

Erlich doubted that either Zinoviev or Kamenev, or any others of the accused men, was guilty of plotting against the Soviet Union or was implicated in the murder of Kirov. Moreover, Erlich questioned whether there had been, in fact "a Zinoviev clique" within the Soviet Communist Party, as the Stalinites maintained.[16]

It remained for Alter to state, most succinctly, the case against the trials and executions: Assuming that the verdicts were just, then the revolution had been made by unworthy betrayers; conversely, if—as Alter suspected—the verdicts were unjust, then the rulers of the Soviet Union had committed a horrible crime against the revolution and the men who made it. In either event, he said, the trials were a tragedy not only for Russia but for the whole revolutionary world. "The shots have hit not only the condemned, they have severely wounded the revolution itself." [17]

The executions led the Bund leaders to re-examine many of their beliefs. It was true that so-called reformist Socialists had failed in Germany, and that they had been guilty of some unsavory machinations in Poland; but this did not mean that democracy was not worth fighting for. Thus the Bund departed from its extreme revolutionary position, and again became a spokesman for social democracy.

Totalitarianism, Alter declared, meant a "return to the barbaric traditions, to the unlimited power of the individual who stands above 'human and divine law'—to the tradition of the Mongol Khan, Ivan the Terrible, and Peter the Great." Totalitarianism thus represented a negation of thousands of years of human striving for freedom and for an end to the oppression by such rulers; and he labeled Stalin's brand of communism a form of this totalitarianism.

> We must revise the old theory that communism and socialism, growing from the same root—and even the same branch—are divided only on matters of tactics and methods of struggle,

[16] *Ibid.,* p. 264.   [17] *Ibid.,* pp. 369–370.

[and that they] should unite in a joint stand in a struggle for the society of tomorrow.

So it was once; now it is different. Even the ends have changed. If socialism has remained true to the concepts of a society of tomorrow based on freedom, communism has gone further and further away from it, until it has reached the present Stalinist antilibertarian totalitarianism.[18]

The Soviet regime was, he now insisted, a radical antithesis of the Socialist society of tomorrow. It was, instead, an oppressive totalitarian state in which anyone who strove for a genuinely Socialist society would face prison or the death penalty.[19]

A side effect of the trials was the beginning of a doubt among some Bund leaders about the infallibility of Marxian dogma. Alter, in particular, began to depart from the Marxian philosophy, particularly the assumption that the Marxist state would be the ultimate Utopia.

The moment of the final triumph of Marxism will also be the moment of its demise. There will then, automatically, arise a new ideology, related to those times, when the drive for bread will cease to be the driving force of human life. The Marxian methods will remain a part of the new ideology. They will be needed to study the past, but the future will be the object of more general [natural] laws.[20]

The Bund had returned to its original position as a social-democratic party, with the Marxism diluted but the myth unsullied.

PERSECUTION AT HOME

Poland's final departure from democracy came in April 1935, when the new, so-called Pilsudski Constitution was adopted. It limited the powers of the Sejm, increased the

[18] Victor Alter, *Czlowiek w. Spoleczenstwie* (Warsaw; Swiatlo, 1938), as reprinted in *ibid.*, pp. 419–420.
[19] *Ibid.*, p. 419.   [20] *Ibid.*, p. 433.

power of the president, and laid the basis for control of the
elective and nominating processes by the regime. But Pilsudski's moment of glory was to be short-lived. Within three
weeks after the adoption of the new constitution he died.

In July 1935, faced with an election in which they would be
leaderless, Pilsudski's followers enacted an election law which
made it virtually impossible for the opposition to nominate
candidates. Under such conditions the anti-Pilsudski parties
could do little to prevent a victory by the government forces,
but they could register a popular protest. The election aroused
little enthusiasm; the Socialists and the peasant parties called
for a boycott. Despite police repressions, including the arrest
of pro-boycott agitators, the electorate of Poland registered
a resounding protest: 50 per cent of the eligible voters boycotted the elections; in urban working-class districts, 80 per
cent stayed away from the polls. The election was seen by
most observers as a vote of no-confidence in the regime.[21]

But the ruling group was unwilling to yield power despite
the obvious lack of popular support. After a year and a half of
crises, the Pilsudski followers who made up the government
—colonels Slawek, Koc, Kowalewski, and Smygly-Rydz—
formed a new political organization, the Camp of National
Unity (commonly abbreviated to "Ozon"). Technically not
a party, it had most of the attributes of a group intent upon
holding onto power and upon winning popular support. The
Ozon program, which was similar to that of the nationalist
fanatics among the National Democrats, offered the Catholic
Church a privileged position, hailed the army as the unifying
force of the nation, assailed communism as something alien
to Poland and—almost as an afterthought—promised distribution of the land among the propertyless peasants.[22]

[21] *Ibid.*, p. 95; *The New York Times*, September 8, 1935, p. 35; also
September 9, 1935, p. 8; and September 10, 1935, p. 10.
[22] A speech by Colonel Adam Koc announcing the formation of the
organization appeared in *Gazeta Polska*, February 21, 1937. A full
report was published in *The New York Times*, February 22, 1937, pp.
1, 9.

The formation of the "non-party" was followed by intensified oppression of its political opponents. An English reporter found "an atmosphere tense with anxiety and fear" throughout the country. Attacks upon Socialist headquarters became an almost daily occurrence; time bombs were set in Bund offices; hooligans organized by the Ozon assaulted Socialists and particularly Bundists.[23] In September 1937, an incendiary bomb was hurled into Bund headquarters in Warsaw; this was followed by a hail of bullets which wounded four people. The attack was believed to be the work of members of the Ozon. No arrests were made and no one was punished, although "police knew in advance of the impending assaults and were well aware of the identity of their perpetrators." [24]

On May Day 1937, a gang attacked the Bund section of the Socialist and labor parade; several bystanders were severely injured, and a five-year-old child was killed. In Kalisz a nineteen-year-old member of "Tsukunft," the Bund youth group, was murdered by a gang as he left the organization's headquarters. Other attacks occurred throughout Poland during the next year.[25]

Opposition newspapers were closed, "with alarming frequency, for publishing news and opinions hostile to the government." Socialist newspapers in particular were victimized; their buildings were regularly inspected and declared technically unfit for use as printing plants. Publications that were not shut down completely contained blank spaces where censors had deleted uncomplimentary articles; editors' notes would merely declare: "We have been unable to print the intended article owing to unexpected circumstances." [26]

The growing political oppression came at a time of eco-

[23] A. L. Easterman, "Poland, Land of Whispers," *Living Age*, CCCL (January 1938), 434; *Warszawer Radio*, May 1, 1936.

[24] Easterman, *loc. cit.*, p. 434.

[25] *Najer Folkscajtung*, May 2, 1937; May 6, 1937.

[26] Easterman, *loc. cit.*, p. 434.

nomic crisis, which affected the Jewish section of the population most adversely. The Bund Central Committee reported: "These are difficult times. The economic crisis grows worse. . . . The economic situation of the Jewish working masses, which prior to the crisis had been seriously painful and unsure, has, in the course of the past years, worsened catastrophically." [27]

The economic plight of the Jews was particularly serious because of their position in Polish society. Of 3,500,000 Jews living in Poland in the 1930's, 75 per cent were in the urban areas. In Warsaw more than 30 per cent of the population was Jewish, in Łodz 35 per cent, and in Lwów 25 per cent. Moreover, the Jews were so much alienated from their Polish neighbors that only 381,000—slightly more than 10 per cent—considered themselves to be Poles of the Jewish faith; the rest described themselves as Jews resident in Poland.[28] Most of the Jews were artisans or workers, with a sizable lower middle class of small storekeepers; the Bund in 1937 reported a total of 700,000 wage-workers and 400,000 artisans among Poland's Jews.[29]

The economic crisis was only one of the problems faced by the Jews. Anti-Semitic attacks and discrimination, both economic and social, were becoming commonplace—and were being sanctioned officially. As early as 1931 Jewish students in the universities were attacked. They were practically barred from admission to most universities, particularly those for technical and medical studies. Most Jewish students found it advisable to go abroad to study; there were 8,000 Polish Jews in foreign universities by 1932.[30]

[27] *Barikht*, p. 3.
[28] Stefan Litauer, "Poland's Problems in 1939," *Fortnightly* CLI (February 1939), 167–168. Litauer's article was an apologia for Poland's anti-Jewish policies.
[29] *Vegn Bund in Poyln* (New York: Bund Club of New York, 1937), p. 2.
[30] Boris Smolar, "What Polish Jews are Facing," *The Nation*, CXXIV (January 27, 1932), 99–100.

With Hitler's accession to power in Germany, the anti-Semitic movements became more extreme. A group of young fanatics who had been members of the National Democratic Party broke off in 1934 to form an anti-Jewish organization called the National Radical Party (commonly known as "Nara"). They wanted all Jews to lose their rights as Polish citizens, all Jewish property to be expropriated, and all Jews finally to be expelled from Poland. This was in contradistinction to Nara's position regarding other national minorities, who were to be assimilated as Poles.

The Naras were mainly city youths, especially university students. They showed terrorist leanings from the outset, but did not use terrorism as their major tactic until after the organization had been outlawed in 1936.[31]

The army colonels, who had succeeded Pilsudski, discovering that they lacked the charismatic appeal of their predecessors decided to maintain power by acting upon the anti-Semitic policy of the Ozon, which they had founded. Thus they ignored Pilsudski's revulsion from the anti-Semitic tendencies among the Poles. The first hint of the new policy came in Colonel Koc's speech announcing formation of the Ozon: "The position toward the Jewish minority is the following: We can never approve violence and brutal anti-Semitic outrages, which degrade our national dignity and honor. Calm, order, and security must be upheld, but we understand the instinct of legitimate self-defense of our people in their aim toward economic independence."[32]

The Ozon's answer to the Jewish problems was to call for a forced mass exodus of the Jews from the home that has been theirs for some six hundred years. Before the Jews could be expelled, however, Poland was to force them out of its economy and replace them with Poles. Colonel Jan Kowalewski, a

---

[31] *Barikht*, p. 33; Buell, "Political Conflicts in Poland," XV (April 1939), 238–239.

[32] Quoted in *The New York Times*, February 22, 1937, p. 9.

leader of the Ozon, set forth the organization's position in a radio address:

> The Jewish question in this country is one of the most important problems. The Jews are too numerous. The answer is mass emigration . . . and we shall seek it in that direction.
>
> We can, however, not wait for the problem to solve itself with the disappearance of the Jews; we must without delay find work for the Polish population in trade, industry, and the handicrafts. We must spare no effort to Polonize the main branches of the national economy and make our main cities capable of playing their part in the economic and cultural life of Poland.[33]

For several years the economic condition of the Jews had already been undermined by a policy of discrimination in taxes and employment. In order to maintain its disproportionately large army, Poland developed an intricate system of direct and indirect taxes, the burden of which fell primarily on the urban population. The Jews were the group most adversely affected, since most of them lived in cities or towns. Thus a group who made up 10 per cent of the Polish population paid 40 per cent of the taxes.

Jobs were likewise made more difficult for Jews to obtain, and those who had employment were dismissed in great numbers. This was particularly true in the nationalized industries, where the policy of Polonization was ruthlessly carried out. In 1922, for example, the privately owned tobacco industry had employed about 3,000 Jews in Warsaw, Białystok, Lublin, and Grodno; nine years later, with the industry owned and operated by the Polish state, almost no Jewish employees remained. The same was true of the alcohol and oil industries.

---

[33] *Gazeta Polska*, April 22, 1937. Pilsudski's successors were primarily his fellow legionnaires of World War I days. Most had been raised to the rank of colonel in the Polish army after 1918. Although some had at one time been Socialists, they almost invariably became militarists with little or no faith in democracy.

And municipalities almost invariably refused, to employ Jews in their civil service—even in the most menial of jobs.[34]

For Jewish artisans the situation was at least as difficult as it was for those who were factory workers. In 1927, the Pilsudski regime, in an effort ostensibly to raise the population's education level, had passed a law that required the licensing of artisans, and that set standards for qualifying examinations; these had included a knowledge of Polish language, history, and geography, and proof of literacy in the dominant language of the state. Without a license an artisan could not employ an apprentice, and would thus be unable to perform his work. Since most of the Jewish artisans were grown men who had been schooled in Yiddish and Hebrew during the Czarist period—when Polish history was a forbidden subject—they found it extremely difficult to pass the examinations. The result of the licensing order was the near elimination of Jewish artisans.

Because of this law, moreover, it was almost impossible for Jewish youths to be trained for the more skilled crafts. The disappearance of Jewish artisans from the ranks of masters under whom apprentices could learn their craft erected one barrier; the lack of trade schools erected a second. Even where there were trade schools, Jewish students found difficulty in being admitted, and in the unlikely event of succeeding, they faced the risk of physical assault from anti-Semitic Polish students incited by the Naras and Endeks.[35]

The official support for anti-Semitism came at a time when, in the face of economic extinction, the Jews of Poland were already without hope. The International Missionary Council of New York reported that at least a million Jews in Poland were close to starvation. A correspondent of the *London Daily Herald* wrote that they had "been living under physical

[34] Smolar, *loc. cit.*, pp. 99–100, notes that by 1931 Warsaw's tobacco industry had only three Jewish workers. In Grodno, where formerly almost all tobacco workers were Jewish, none were employed by 1931.
[35] *Ibid.*, p. 99.

terror and are threatened with mass expulsion from Poland. They cannot organize for defense and even hope seems denied them." [36]

The Bund assumed leadership in the fight to save the jobs of the Jewish workers and the position of the artisans. In Łodz an attempt to fire eleven teachers was answered by a threat of strike action by the Bund and the PPS, and the teachers were retained. Two PPS members of the Sejm, elected on a joint ticket with the Bund, put pressure on the postal authorities to make jobs available for Jews. And in the tobacco and other industries the unions led demonstrations and strikes in a vain effort to save the jobs of the displaced Jews. In an attempt to save the artisans' economic lives, the Bund organized a Jewish Socialist Artisans Union, which worked closely with the PPS-affiliated organization of Polish artisans in fighting anti-Semitic attacks.[37]

FROM PERSECUTION TO TERROR

By 1936 the economic struggle had become a fight against physical extermination by the Nara and Endek gangs. The first in a series of physical assaults occurred on March 9, 1936, in the small city of Przytyk. In the violence, led by Endeks, at least two Jews and one of the attackers were killed. The assault was preceded by an Endek leaflet, which read:

> Don't be afraid of blood!
> Hit! Hit Steadily!
> Hit Steadily with whatever is available!
> Hit the Jews! [38]

---

[36] *Report of International Missionary Council*, New York, August 1937; see also *Commonweal*, XXVI (September 3, 1937), 440, for an abstract of the report; Easterman, *loc. cit.*, p. 436.

[37] *Barikht*, pp. 44–45; *Vegn Bund in Poyln*, p. 4.

[38] *Der Jidiszer Arbeiter Klas in Jor 1936* (Łodz: J. Kiersz, 1937), p. 12; Jacob Pat, *Der Oysveg in Poyln* (New York: Jewish Labor Committee, 1938), p. 5.

As soon as news of the incident reached Warsaw, a special meeting of the Bund Central Committee produced a decision to call a half-day general strike, which was set for the morning of March 17; and on March 13 the Landrat of the Jewish unions voted to become co-sponsor. The official strike call, which was issued the day after the Central Committee meeting and distributed widely throughout Jewish working class areas, read as follows:

> As an answer to the horrible . . . assault on the Jewish population in Poland we have decided to call a half-day protest strike by the entire Jewish working-class population in Poland for Tuesday, March 17.
>
> Our chief aims for Tuesday's strike are:
>
> (1) Against the anti-Semitism of the Endeks and the Sanacja, against the continuing pogrom agitation and physical extermination of the Jewish population.
>
> (2) Against Jewish nationalist and clerical reaction.
>
> (3) Against the boycott of Jewish workers, against the elimination of Jews from all positions in the economy, against the policy of starving the Jewish masses.
>
> (4) Against persecution of the Yiddish schools and [discrimination against] the culture of the Jewish masses; against attempts to create a Jewish ghetto in the colleges, against all forms of national persecution.
>
> (5) Against reaction, fascism, and capitalism.
>
> (6) For full equality for the Jewish population at all levels of economic, political, and social life in Poland.
>
> (7) Work, bread, and freedom for all nationalities in Poland.
>
> (8) For international proletarian solidarity.
>
> (9) For an effective self-defense by the Jewish population against all attempts at pogroms.
>
> (10) For a workers and peasants government, for socialism.[39]

The call was virtually ignored in the non-Socialist Yiddish press; *Der Moment*, the most popular Yiddish newspaper in

[39] *Najer Folkscajtung*, March 14, 1936; *Circular Number 36*, Central Komitet, Algemajner Jidiszer Arbeiter Bund in Poyln, dated March 13, 1936; copy in Bund Archives.

Poland, did mention it, but reported erroneously that the strike has been called for only one hour, and criticized the Bund and the unions for not calling on intellectuals and professionals to support the action. The Right Poale Zionists ignored the strike call completely; though they declared a one-hour stoppage by the slaughterers, the only major union they controlled, the sole issue was a proposal to do away with ritual slaughter. The small Socialist Workers Party and the "Left" Poale Zion were the only organizations to join the Bund and the Jewish unions in the strike, which was thus in essence a Bund action.[40]

The strike paralyzed business in the Jewish areas of Warsaw, Białystok, Czenstahowa, Vilno, Cracow, Lwów, Tarnow, Łodz, Lublin, and all other centers of Jewish population. In these cities the PPS-controlled unions joined their Jewish co-workers in the stoppage and the strike was more effective than even the Bund had dared hope. Newspapers that had ignored the call reported the strike's success in glowing terms. According to the pro-Zionist *Hajnt*,

> In all businesses where Jewish workers and staff are employed, the strike was a total success. All Jewish businesses— almost without exception—were closed.
>
> In the municipal slaughterhouse no Jewish workers appeared, nor did any Christian workers who are under the influence of the PPS. A meeting of Jewish and non-Jewish workers there heard fiery speeches.[41]

The popular *Warszawer Radio* commented: "Sabbath of Sabbaths! That is the only way to describe today's loud silence, the protest by the Jewish populace of Poland against Przytyk and against the uncontrolled anti-Semitism generally."[42]

[40] *Der Moment*, March 16, 1926; *Der Jidiszer Arbeiter Klas in Jor 1936*, pp. 61–62, 29.
[41] *Ibid.*, pp. 86–157; *Hajnt*, March 17, 1936.
[42] *Warszawer Radio*, March 17, 1936.

The Polish Socialist daily joined the chorus, noting especially the unity between the Jewish and Polish workers in the establishments where they worked side by side.[43] The strike had been successful in demonstrating the growing strength of the Bund.

Heartened by the success of the strike, and the solidarity shown by the Polish workers, the Bund called a conference against anti-Semitism, to be held jointly with the PPS and the unions. The call made it clear that this was to be a Socialist meeting, and that the aim was to launch a united Socialist drive against the government, which the Bund considered the source of pogroms. But the government prohibited the meeting, and confiscated the leaflets issued by the Bund.[44]

Though the Socialist drive did not markedly reduce the anti-Semitic acts it did solidify the growing fraternity between the Jewish and Polish Socialist parties, and it further separated the Bund from the other Jewish organizations. In May 1937 another assault occurred, this time in Brześć (Brest-Litovsk). One Jew was killed, and almost all the city's Jewish stores were destroyed by explosions. A joint statement issued by the Bund, the Social Democratic Party of the German minority in Poland, and the PPS denounced the attacks:

> The Brzesc pogrom is the fruit of the systematic nationalist instigations. It became ripened in the atmosphere of continual concessions of the Sanacja to the so-called Nara. The concessions take the form of the Sanacja accepting for its own the most reactionary and anti-Semitic postures of the Nara and also [takes the form of] allowing the Nara-perpetrators of the anti-Jewish excesses to go unpunished.[45]

Significantly, the Bund refused to participate in a two-hour general protest strike called by the non-Socialist Jewish

---

[43] *Robotnik*, March 18, 1936.

[44] *Der Jidiszer Arbeiter Klas in Jor 1936*, pp. 160–162; *Najer Folkscajtung*, June 11, 1936.

[45] *Najer Folkscajtung*, May 15, 1937, June 9, 1937, June 15, 1937.

parties. It argued that the strike, having been called by Zionists and other "bourgeois" elements, was nationalist and therefore reactionary. But the real reason for refusing to join the strike was not mentioned—namely that the Bund was now becoming a part of a mass multinationality movement.[46]

Other assaults followed in rapid succession, the most violent in Czenstahowa, a major textile city. In August 1937 there were four hundred attacks on Jews in seventy-nine cities and towns throughout Poland.[47]

Besides the physical assaults, an intensified campaign to segregate the Jews and to force them out of Poland was undertaken by the Ozon and the two openly anti-Jewish parties, Nara and Endeks. The medical society voted to bar Jews from membership, as did the bar association. One American observer reported of the conditions in 1938: "The ghetto which the 'Real Russians,' an extremely nationalistic anti-Jewish, anti-Polish party closely tied to the Czarist regime, demanded and the Czarist government did not introduce for the Poles, the Polish Nationalists are now demanding for the Jews. And the government has started to introduce it." [48]

The ghetto was first introduced in the universities, where there were believed to be many adherents of Nara. At the instance of the Ministry of Education, rectors of Polish universities officially established "ghetto benches," seats segregated from the rest. Jewish students who refused to accept these seats were beaten by anti-Semitic students and then expelled from the schools. There were protests by labor unions and leaders of the Polish intelligentsia, among them distinguished scientists, professors, and men of letters, as well as from Socialists and democrats among the students themselves. Fights between the anti-Semitic and democratic students were an almost daily occurrence.

[46] *Ibid.*, June 22, 1937.
[47] *Ibid.*, June 23, 1937; Pat, *op. cit.*, p. 5.
[48] William Zukerman, "Jews and the Fate of Poland," *The Nation*, CXLVI (April 2, 1938), 379.

The Bund, to protest the segregation, called a two-day general strike. The PPS and many academicians joined in the call, and the strike was highly successful; Poles joined their Jewish co-workers in fighting off attacks by nationalist gangs. The reporter for *The Nation* wrote: "Never before has the Polish Socialist Party worked so harmoniously with the Jewish Labor Party (Bund) against anti-Semitism." [49]

RESISTANCE

The Polish regime's proposed solution for the "Jewish problem" was similar to the Zionists': namely, mass emigration. An apologist for the regime wrote: "The organization of large-scale emigration of Polish Jews for settlement in overseas countries, and in particular in Palestine, is just as important to the Jews as it is to the Poles, and the Polish government will have to devote to it much of its time. . . ." [50]

The Bundists were quick to note the similarity; the Zionists and the Polish anti-Semites, they cried, took the same stand. A Bund leader noted that Ben Gurion, leader of the world Labor Zionist movement, along with Greenbaum, leader of the liberal General Zionists, and Jabotinsky, leader of the extremist and nationalist Revisionists agreed with the enemies of the Jews. The Ozon had declared it necessary to get the Poles into trade, and this could be done only by forcing the Jews to leave the country. The World Jewish Congress, a pro-Zionist body, had said that for economic reasons, or because of the economic crisis, or because of the social structure of East European states, it was necessary for the Jews to emigrate. The Bundists called this treason to the Jews, "who have no interest in leaving Poland." The Jews,

---

[49] *Ibid.*, pp. 379–380; *Tsu di Idishe Arbeiter un Folkmassn fun Varshe* (Warszawer Komitet, Algemajner Jidiszer Arbeiter Bund, October 1937); copy of leaflet in Bund Archives, New York.

[50] Litauer, *loc. cit.*, p. 169.

said Alter, were as vital to the Polish economy as the Poles. "The theory of Greenbaum that Jews are 'excess baggage' in Poland is dangerous nonsense, which must be strongly rejected." [51]

The whole idea of mass emigration, the Bund insisted, was based on fraud, and was itself a delusion. It was being proposed by the regime to cover up its own failings; but it would solve none of the problems besetting Poland's economy or its social problems—it was pure nonsense, knowingly perpetrated on the population. Vladimir Kossofsky, a Bund leader, said that "the conditions of mass emigration are totally lacking and this is known quite well by the proposers of emigration." [52]

The anti-Semitic press declared that the Bund was against Poland, and that all Jews were enemies of the state. The Ozon proposed that the Bund be declared illegal because of this enmity toward Poland. The Bund charged in reply that it was not the real target of the attack, but that the whole of the Jewish population, and the labor movement generally, were endangered by it. The trade union federation agreed with the Bund, and denounced both the proposal and anti-Semitic agitation generally.

In defense of its stand, the Central Committee of the Bund asserted its own loyalty to the Polish state:

> No, it is not we who create among the Jewish masses a feeling of estrangement from Poland; this is attempted by those who have always, and everywhere, supported the Jewish reaction which strives to turn the Jewish masses into a . . . fanatic group which is alien to the ideals and struggles of the Polish working people; this is being attempted by the Polish nationalists who plead, before the whole world, that Poland is only a temporary home for the Jews and that they must leave,

[51] Victor Alter, *Antysemityzm Gospodarczy w Swietle Cyfr* (Warsaw: Mysl Socjalistyczna, 1937), pp. 8–9, 36; also *Henryk Erlich un Victor Alter*, pp. 404–405, 406–407.
[52] *Najer Folkscajtung*, May 7, 1937.

the sooner the better, because Poland can be nothing but anti-Semitic.

. . . Our party has roused, and still rouses, an awareness among the Jewish masses of the inseparability of their fate and the fate of the land in which they live; [the Bund] has developed and is still developing in the Jewish masses the feeling that they are citizens of Poland, who are not only entitled to equal rights with others, but are also obligated to equal responsibility with others; [the Bund] has linked, and still links, the Jewish masses ever closer with the life of Poland and with the struggles of the Polish working masses for a better tomorrow and for a fuller liberation in their joint fatherland.[53]

Poland's troubled situation was not caused by the Jews or by the Socialists, according to the leaders of the Bund; it was caused by those who "fill the nation with cannibalistic agitation, those who have for many years supported the most unenlightened parts of the community, those who excuse murder and rape . . . who say the Jews must leave Poland . . ." The charge was aimed at the Ozon rulers of Poland, and it hit its mark; they confiscated the issue of the Bund daily in which it appeared.[54]

The Bund offered the Jews an answer to anti-Semitism: that they could expect no liberation from persecution unless there was a "simultaneous freeing of the Polish masses from social oppression." It was therefore necessary for the Jewish and Polish workers to unite in a common struggle against the authoritarian regime, and for democracy and socialism. "Your liberation," Alter wrote, "can only be a side product of the universal freeing of all oppressed peoples." [55]

The Bund's view that anti-Semitism was only a side issue,

---

[53] *Najer Folkscajtung*, June 20, 1937; see also issues for June 11, 1937 and June 14, 1937.

[54] *Najer Folkscajtung*, June 18, 1937. The copy presented to the censor, with the stamp of the censor who confiscated it, is in the Bund Archives.

[55] Victor Alter, *Tsu Der Idn Frage in Poyln* (Warsaw: "Monografja," 1937), p. 24; reprinted in *Henryk Alter un Victor Alter*, p. 402. See also *Najer Folkscajtung*, March 15, 1936.

and that the real targets of the Ozon were the labor and democratic movements, was shared by many observers. According to *The Nation*'s correspondent, "It may sound strange abroad, but in Poland it is generally true that the present anti-Jewish drive, with all its terror, barbarism, and revival of medievalism is directed more against Polish democracy than against the Jews." [56]

The threat posed to each by anti-Semitism tended to draw the Bund and the PPS closer. In Warsaw they issued a joint daily newspaper; they united for the 1937 May Day parade, and formed joint defense units. Their trade-union affiliates held joint conventions, and there was even talk of uniting into one party. The only impediment to union was fear on the part of the PPS that Polish voters might hesitate to support a party with a major Jewish component. The PPS on the one hand was becoming an effective force against anti-Semitism, and the Bund on the other was thinking of itself as the Jewish section of the Socialist movement in Poland. It was agreed that the only solution to the common threat must be "a fraternal unity of struggle of Jewish and Polish workers, to root out anti-Semitism, by establishing a genuine democracy of the people, because there can be work and freedom for all its citizens." [57]

Although the government was now officially anti-Semitic, and despite the attacks, both economic and physical, by a noisy, rowdy, and apparently large segment of Poland's population, there were also signs by early 1938 that a majority of the working people and the peasants opposed the anti-Jewish actions. The unions and peasant groups declared that the attacks against the Jews were really aimed against themselves, and the Jews were accepting the Bund's position, that their only real defense was in cooperation with the Polish

[56] William Zukerman, "Jews and the Fate of Poland," *The Nation*, CXLVI (April 2, 1938), 380.

[57] The joint newspaper was called *Dziennik Ludowy*. The issue for May 6, 1937, is in the Bund Archives in New York. See *Najer Folkscajtung*, May 2, 1937; also Pat, *op. cit.*, p. 7.

working people. Multinational self-defense units were formed in Warsaw, with the chief objective of shielding Jews against attack. When Nara pickets tried to prevent Poles from shopping in Jewish-owned shops, they were routed in many towns by PPS workers and peasants. In some areas the Endeks tried to keep Poles out of Jewish shops by photographing them as they entered; whereupon the PPS and the peasant organizations again formed groups to prevent the anti-Semitic photographers from doing their work.[58]

In August 1937, the peasants of Poland staged a ten-day general strike for "freedom, democracy and an end to the dictatorship." Despite opposition by the Endeks and the government, the stoppage was almost complete. Police were sent in to put down the strike; in many areas they opened fire into crowds of peasants, and at least fifty strikers were killed. The PPS and the Bund helped the peasant leaders in the action, raised funds for the strikers, and arranged for protest memorials after the massacre.[59]

The growth of unity among the democratic parties was now evident. The PPS and the peasant groups had come to recognize the threat to their existence in the authoritarian, anti-Semitic regime; the Bund had begun to recognize that it could not be effective without support from the ethnic majority. A party that had been only mildly interested in Polish independence, and that had backed it lukewarmly in 1920, by 1937 had become the most important supporter of the Jews of Poland, at the same time insisting "that in this land we were born, and to this land we give our loyalty." [60]

VICTORY AT THE POLLS

After 1935 the Bund showed a growing strength in election after election. Its increasing power was the logical outcome of the situation among the Jewish parties. Although the Zion-

[58] *Ibid.*, pp. 16–17.   [59] *Ibid.*, pp. 7–8, 13–14, 20.
[60] *Ibid.*, p. 20.

ists favored mass emigration from Poland to Palestine for reasons completely antithetical to those of the anti-Semites for wanting to be rid of the Jews, they were nevertheless open to the charge that they were in alliance with those anti-Semites. The so-called bourgeois non-Socialist parties were by their very nature unable to call strikes or lead militant action or mass protest against the anti-Semites; moreover, they had no allies among the Poles since their Polish counterparts supported the Ozon regime. The religious parties, on the other hand, were too closely tied to the mystical Chasidic theology which rejected militant action, to be effective. Only the Bund could point to a clear antipathy toward the proposals for an exodus, could ally itself with a major Polish party or bloc of parties, and could take the lead in militant action.[61]

The first indication of the Bund's strength came in the *Kehilla* elections of 1936. In most cities the Bund locals entered these elections, against the advice of the national organization, merely to demonstrate their strength, with results that were more than even the local leaders of the party had hoped for. The Bund emerged as the largest Jewish party in Vilno, Lublin, Grodno, Piotrkow, and Warsaw. In the capital, it polled a clear majority of the Jewish vote, winning twenty seats as against three for the joint Poale Zion ticket.[62]

A second indication of the Bund's growing strength came with the elections to the Łodz city council in October 1936. Anti-Semitism was almost the only issue. The Socialist parties were split; the Łodz PPS worked feverishly to obtain support from conservative Jewish voters, on the assumption that the Jews would support the Socialists in preference to the Endeks, thus assuring a PPS majority in the council. But the

---

[61] See, for example, Horace M. Kallen, *Frontiers of Hope* (New York: Horace Liveright, 1929), pp. 164–210; also Segal, *op. cit.*, pp. 181–185.

[62] *Der Jidiszer Arbeiter Klas in Jor 1936*, p. 221; *Vegn Bund in Poyln*, p. 3.

PPS refused either to support the Bund or to join a united bloc. Indeed, it considered the Bund an opponent and campaigned against it. Despite the Socialist rift, the Bund polled 23,692 votes; its nearest Jewish non-Socialist rival polled 14,947. Although the PPS received nearly four times as many votes as the Bund, almost all of its voters were in non-Jewish districts.[63]

Immediately after the election the national leaders of the PPS chided their Łodz organization for its campaign against the Bund, and insisted successfully that the local PPS and Bund work together on fraternal terms. In late November the Socialist parties of all the nationality groups in Poland decided on joint action to end the authoritarian regime and to work toward a stronger Socialist movement in Poland. Among other planks in the platform of the Socialist parties was one calling for cultural autonomy for each of the nationalities. At last the Socialist parties of Poland—primarily the Bund and the PPS—were on the verge of unity; forty years of internecine strife was finally at an end.[64]

By mid-1937, further signs of strength began to emerge. Elections for delegates to the Jewish labor congress in Warsaw went overwhelmingly for the Bund, which carried 193 of 253 delegates. Socialist spirits were buoyed up, with victory in the air. The PPS, speaking for all Socialist parties in Poland, called for new democratic elections and dissolution of the Sejm.[65]

The policies of the Ozon regime were not winning popular support, nor were they solving the nation's economic problems. Official statistics submitted by the government to the League of Nations indicated that 6,000,000 residents of Poland were on the verge of starvation. The government, as it faced the possibility of open rebellion by the peasants, was

[63] *Ibid.*, pp. 3–4; *Der Jidiszer Arbeiter Klas in Jor 1936*, pp. 230–231.
[64] *Najer Folkscajtung*, December 17, 1936.
[65] *Vegn Bund in Poyln*, p. 3; *Najer Folkscajtung*, May 11, 1937.

no longer a viable regime. Koc, who had led the Ozon from its formation, resigned at the end of 1937, and General Skwarcynski, a more liberal friend of Pilsudski, took over the organization. One of his first actions was to oust a violently anti-Semitic, pro-Nazi deputy, M. Budzynski, from the party and the Sejm. By 1938 the Ozon had split into two distinct and warring factions. The struggle within the Ozon forced the dissolution of the Sejm, and new elections were held on November 6 and 13.

President Moscicki, a former PPS member and leader of the democratic wing of the Ozon, failed in an effort to rewrite the election laws so as to allow the democratic parties to join the government. The PPS, the Bund, and the Endeks all boycotted the election, each for its own reasons. Under pressure from the government to vote, however, a total of only 35 per cent of the populace stayed away from the polls—a much smaller number than had done so in 1935.[66]

Though the Ozon leaders now assumed, on the basis of the election, that they had public approval, events were to prove them in error. The municipal elections called for December 1938 and January 1939 were to be open to all parties; moreover, they were to be the first "fair plebiscite of Polish opinion on the regime . . . for these elections were relatively free of interference by the administration."[67]

In these elections both the Bund and the PPS offered candidates, but each ran as a separate party. Although the Bund had proposed unity, the PPS had rejected the proposal because it feared Jewish candidates might hurt the vote and cloud the basic issues. The Bund considered the possibility of backing the PPS candidates, but decided it would do better if it ran a separate ticket. As Alter explained the decision,

> The PPS wanted to uphold the purely Polish character of her ticket, maintaining that this would make it easier to fight Polish nationalism; therefore it was necessary for the Jewish workers

[66] Buell, *loc. cit.*, pp. 240–243; Easterman, *loc. cit.*, p. 435.
[67] Buell, *loc. cit.*, p. 244.

to go to the polls independently. To suggest that Jewish workers deny themselves [candidates] indicates an attitude of surrender on their part. Should the chief role in the battle for
the rights of the Jewish masses be transferred to the Polish
Socialists, it would indicate a dependency-complex. . . . The
anti-Semitic press insists on the exclusion of Jews from political life. If the Jewish workers had no choice but to vote for
the PPS list they would be doing precisely what the anti-
Semites want: [they would be making] the city council free
of Jews.[68]

Nevertheless, relations between the PPS and the Bund were
close during the campaign. Erlich asked Bundists who lived in
districts with no Bund tickets to support the PPS instead of
one of the other Jewish lists. The PPS, likewise, asked its
members in predominantly Jewish districts to support the
Bund.[69]

The elections surprised even the Socialists, whose victory
was greater than anyone had anticipated. The anti-Semitic
parties were severely weakened; the vote of the Ozon fell
sharply; the PPS showed remarkable gains, and the Bund
emerged as the strongest party among the Jews of Poland. In
Warsaw the Bund carried 17 of the 20 Jewish seats, and in
Łodz it carried 11 out of 17. The PPS elected 33 councilmen
in Łodz and 27 in Warsaw; as a result, in both of Poland's
largest cities there was now a Socialist majority in the ruling
bodies. The same was true in Lwów, Piotrków, Cracow,
Białystok, Grodno, Vilno, and other cities.[70]

The Bund had reached its high point. It awaited the revi-
sion of election laws and a new election, in which its leaders
were sure it would become the official voice of Poland's
3,500,000 Jews. But war intervened.

[68] *Najer Folkscajtung*, December 16, 1938.
[69] *Ibid.*, December 17, 1938.
[70] *Henryk Erlich un Victor Alter*, p. 39; Buell, *loc. cit.*, pp. 243–
244; Hertz, *Geshikhte fun Bund in Lodz*, p. 429; *The New York
Times*, December 20, 1928, p. 16; *Najer Folkscajtung*, December 19,
20, 21, 1938.

X

Catastrophe

THE destruction of the Jewish community of Poland by the Nazis during the five-year occupation of the country has been well documented.[1] It is an episode in history without equal, a study in the depravity of man that is almost beyond belief. Though the chronicle bears repeating, in this study it will be restricted to events concerning the Bund.

Faced with the tragedy which befell them as Jews, the Bundists reacted with heroism—born, perhaps, of despair— and a stubborn refusal to yield on any of their basic ideals. Whether these ideals should have been upheld is a matter in which judgment must depend upon values; that they were upheld under horrifyingly brutal conditions is a further indication of the power of the myth that pervaded the Bund, and of its unique role as a Jewish Socialist party in a hostile land.

THE BEGINNING OF THE END

Hitler's invasion of Poland was not unexpected; the negotiations that preceded it had gone on for months. Only the Polish government failed, until the last days, to recognize the immediate danger in which the country had been placed; it did not order its army mobilized until August 30, 1939, less than two days before the invasion. The Polish regime still hoped that somehow Hitler's appetite would be appeased;

[1] For a description by a Bund leader see Bernard Goldstein, *The Stars Bear Witness* (New York: Viking Press, 1949); for official documents of the Nazi extermination of the Jews see mimeographed transcripts of the Trial of Major War Criminals, Library of Congress, Washington. Original materials may be found at the YIVO-Institute for Jewish Research in New York, and in the Bund Archives.

certainly he could not be foolish enough to invite a two-front war, against Britain and France to the west, and against Poland and Russia to the east. But Poland's rulers had under-estimated Germany's diplomatic maneuverability, as well as Stalin's ability to rationalize any action he took. Eight days before the invasion, the Poles last hope was destroyed when Soviet Russia and Nazi Germany signed a nonaggression pact.[2]

Socialists throughout the world were shaken by Stalin's agreement with Hitler. The "glorious" Russian Revolution had in twenty-five years gone full circle; the new Bolshevik line had become an alliance with the "worst enemy the working class had ever known." The pact, said the Bund organ, was an immoral and inexcusable betrayal of all the hopes of the working class; "the friendly handshake between the representatives of the Moscow government and the organizers of the anti-Comintern pact was a genuinely shattering experience." [3]

> What do the Communists in England and France now think? How do the Communists in Germany feel—they and the Socialists who have dreamt of a military and political defeat for Hitler? How do the workers in the concentration camps of Germany and Czechoslovakia . . . feel as they see the club of their persecutor made more powerful by . . . Moscow? [4]

A day after the pact was announced, it was clear that Poland had no alternative except war or total surrender. The British ambassador, Sir Arthur Henderson, was told by Hitler that Germany would not compromise, that all of its demands would have to be met or the German war machine would go into operation. Possibly, a Bund spokesman conceded, Hitler would have acted in the same manner regardless of the Russians; but the fact was that the nonaggression pact had given

[2] See Buell, *Poland: Key to Europe* (New York: Alfred A. Knopf, 1939), pp. 364–386.
[3] *Najer Folkscajtung*, August 24, 1939.
[4] *Ibid.*

him the leverage he needed to feel secure in his position. "Who in his right mind would believe it an accident that this answer was given by Hitler in the same hour that the airplane which had carried Ribbentrop to Moscow had landed at the Moscow Airport?" [5]

The German attack forced the ill-prepared Polish army into headlong, breakneck retreat. The army that had been Poland's pride proved to be no match for the Germans; within five days the German army was at the gates of Warsaw. The Polish government declared it an open city, and proceeded to evacuate; all the political parties followed suit. The Bund's Central Committee, realizing the danger faced by Warsaw's 300,000 Jews once the city fell into the Nazis' hands, considered calling for resistance, but decided almost at the last hour to accept the order to evacuate, lest Jews be blamed for the death and destruction that resistance would entail.[6]

The Polish Socialists decided, however, that capitulation of Warsaw without a struggle would mean a greater catastrophe than resistance, however hopeless. Niedzialkowski and Zygmunt Zaremba, two of the chief leaders of the PPS, persuaded Mayor Starzinski and the general in command of the Warsaw garrison not to accept the central government's order for surrender. The declaration that Warsaw was an open city was rescinded, and preparations were begun for its defense. During the twenty-one-day siege that followed, the whole might of the German army and Luftwaffe was aimed at the city, turning it into an island of rubble. The Bund and the PPS worked in close accord during the siege, forming front-line companies from among their members, under command of the Polish military, and labor battalions which erected defense installations. Shmuel Mordechai (Arthur) Zygelboym, a leader of the Bund, met daily with Niedzialkowski and Zaremba to arrange liaison between the Jewish

[5] *Ibid.*, August 26, 1939.
[6] Goldstein, *op. cit.*, pp. 26–27.

and Polish segments of the city's population. The Bund's *Folkscajtung*, and the PPS newspaper *Robotnik*, appeared in the beleaguered city; they were the only newspapers published during the siege. But in the end the German military leviathan overcame the spirited resistance, and the city capitulated; a single member of the defense committee, Niedzialkowski, refused to sign the document of surrender. He declared "The working class does not capitulate." [7]

THE BUND REORGANIZES

Within two weeks after the fall of Warsaw the Bund was reconstituted as an underground organization, at a secret conference of twenty delegates from all sectors of the Jewish working class. From the outset, the organization was divided into three groups, under the over-all direction of the Warsaw committee. Their work was apportioned along functional lines. The central body was made up of the trade union committees, and was the first to be organized. Their primary job was to organize soup kitchens, with the twofold purpose of offering nourishment to union members and a meeting place where mutual problems could be discussed despite the Nazis' prohibition of meetings. Political committees were kept small to avoid detection, and few of their leaders knew the leaders of the other groups; in this way there was little danger that they might be tortured into disclosing information to the German secret police. [8]

Besides the party organization, the Bund set up ancillary groups, most important of which was the Socialist Red Cross. It was assigned three jobs: (1) to arrange for medical aid to sick and needy members and affiliates of the Bund; (2) to secure hiding places for leaders of the Bund who might be sought by the Nazi authorities; and (3) to maintain contact

[7] *Ibid.*, pp. 31–32; *Zygelboym Bukh* (New York: Ferlag Unser Tsait, 1947), pp. 25–27.

[8] *Ibid.*, pp. 28–29; Goldstein, *op. cit.*, pp. 42–43, 45.

with and supply food and clothing to members of the party, or affiliated organizations, who were arrested and placed in concentration camps.[9]

One of the most delicate operations performed by the Bund was the publication of a newspaper. Even though all printing plants and duplicating equipment had been seized by the Germans to prevent an underground press from being organized, the leaders of the Bund, anticipating this move, had hidden a mimeograph machine in the home of one of its members. It was on this machine that a weekly newspaper and four monthly journals were produced. The chief difficulty was in obtaining paper, stencils, and ink for the operation. They were obtained—at great cost in money and lives—and so during the occupation Bund organs appeared regularly in Yiddish and Polish. To help maintain secrecy, the editorial and mechanical operations were completely separated; the writers and editors did not know where the plant was located, or who operated it; nor did the mechanical staff know who the writers were or where they were to be found. The distributors, likewise, were kept completely apart from the editorial and mechanical staff.[10]

Another vital work which the Bund soon undertook was to organize a system to offer some schooling to the Jewish children of the city. The Nazis, almost as soon as they occupied Poland, had prohibited any Jewish schools, secular or religious. The Bund, defying the order, set up two illegal schools for children which offered education, some minimal

[9] Goldstein, *op. cit.*, p. 45.
[10] *Ibid.*, pp. 44–45; Barikht fun Tsentral Komitet fun Untererdishn Bund Vegn Lebn in Ghetto: coded message sent by the underground Bund to its representatives in New York. A copy and a translation into Yiddish (without pagination) are in the Bund Archives. Part of the message is reproduced in *In di Yorn fun Idishn Khurbn* (New York: Ferlag Unser Tsait, 1946), and footnote references throughout the rest of this chapter are to this source. The message, delivered by secret courier for the Polish Government-in-Exile, is dated March 16, 1942, and covers the period between September 1939 and that date.

entertainment, play, and food. At one time more than 20 per cent of the children in the Jewish area were attending the Bund schools. Youth clubs were also organized, offering seminars, discussions, choirs, and dramatic groups—all secret. Rudimentary medical courses, to meet one of the chief needs of a Jewish population hampered by disease and a lack of physicians and nurses, were also organized by the Bund under Dr. Ludwig Hirschfield, who had won the Nobel Prize a few years before. Physical education courses and adult education work were also organized.[11]

THE JUDENRAT

Whenever the Nazis captured a city, they insisted that the local authorities name a group of hostages whose lives were to be forfeited should the citizens offer serious resistance to the German rulers. The demand in Warsaw came on the first day after the capitulation, and the Nazis wanted the hostages to be representative of the entire population, Jewish and Polish. The mayor asked the Bund, because it represented the Jewish working class, to name one of the hostages. This posed a serious problem, since most of the Bund leaders were already sought by the Gestapo; only one leader, Zygelboym, could possibly have escaped immediate arrest. He had been a resident of Warsaw until 1937, but had gone to Łodz in that year and in 1938 had been elected a city councilman there. He had arrived in Warsaw a few days before the siege, and was virtually unknown to the police in the capital. His choice as hostage—a choice for which he had volunteered—was based on his anonymity alone. Fortunately, the Nazis did not kill the hostages.[12]

Zygelboym was also named by the Bund as its delegate to the Judenrat, a body of Jewish leaders who were expected to carry out the orders of the Nazis. By fostering resistance

[11] *In di Yorn fun Idishn Khurbn*, p. 14; Goldstein, *op. cit.*, p. 47, 84.
[12] *Zygelboym Bukh*, pp. 27–28.

rather than timid compliance, he soon became a persistent thorn in the Nazis' side.[13]

The Judenrat had been expected to do little more than carry out orders; there was to be no opposition and no appeal. But Zygelboym refused from the outset to accept this edict, and his defiance became overt in October 1939, when the Germans directed the Judenrat to order all Jews moved into a closed ghetto. Aside from its medieval character, the order would have meant the uprooting of more than a fourth of the city's Jewish population, who lived outside the designated area. The Judenrat decided to obey the directive, despite Zygelboym's impassioned plea for refusal to carry it out. As soon as the decision was made, Zygelboym told the delegates:

> You have reached here an historic decision. It appears that I have been too weak to convince you that we must not do this. I do not, for my own part, feel enough strength to be able to participate in the undertaking. I feel I would not have the right to live if . . . the ghetto should be established and my head remain unscathed. I therefore declare that I resign my mandate. I recognize that the chairman has an obligation to report this to the Gestapo, and I know the consequences this can have for me personally. I cannot act otherwise.[14]

The speech persuaded the members of the Judenrat to reconsider their action, and the discussion was renewed. In the end the council accepted a compromise: the Judenrat would not order the Jews to go into the ghetto, but it would inform the Jews throughout the city of the Nazi order. Although the situation was not changed in any way, the Judenrat itself was absolved of blame.

As soon as the order had been made known, Jews who lived outside the designated ghetto came in bewilderment to the Judenrat building. Zygelboym, deciding to seize the opportunity to defy the Nazis, clilmbed onto the balcony and addressed the throng, estimated at 10,000. He urged them not

[13] *Ibid.*, p. 30.   [14] *Ibid.*, p. 30.

to leave their homes, but to remain where they were until the Germans removed them by force.[15]

The speech did not escape the notice of the Gestapo, whose chief ordered Zygelboym to come down to police headquarters the next morning. As Zybelboym knew, this meant probable imprisonment, torture, and death. The Bund Central Committee met as soon as the news reached its members; the committee decided Zygelboym could no longer remain in Poland, and voted to send him abroad. After some delay, much effort, and close contact with the Polish underground, Zygelboym managed to escape to Belgium by a long and circuitous route. Thence he went to the United States and finally to Britain, where in 1942 he became a member of the Polish Parliament-in-Exile.[16]

THE GHETTO

Despite Zygelboym's appeal, the Jews went into the Ghetto, and by 1940 "a high brick wall and barbed wire separated the Jews from the gentiles. There was no intermingling, no communication, no contact." [17]

The Bund continued its activity after the Ghetto was instituted, but now its work became somewhat more complex. Besides continuing to hold regular meetings of party groups, it was necessary to maintain contact outside the Ghetto. A liaison was soon established with the Polish labor movement through Antoni Zdanowski, the leader of the Transport Workers' Union. Moreover, Leon Feiner, a Cracow attorney and Bund leader who could easily pass for a Pole, was detailed to live outside the Ghetto so as to maintain direct contact with the Polish community.[18]

---

[15] *Ibid.*, pp. 30–31.   [16] *Ibid.*, p. 31.
[17] Goldstein, *op. cit.*, p. 48.
[18] *In di Yorn fun Idishn Khurbn*, p. 13. Feiner used the pseudonym of Berezowski.

A party executive and council was instituted to direct the work of the Bund in the Ghetto; "Tsukunft," the youth federation of the Bund, and "Skif" (Sotsialistisher Kinder Ferayn), the children's group, were also active. The press was enlarged to include a Yiddish weekly with a large readership, a monthly theoretical organ, a Polish monthly, and youth publications in Yiddish and Polish. Nor was the activity limited to the Warsaw Ghetto; there were organizations in almost all other Polish cities.[19]

There was considerable danger in being an active Bundist—many ended their lives on the gallows for spreading propaganda—but there was no paucity of volunteers. The *Hamburger Tageblatt* reported that a special court in Zwiazkowiec had condemned three men captured while distributing the underground weekly with news from abroad. "The journal had many subscribers," the Nazi daily reported, "who paid a regular fee to meet its costs of production." In Lublin a Bundist was captured with illegal leaflets and documents, and died on the gallows.[20]

Relations between the Ghetto's inhabitants and those outside were maintained through the Polish Socialists, with whom the Bund's previous affiliation now stood it in good stead; it was the only Jewish party with such contacts on the other side of the wall. When the Polish Socialist movement itself split over issues of tactics and goals, the Bund became closely allied with the newer and more radical group, the "Polish Socialists" rather than the more conservative PPS. The original cause of the split, which became serious after Hitler's invasion of Soviet Russia in 1941, was the issue of the Soviets. Whereas the radical Socialists wanted to drop all propaganda against the Soviet Union and devote full time to fighting the Nazis, the PPS could not forget the long history of Polish oppression by the Russians or the Hitler-Stalin Pact of 1939.

[19] *Ibid.*, pp. 13-14.
[20] Emanuel Novogrodski, "Mai Blumen Iber di Ghetto-Vant," *Unser Tsait*, II, May 1942, pp. 10-11.

Although relations of the Bund with the PPS were described as "loose and cool", they entailed no animosity. On the other hand, contact between the Bund and the more radical Socialist group was close, and it was through this group that the Bund in Poland maintained contact with the Government-in-Exile. Moreover, since they were Poles rather than Jews, the members of the Polish Socialist group were able to move about the country, maintain contact with the Bund groups outside Warsaw, and distribute messages and publications for the Warsaw Bund.[21]

Animosity toward the German invaders on the part of the Polish anti-Semitic parties did not lessen their hatred toward the Jews. Though the Endek, Nara, and Ozon all maintained underground organizations opposed to the Nazis, they did not object to the Nazis' treatment of Poland's Jewry. An underground paper published by the Ozon openly expressed pleasure at the extermination of the Jews; it objected only to the methods used. Ten of the forty underground newspapers published by the Poles were overtly anti-Semitic, and most of the others ignored the plight of the Jews. Only the few papers published by the Socialists and the Wyzwolenie, liberal peasants' party, were friendly to the Jewish cause.[22]

The relations of the Bund with the other Jewish parties also were strained; its central committee accused them of ignoring the plight of Poland and of dreaming of impossible schemes. According to the report from the Bund's underground organization in early 1942,

> The [Jewish] opponents of the Bund . . . show no major interest in the fate of Poland.
> The Poale Zionists . . . are even prepared to yield Poland to its eastern neighbor. In their occasional publication they speak of only one dream—to depart to Palestine.

[21] *In di Yorn fun Idishn Khurbn*, p. 18; Goldstein, *op. cit.*, p. 97.
[22] *In di Yorn fun Idishn Khurbn*, p. 18; S. Mendelson, "Es Muz Kumen Maysim," *Unser Tsait*, II, November 1942, p. 3.

They minimize the importance of the [Western] Allies to our future. Their only hope is tied to Russia.

Our other opponents are waiting passively for a solution.

The Bund remains hopeful and remains a believer in the existence of Poland.

The Communists have organized here lately and carry on work on a generally . . . patriotic basis. As of now, their influence in the Ghetto is minimal.[23]

Despite persecution and slaughter, the Bund maintained its belief in eventual victory. "We stand fast in favor of a free, independent Socialist Poland in a voluntary federation of Socialist republics in Europe," it proclaimed. Moreover, the Polish Bund rejected all talk of emigration from Poland, and insisted that the Jewish problem could be solved in Poland only on the basis of social and political equality. Nor was the Bundists' interest in Socialist issues dampened in their own moment of tragedy; the Bund's Central Committee asked for information from its representatives abroad about such matters as the conditions in the Soviet Union and relations between the various Socialist and Communist parties, particularly with regard to Soviet Russia—whether there were signs of a change in the totalitarian nature of the Soviet regime, whether the Polish Government-in-Exile had arrived at a rapprochement with the Soviets, whether the Bund had amicable relations with the London government, and about Socialist and Jewish problems generally.[24]

The Bund's representatives abroad served several useful purposes: they kept the Polish movement apprised by secret couriers of the situation in the world at large, and they arranged for financing the Bund's operations in Poland. These arrangements were a complicated affair, replete with secret transactions worthy of a spy thriller. Many Poles wanted to exchange their Polish zlotys for American dollars, since they had little faith in Poland's future, whereas the Bund needed

[23] *In di Yorn fun Idishn Khurbn,* p. 18.
[24] *Ibid.,* p. 19.

Polish money. The Poles thus gave the zlotys to the Bund, which arranged to have dollars—raised mainly by the Jewish Labor Committee in New York—deposited in American banks to the account of the Poles who had given the Bund the zlotys.[25]

ERLICH AND ALTER

When Warsaw was declared an open city, the Bund directed its two most prominent leaders, Erlich and Alter, to leave and establish headquarters in the new capital, wherever it might be. Alter asked to remain behind as leader of the underground, but the Bund refused; he was too well known as the leader of the Jewish trade unions, and would endanger himself and the Bund. Alter got as far as Kowel, at the eastern end of Poland, and Erlich reached Miedzyrzec, on the Lithuanian border. In the meantime, the Soviet Army had occupied the eastern portions of Poland as part of the agreement with Germany.

Alter was not well known to the Soviets; he was therefore not disturbed by the secret police (NKVD) until after he induced several other trade union officials to join him in a memorandum to the Russian authorities, warning that Germany would attack it as soon as the Nazis were through with Poland. The memorandum was turned over to the Russian secret police, and Alter was arrested.

Erlich had been a member of the St. Petersburg Soviet in 1917 and was known to the Communists as an opponent. He was spotted at the railroad station at Miedzyrzec, and arrested immediately.[26]

[25] Goldstein, *op. cit.*, pp. 50–51.

[26] Lucien Blit, "Erlich un Alter in Soviet Rusland," *Henryk Erlich un Victor Alter*, pp. 96–100. Blit had been a Bund member of the Warsaw city council in 1939; then he fled to the Russian Zone, where he was arrested in 1940. He was released in the amnesty of 1941, and shared a room with Erlich and Alter while they were temporarily free. See his testimony in United States House of Representa-

It was apparent that Erlich and Alter, as democratic Socialists and potential leaders of the large Polish-Jewish population that had been absorbed into the Soviet Union, were
regarded by Stalin as threats to his power. Moreover, Erlich,
as leader of the Menshevik faction in the St. Petersburg Soviet
in 1917, had been opposed to the Bolsheviks' seizure of
power, and Alter had been arrested on his previous visit to
the Soviet Union in 1921. The Great Purge had only recently
ended, and Stalin wanted no potential rivals or enemies on
Soviet soil.

The two Bund leaders were separately held at the Batirka
prison in Moscow, where they were questioned for long
periods. They were accused of being agents of the Polish
intelligence, of plotting to blow up Soviet rail lines, "and all
such kinds of rubbish as is put into a thriller but probably
rarely happens in Russia." According to their roommate Lucien Blit, Erlich in particular was subjected to intensive
questioning by, among others, Lavrenti Beria, chief of the
secret police.[27]

Although both refused to confess, in July 1941 they were
condemned to death as Polish spies. Neither would ask for
clemency, which might have indicated his guilt, but both had
their sentences commuted to ten years at hard labor. In
September, a general amnesty was proclaimed for Polish
citizens, and they were freed.[28]

The Polish government immediately proposed to make
Erlich a member of the Polish Parliament-in-Exile, and began
arrangements for him to reach England. Alter was to become
a member of the staff of the Polish Embassy in Moscow, in
charge of relief work among Polish citizens in Soviet Russia.
Meanwhile, the Soviets induced Erlich and Alter to begin the

---

tives, Select Committee on Communist Aggression, *Third Interim
Report* (Washington: Government Printing Office, 1954), pp. 1201–
1203.

[27] *Ibid.*, pp. 1201–1203.
[28] *Ibid.*, pp. 1203–1204.

formation of an international anti-Fascist committee, aimed at uniting all of the world's Jews for a fight against Hitler.[29]

Why Stalin had so suddenly changed his attitude, and now wished Erlich and Alter, whom he had imprisoned only two years before, to lead so important a committee is not difficult to understand. This was a period of grave danger to the Soviet Union, and thus to Stalin's rule. Moreover, there was considerable doubt in some quarters whether Stalin was genuinely interested in fighting for democracy. By forming such a committee, with two men whose opposition to his rule was established, he must have hoped to allay such doubts.

The two Bund leaders soon showed their independence, however, by insisting that the sponsorship of the new committee be divided between Soviet Russia, the United States, the United Kingdom, and Poland; moreover, they insisted that the leadership would have to be non-Russian. The final decision concerning Erlich and Alter's terms had to come directly from Stalin. After a three-month delay, during which there was little contact between the Bund leaders and the Russians, the former were called, after midnight, ostensibly to a conference on the proposed organization. Their roommate expected them to return in half an hour, but he waited in vain. The pair were again arrested by the secret police; all efforts at locating them failed.[30]

Seven months after their arrest, Stanislaw Kot, the Polish ambassador to Moscow, attempted to discuss the fate of Erlich and Alter with Andrei Vyshinsky, Soviet Deputy Commissar for Foreign Affairs. Kot based his interest in the case on the fact that they were both Polish citizens and Warsaw city councilmen. "I understand your intentions and feel-

[29] Polish Foreign Minister Raczynski to Russian Ambassador Bogomolov, June 10, 1942; Document 298, Sikorski Documents, published in General Sikorski Historical Institute, *Documents on Polish-Soviet Relations, 1939–1945* (London: Heinemann, 1961), pp. 503–504.

[30] Blit testimony, in United States House of Representatives, Select Committee on Communist Aggression, *Third Interim Report* (Washington: Government Printing Office, 1954), pp. 1204–1207.

ings, Mr. Ambassador," the Russian replied. "But I cannot discuss the case of Erlich and Alter with you, because, as you know, in the view of the Soviet Government those men are Soviet citizens." [31]

The protests against the arrests of the two Jewish Socialist leaders were world-wide. Among those pleading for them were Sir Stafford Cripps, a leader of the Labor Party in Britain, and the Republican presidential candidate Wendell Willkie. Finally, on January 27, 1943, more than a year after the arrests, a group including the theologian Reinhold Niebuhr; William Green, president of the American Federation of Labor; Philip Murray, president of the Congress of Industrial Organizations; and David Dubinsky, a onetime Bundist who was now president of the International Ladies' Garment Workers Union, cabled Stalin asking him to free the two men. A reply addressed to Green came from Ambassador Maxim Litvinov:

Dear Mr. Green:

I am informed by Mr. Molotov, People's Commissar for Foreign Affairs, of receipt by him of a telegram signed by you concerning two Soviet citizens, Alter and Erlich.

I am instructed by Mr. Molotov to inform you of the following facts:

For active subversive work against the Soviet Union and assistance to Polish intelligence organs in armed activities, Erlich and Alter were sentenced to capital punishment in August 1941.

At the request of the Polish government, Erlich and Alter were released in September 1941.

However, when they were set free, at the time of the most

[31] Report of conversation between Stanislaw Kot, Polish ambassador to the Soviet Union, and Deputy Commissar of Foreign Affairs Andrei A. Vyshinsky, in Kuibyshev, USSR, June 2, 1942. Document 224, Sikorski Archives, General Sikorski Historical Institute; *loc. cit.*, p. 363. The claim that Erlich and Alter were Soviet citizens was based on the assumption that this was the status of all persons on Soviet-occupied Polish territory at the time of occupation. The claim was, at best, tenuous since both men were born in Poland and themselves claimed Polish citizenship.

desperate battles of the Soviet troops against the advancing Hitler army, they resumed their hostile activities, including appeals to the Soviet troops to stop bloodshed and immediately to conclude peace with Germany.

For this they were rearrested and in December 1941, sentenced once more to capital punishment by the Military Collegium of the Supreme Court. This sentence has been carried out in regard to both of them.[32]

Thus the world learned that Stalin had executed two political opponents, the leaders of the Bund.

LIFE IN THE GHETTO

The Ghetto became a death trap for 400,000 Polish Jews— 300,000 pre-war inhabitants, plus the thousands who had fled to Warsaw from the provincial cities. The Polish Government-in-Exile's courier thus described a visit to the Ghetto, after a meeting with Feiner and a Zionist leader in 1942:

What I learned at the meetings . . . and later, when I was taken to see the facts for myself, was horrible beyond description. I know history, I have learned a great deal about the evolution of nations, political systems, social doctrines, methods of conquest, persecution and extermination, and I know, too, that never in the history of mankind did anything occur to compare with what was inflicted on the Jewish popoulation of Poland.

The first thing that became clear to me . . . was the complete hopelessness of their predicament. For them, for the suffering Polish Jews, this was the end of the world. There was no escape for them or their fellows. This, too, was only part of the tragedy, only partially the cause of their despair and agony. They were not afraid of death itself, and, indeed, accepted it as something almost inevitable. Added to this realiza-

---

[32] Blit testimony, *loc. cit.*, pp. 1204–1207, Maxim Litvinov to William Green, February 23, 1943; copies in Bund Archives, New York, and in files of American Federation of Labor–Congress of Industrial Organizations.

tion was the bitter knowledge that in this war, for them, there could be no hope of any victory whatsoever, none of the satisfaction which sometimes softens the prospect of death.[33]

In October 1942, the Polish courier reported that 300,000 of the ghetto's 400,000 residents had been killed. And Feiner estimated that 3,000,000 Polish Jews, including the 300,000 in Warsaw, had been murdered by the Nazis between October 1939, and June 1943, half of them in the last ten months of that period. He reported that only 75,000 Jews were still alive in German-occupied Poland, 10,000 of them hiding in Polish sections.[34]

The Bund leaders realized early that the Nazis planned total extermination of the Jews, and called on the Jewish population to resist with whatever means were at their disposal. In mid-April, the Nazis forced the leading Jewish professionals from their homes and shot them in full view of the population. The Bund organ *Der Vecker* warned the Ghetto population that this was only the beginning of an action aimed at wiping out Jewish resistance; the object, the Bund warned, was to frighten them into passive submission.[35]

One of the techniques of mass murder employed by the Nazis was the recruiting of workers for "labor camps," which turned out to be centers for mass extermination. Although the technique had been used early in the occupation, it did not become general until 1942. At the outset the Jews accepted the Germans' word that the camps were places of employment, but in a short time the Bundists discovered

[33] Jan Karski, *Story of a Secret State* (Boston: Houghton Mifflin, 1944), pp. 320–321.

[34] *Ibid.*, p. 324; Berezowski (Feiner) to E. Sherer, representative of the Bund in the Polish Parliament-in-Exile; see also *In di Yorn fun Idishn Khurbn*, pp. 52–53. Raul Hilsberg, *The Destruction of the European Jews* (Chicago: Quadrangle Books, 1961), estimates on the basis of official German documents that 50,000 of Poland's 3,350,000 Jews lived through the war.

[35] Marek Edelman, "Di Ghetto Kampft," in *In di Yorn fun Idishn Khurbn*, p. 171.

that they were in reality extermination centers. "Don't be deceived! Throw off your illusions. You are being taken to death by extermination," the Bund warned. "Do not give yourselves voluntarily into the hands of your executioners." The Bund issued leaflets and proclamations urging the Jews to refuse to go voluntarily: "No matter how great the feeling of powerlessness, don't allow yourselves to be caught. Fight with your hands and feet." [36]

Attempts at resistance proved futile, however, and those who fought the Nazi orders inevitably died; unarmed multitudes are helpless against an armed enemy. In January 1943, a Bundist appealed to a group of Jews en route to an extermination camp to refuse to board the train. When they followed his advice and resisted the Nazis, the Germans opened fire and killed them all. They had been spared the horrors of slaughter in a concentration camp; they had died resisting, but they were dead nevertheless. Nothing, clearly, was to deter the Nazis from their drive to exterminate the Jews of Poland.[37]

In destroying the entire Jewish community, with it the Nazis destroyed as well all of the institutions built by the Jewish population in its six-hundred-year sojourn in Poland. All of the Bund institutions, schools, clubs, libraries, and cultural centers were wiped out, none more tragically than the Medem Sanatorium at Medzieczyn. The Sanatorium housed one hundred sickly children from working-class homes in Polish cities. Besides the children there were teachers, technicians, and a medical staff who had served for years at great sacrifice. In August 1942, the Nazis sent a detachment there and ordered the children to board trucks for "evacuation," a word whose real meaning everybody knew. The youngsters resisted; they cried, kicked, and fought back, but in vain. They were dragged into the trucks and taken to the death camps,

[36] Karski, *op. cit.*, pp. 339–354; Edelman, *loc. cit.*, p. 127; Goldstein, *op. cit.*, p. 118.
[37] Edelman, *loc. cit.*, p. 132.

comforted all the way by the teachers, nurses, and doctors, who died with them in the gas chambers. Among the victims of that raid were Zygelboym's wife and son.[38]

THE BUND IN EXILE

The Bund had two organizations during the war, one in Poland and the other in the United States and Britain. The latter was in effect a Bund-in-Exile, and it became the voice of the Jewish Socialists in their dealings with the Polish Government-in-Exile. Relations between the two were not always friendly, although there was a close liaison between the Bund and the exiled leadership of the PPS, particularly in Parliament.

Though during the first years of the war there was considerable disagreement between the Bund and the London government, the Bund had no tribunal through which to make known its opposition other than its own press. In early 1942, at the suggestion of the PPS, the Polish Parliament voted to name one Bund member as a delegate—the first Bundist to serve in any Polish Parliament. The basis for the decision was that in the last free elections—to the city councils in 1938 —the Bund had polled a clear majority of the Jewish vote. The original delegate named was Erlich, but he was at that time supposedly in a Russian prison (and in fact had already been executed). As an alternate the Bund chose Zygelboym, who had been its representative at Socialist meetings throughout the United States since his escape from Warsaw.[39]

Zygelboym foresaw a hard fight against both the Polish

[38] Goldstein, *op. cit.*, pp. 127–128.
[39] "Kh'Arthur Zygelboym in Poylishn National Rat," *Unser Tsait*, II, March 1942, p. 7; *Zygelboym Bukh*, p. 32; interview with Emanuel Sherer, coordinating secretary of the Bund, in New York, February 26, 1965. Sherer succeeded Zygelboym in the parliament. Zygelboym adopted the name Arthur as a "party name" during the repressions of the 1920's. The PPS-in-exile had not split into left-wing and right-wing organizations, as the party had in occupied Poland. The relations between the Bund-in-exile and the PPS-in-exile were thus cordial.

"reaction," the dominant nationalist parties with anti-Jewish bias, and the Jewish groups "who speak of emigration"—the Zionists, who also had a representative in the Polish Parliament-in-Exile. His role, as he saw it, was more than that of a mere reporter of the sufferings of the Jewish workers under Hitler; he also hoped to speak on behalf of their hopes for a better future in a free Poland. He thus took a position of opposition within the new Parliament, and even voted against the budget to show his opposition to the presence of parties like the Endek in the government.[40]

At the same time that Zygelboym entered the Parliament, the Endeks returned to the cabinet-in-exile after a four-month absence. In late 1941, immediately after the Polish and Russian governments had reached an agreement, the Polish Parliament, on the recommendation of the PPS and the Peasants, proposed a declaration of aims for postwar Poland, which included a guarantee of democracy and equality for all minority nationalities. The Endeks had refused to sign the declaration, and after Parliament threatened to upset the government they resigned from the cabinet. Two members of the National Democrats returned to the cabinet in February 1942, after signing a declaration; the Bundists questioned the honesty of their intentions—with good reason. One of the Endek ministers, Marian Seyda, was described by the Bund organ as "an old hard Endek, a reactionary betrayer with a reputation." Moreover, the new cabinet included three members of the so-called unaffiliated right, one of them a member of the violently anti-Semitic Nara, whose London newspaper *Walka* was filled with anti-Semitic articles. The two other delegates from the so-called unaffiliated right were former officials in the post-Pilsudski governing Sanacja.[41]

[40] "Kh'Arthur Zygelboym . . . ," *loc cit.*, p. 7; "Dekleratsye fun Bund in Poylishn Golos-Parliament," *Unser Tsait*, II, June 1942, p. 9; *Zygelboym Bukh*, p. 34.

[41] S. Mendelson, "A Nayer Kurs," *Unser Tsait*, II, March 1942, pp. 4–5.

National Democrat, Nara, and Sanacja leaders were included in the cabinet in an effort to create a wartime government of national unity. Such a government was contrary to the desire of the Bundists, who regarded an all-party national unity government as one made helpless by its lack of direction, or inevitably dominated by the reactionary parties. "The Sanacja and Endeks carry joint blame for taking Poland down to defeat," a Bund leader said. Now, when Poland needed world-wide support from labor and liberal elements, inclusion of these elements could only hurt Poland's cause: "Endek, Sanacja, and Nara elements are only capable of besmirching Poland's name, and discrediting the land in the eyes of the world." The new Poland, he said, would be built by the "proved and struggle-hardened masses" who were fighting daily against the Nazi occupiers of the homeland, and not by the Endeks, Naras, or Sanacja rulers in London.[42]

The Bund's position was stated succinctly by Shloyme Mendelson, one of its cultural leaders resident in New York:

> The thousands and thousands who end their lives on the gallows or in concentration camps and cry out with their dying breaths, "Long live free Poland," do not believe that the new Poland will be built by the Hallers, Kocs, Haleckis or their ilk. [The three were leaders of the pre-war government now serving on the cabinet-in-exile.]
> The gravediggers of yesterday's Poland cannot build the Poland of tomorrow.[43]

By March it became apparent that the declaration which had been signed by the five new members of the cabinet whom the Bund delegate had opposed was a different declaration from the one they had refused to sign the year before. It contained seven points setting forth the government's view of the future order in Poland; and at least four of them, in the

---

[42] *Ibid.*, p. 5.
[43] S. Mendelson, "Vuhin Geht di Sikorski-Regirung?", *Unser Tsait*, II, June 1942, p. 5.

words of Emanuel Sherer, spokesman for the Bund's New York organization, were "contrary to the true needs . . . of the new, free, and independent Poland." The first point, that Poland would be "true to Christianity and culture," was ambiguous. Since Christianity meant different things to different people, and since to the Nara and the Endeks, it meant anti-Semitism, it was either meaningless or dangerous, and Sherer assumed it was the latter. Moreover, "tying the state to a religion denotes clericalism with its many types of limitations on freedom—and never means progress or true democracy." [44]

The second point at issue was the declaration that elections were to be fair, equitable, direct, and secret. Sherer charged that this evaded a central necessity—that they also be proportional. He conceded that proportional representation might not be necessary in the United States or the United Kingdom; but in Poland, where at least 35 per cent of the population was not Polish by nationality, the matter was otherwise. Particularly hard hit by such a ruling, he said, would be the Jews, who were spread throughout the country and would thus be underrepresented. [45]

The third point, which guaranteed full rights and freedoms to all national minorities that had been loyal to Poland, was particularly difficult for the Bund to accept. In the first place it might react directly against the Jews, and second, it was based on the assumption of collective responsibility. The requirement of loyalty to Poland was aimed particularly at the *Volksdeutsche*, the German minority, many of whom had

[44] E. Sherer, "A Brik Tsum Morgn Oder a Shtrik Tsurik?", *Unser Tsait*, II, April 1942, pp. 3–4.

[45] *Ibid.*, p. 4. Sherer's premise was based on an erroneous analysis of the Jewish position. Most Jews lived in the larger cities where they were congregated in specific areas and where they represented from 20 to 35 per cent of the population. Fair representation could thus be possible for the Jews without proportional representation, if districts were so divided that the Jews would be dominant in several of them.

generally supported the Nazis before and during the invasion and occupation. But Sherer feared that it could be turned against any minority, including the Jews, by an unfriendly government. He also opposed condemning all *Volksdeutsche*, some of whom were Social Democrats suffering death and imprisonment along with their Jewish and Polish compatriots. Disloyalty was an individual matter, which required judicial action and could not be assumed on the basis of edicts.[46]

The fourth point assailed by Sherer was the socio-economic plank, which favored a return to the system of private-enterprise capitalism. This, he said, was a return to the past, whereas Poland needed a new economic system—socialism.[47]

Sherer wanted a firm declaration promising a democratic and Socialist Poland, in which each of the nationalities would be treated as an integral part of the state.

> If we genuinely want the present world war to be the last, we must abandon completely the bankrupt yesterday and build a new postwar Europe on the basis [of] a free Socialist society and cooperation between all free and equal peoples in a European federation.
>
> An upstanding and consequential democratic program—just as a completely honest and democratic Poland—can be created only through a genuinely democratic government.[48]

That the Bundists' fears had substance became apparent almost immediately after Zygelboym entered the Parliament. The National Democrats introduced, and the Parliament passed, a proposal that a Jewish homeland be organized outside Poland, to which the Polish Jews would be asked to emigrate. The motion, which continued the pre-war government's policy of ridding Poland of its Jews, was made by Mme Zaleska, an anti-Semitic representative of the National Democrats. A suggestion by Dr. A. Schwartzbard, the Zionist member of the Parliament, that Palestine be specifi-

---

[46] *Ibid.*, p. 5.   [47] *Ibid.*, pp. 5–6.   [48] *Ibid.*, p. 6.

cially named, was rejected before the bill was passed. Only Zygelboym and one Polish Socialist voted against it; Schwartzbard abstained, and Adam Ciolkosz, another Socialist, declared against it but was absent. The representative of the Bund protested the proposal; he refused to consider anything but Poland as the home of the Polish Jews. According to the Bundist formal protest, "The Jewish masses consider Poland for the joint home of the entire population of the country. The vote in the National Parliament is a warning to the Jewish masses. It shows that the Polish reaction has not give up its anti-Semitic position." [49]

The Bund was also at odds with the Zionists, who wanted the war to result in the establishment of a Jewish national home in Palestine. For this reason, the Zionist delegate refused to vote against the Zaleska proposal in the Polish Parliament. To accomplish this end, the Zionists wanted a separate Jewish army of 10,000 men to be established in Palestine, with 3,000 Palestinian Jews forming the core of the force and 7,000 from other countries to be added. The proposed army was rejected by the British government, which feared that it would turn the Arabs against the Allies. The Zionists continued to agitate for a Jewish army even after the British government had turned down their plea. The Bund spokesman charged, however, that a separate Jewish army would do more harm than good, and would lead, in the end, to Middle Eastern warfare.[50]

> The idea of a separate Jewish army is harmful to the Jews wherever they may be; it is even harmful to the Jews in Palestine. Are the Jews of Palestine really interested in rousing distrust . . . among the native population? Are they interested

[49] "Protest fun Algemaynem Idishn Arbeiter Bund Kegn dem Anti-Semitishn Bashlus fun Poylishn Natsional-Rat Vegn a Idisher Milukhe," *Unser Tsait*, II, July 1942, p. 3.

[50] H. Lezgin, "A Shedlekher Tuml," *Unser Tsait*, II, April 1942, p. 12; *The Times* (London), November 11, 1941.

in having a separate Jewish army in Palestine against whom will stand a separate Arab army? Who would benefit from this?

The idea of a separate Jewish army was preached by the most reactionary forces in Czarist Russia and Poland. They wanted to carry this out as a sign of inequality. And the Jewish masses were always on guard against this, and they will undoubtedly guard themselves against this in the future.

Thus when the Zionists raise the issue of a Jewish army today . . . they create serious harm . . . They are feeding grist to the mill of inequality and reaction . . . They mobilize the energies of the Jewish people in the present tragic, oppressive times when we must expend so much energy to help support the 10,000,000 Jews under Hitler, in useless and quixotic ventures.[51]

The Bundists feared the Jewish army would be only a first step along the path of emigration, and toward a further alienation of the Polish Jews from Poland. Zygelboym made the Bund's position clear in his first major declaration of policy before the Parliament: "The Jewish population of Poland has its fatherland. That fatherland is Poland, just as it is the fatherland of the Polish masses." The emigration of its inhabitants might possibly aid the economy of Poland—although he did not concede, that it would—but any such emigration would have to be multinational, rather than a strictly Jewish affair; Jews and non-Jews would have to be handled as equals. The Jews, he said, had shown that they realized their responsibilities and had fulfilled their duties as citizens from the outset of the war. They had fought well in the defense of the homeland; they were now serving with valor in the Polish army in exile.

The time had come, he said, for Poland to end the "Jewish problem"; and this could be done only on the basis of a three-point program: (1) full equality for the Jewish population in all sectors of the political, social, and economic life of the country; (2) a guarantee to the Jewish population

[51] Lezgin, *ibid.*, p. 16.

permitting free development of its national heritage through the acceptance of national cultural autonomy, and recognition of the Yiddish language throughout the state for educational and legal institutions; and (3) legal prohibition of anti-Semitism in society, politics, and education. Zygelboym wanted anti-Semitic propaganda and activities to be made criminal acts, subject to prosecution.

But such a state could not be achieved in a vacuum; it would require a free and democratic Poland in a free and democratic Europe. And a free, democratic Europe, said Zygelboym, was the goal toward which the Bund was directing all of its efforts. He therefore offered the Polish Parliament a ten-point program aimed at achieving the goal: (1) a regime based on trust of the working masses of all nationalities—a workers' and peasants' government; (2) full democracy with territorial, national, and economic self-determination; (3) prohibition of all discrimination against minorities, with full guarantees of equal rights; (4) an end to all class privileges, distribution of land to the peasantry, and socialization of industry; (5) state aid to artisans, small businessmen, and cooperatives; (6) a guarantee to all citizens of the right to a job, protection of life and limb, fair conditions of work, and a democratic system of social welfare; (7) reconstruction of Poland's economy on the basis of planning, specifically economic rehabilitation of the pauperized Jewish population; (8) free public education for all, with the national minorities using their own languages; (9) secularization of the whole political and social life of Poland; and (10) cooperation with the other states and establishment of a permanent organization of the free nations of Europe on the basis of equality.[52]

The Bundists realized that Zygelboym's programs were idealizations, even if the Polish Parliament were to enact them

---

[52] "Dekleratsye fun Bund in Poylishn Golos-Parliament," *Unser Tsait*, II, June 1942, pp. 6–9.

in good faith. By mid-1942 it had become obvious that there would be few if any Jews left alive in Poland by the end of the war. Zygelboym told a meeting of the Socialist International in London, "It is possible that there may be no one left to rescue." [53]

The Bund organized a militia early in the occupation; this was at best a semi-military organization with a minimum of arms and a maximum of bravado. As early as April 1940, it was involved in protecting the Jews from attacks by Polish and German hooligans. When, in that month, a Polish gang assaulted a group of Jews in Praga, a suburb of Warsaw, the militia came to the Jews' defense and, after a prolonged street fight, drove the hooligans off. Most Jews expected that the Nazis would retaliate, but the retaliation never came.[54]

When, in mid-1941, the ghetto in Lublin was completely wiped out by the Nazis, and it became apparent that the Jews could either go to their deaths passively or die fighting the Nazis, the Bund set up a battle organization and started its effort to acquire arms. Bernard Goldstein, a leader in the militia, recalled later: "The acquisition of arms became the one goal toward which we strained every sinew of our organization. It was clear we would have to fight. How much time we had we did not know, but we knew we did not have enough." [55]

After the slaughter of Jewish intellectuals in April 1942, the Bund decided to organize a nonpartisan Jewish army to fight the Nazis. Only two Socialist-Zionist youth groups agreed to join, the Hashomer Hatsair and the Hakhalutz; the Revisionist Zionists, a militant nationalist group, formed their

[53] "Vaygeshray fun Idisher Bafelkerung in Poyln," *Unser Tsait*, II, October 1942, pp. 18–19.
[54] Goldstein, *op. cit.*, pp. 52–53.
[55] *Ibid.*, p. 88; Edelman, *loc. cit.*, pp. 169–171.

own small para-military group, the Irgun, and the religious groups refused to take part in any military activities.[56]

The three leaders of the underground Bund army were Goldstein, a pre-war union leader; Berek Snaidmill, an intellectual who had been a reserve officer in the Polish Army; and Abrasha Blum, an engineer who had been educated at the University of Liége in Belgium. None of them had been trained in military science, nor had any had experience in guerrilla warfare. Therefore, when the joint Jewish army was formed in October 1942, battle command was given to an official of the Hashomer Hatsair, and liaison with the Polish underground armies was under Feiner of the Bund.[57]

The Jewish military group had considerable difficulty in obtaining arms. The Gwardia Ludowa, the pro-Soviet underground army, sent in the first weapons—a few pistols. The PPS and the more radical "Polish Socialists" smuggled gasoline and other raw materials through to the Ghetto army and sent instructions on the construction of grenades and the primitive fire bombs known as Molotov cocktails. But there were so few arms that the Jewish army would have been unable to offer more than token resistance against the Nazis.[58]

[56] *Ibid.*, pp. 169–171; Berezowski to Sherer, *op. cit.*, p. 55. Hashomer Hatsair was closely related to the "Left" Poale Zion, Hakhalutz to the "Right" Poale Zion.

[57] Edelman, *loc. cit.*, p. 189; Goldstein, *op. cit.*, pp. 45–46.

[58] S. Zachariasz, "The Ghetto Was Not Alone," *Jewish Life*, IV, April 1951, pp. 10–11; Edelman, *loc. cit.*, pp. 190–195. There were at least three underground armies in Poland. The largest and oldest of these was the Armia Krajowa, led by Tadeusz Bor-Komarowski. It dated to the beginning of the war, and was composed of detachments representing most of the Polish parties, including the PPS, the peasant parties, and the National Democrats. The Socialist segment of the Armia Krajowa was friendly toward the Jews; the National Democratic segment was openly hostile, and the others were neutral. The second underground army, the Narodowe Sily Zbrojne, was linked closely with the old National Radicals. It was not a significant factor in the fight against the Nazis. It was, however, violently anti-Semitic, and has been accused of aiding the Germans

The first actions of the new army were mainly terrorist attacks and rescue missions aimed at freeing arrested members. Thus when three Bundists were arrested by the Gestapo, they were rescued by a small group of members of the Ghetto army. Likewise, all members of the so-called Jewish Gestapo—an organization consisting mainly of apostates, who worked as agents for the Nazis in the hope that their lives would be spared—were either murdered or driven out of the Ghetto. Four German Gestapo men, who tried to enter the Ghetto in late 1942, were also murdered by a band of Ghetto army men.[59]

Toward the end of December 1942, the first shipment of arms—a few pistols and grenades—arrived from the official Polish underground army. The arms had come at a fortunate moment, since the Nazis planned to begin in January the evacuation of the last remaining Jews to the extermination centers. The attempts met stiff armed resistance; the Germans lost heavily against the poorly armed Jews, but so did the Jews themselves. The battle did, however, serve another purpose: the Polish underground army recognized the military possibilities in a Jewish resistance force and sent in considerably more arms—including automatic weapons. The Jewish force was now capable of limited resistance against the Nazis.[60]

---

in their extermination of the Jews. The Gwardia Ludowa, the Communist-organized underground army, came into being after the German invasion of the Soviet Union. Although it had good arms, supplied by the Soviets, it did not play a significant role in the war against the Nazis. See Tadeusz Bor-Komarowski, *The Secret Army* (London: Gollancz, 1950); also M. K. Dziewanowski, *The Communist Party of Poland*, pp. 160–161. For a description of the anti-Semitic activities of part of the Armia Krajowa see Oscar Pinkus, *The House of Ashes* (Cleveland and New York: World Publishing Company, 1964), especially pp. 195, 217–218, 221, 223, 225, 226–227. Pinkus maintains (p. 227) that the Armia Krajowa killed Jews on direct orders from the Polish Government-in-Exile. His charges, which bear investigation, are not substantiated.

[59] Edelman, *loc. cit.*, pp. 190, 195–196.
[60] *Ibid.*, pp. 191–193.

In March the prelude to the main battle occurred. The Nazis ordered the brushmakers to prepare to go to "labor camps"; the Bund told the brushmakers—who were almost all Bundists—to ignore the order. The Nazis sent in trucks to take the men to the camps, the battle groups planted bombs in the trucks, and the vehicles were destroyed before any brushmakers could be sent to their doom. At the same time the Ghetto army invaded the Nazi jail in the Ghetto, freed the Jewish prisoners, and showed its defiance of the Germans.[61]

The Germans set the date of April 19 for liquidating the Ghetto. They knew that they would face some opposition, and therefore sent in a full battle group. The German soldiers met with concentrated fire as they entered the Ghetto, and suffered a good many casualties. When the Nazis sent in a tank unit, the Jews destroyed one tank and forced the rest to flee. As the Germans withdrew, the Ghetto army captured a mortar and other arms. After a twelve-hour lull, the battle was resumed when a Nazi platoon tried to enter the Ghetto; its progress was halted by a land mine. German officers now tried to arrange a truce, offering guarantees that the Jews would be evacuated to work and not death. The Jews rejected the offer and continued the fight, which went on for more than two weeks. On May 3, when the Nazis set fire to the Ghetto, the heroic battle of the poorly armed, undermanned Jewish Ghetto army was nearing its end.[62] Marek Edelman, one of the survivors of the battle, described it thus:

> What the Germans couldn't accomplish the all-powerful fire was now doing. Thousands of people die in the blaze. The odor of burning bodies is in the air; on the balconies of houses, in the window niches, on the unburnt stone steps lie coal-black bodies. The fire drives people out of the defense bunkers, forces them to flee the long-prepared "safe" hiding places in cellars and on roofs. Thousands wander about the fields,

---

[61] *Ibid.*, pp. 195–197.   [62] *Ibid.*, pp. 197–200.

placing themselves in danger of being caught at any moment, to face arrest or immediate death at the hands of the Germans.[63]

Fighting continued sporadically in the burning Ghetto; it was obvious that there could be no escape. Those in the bunkers either were killed by German gas bombs or committed suicide. "One thing we can say—we didn't allow the Germans to carry out their plan. They didn't take a single one [of those still fighting] out alive." By May 10 the battle was over. Merely a handful of the resistance force was still alive—only those who escaped to the "Aryan side" of Warsaw. Of the hundreds of Bundists who fought in the battle, five survived. The various estimates of the German losses run all the way from sixteen to 5,000.[64]

The few Bundists who remained alive continued to fight for a free Poland and participated in the 1944 Warsaw uprising; but after May 10 there was no longer a Jewish constituency in Poland for the Bund to represent. Hitler had "solved" Poland's Jewish problem.[65]

THE FINAL BLOW

One of the tragedies of the war was the unwillingness, or the inability, of the great powers to rescue the millions of Jews from the clutches of Hitler. Undoubtedly, military and political considerations made this an almost impossible task, but the prevailing apathy in all the Western world has never been explained satisfactorily.

When the courier for the Polish Government-in-Exile visited Warsaw in late 1942, the representatives of the Bund

[63] *Ibid.*, pp. 201–202.
[64] *Ibid.*, p. 208; Hilsberg, *op. cit.*, p. 326; Hilsberg accepts the German statement that only sixteen Nazis died in the fighting; Nathan Ausubel, *Pictorial History of the Jewish People* (New York: Crown Publishers, 1953), p. 263, places the figure at five thousand. The truth appears to lie somewhere between.
[65] Wireless message from Berezowski to Sherer, October 25, 1944; copy in Bund Archives.

and the Zionists pleaded with him to get word to the Allies that the Jews were facing extermination, and to beg the Allies to do something, somehow, to save them. "The democracies cannot calmly put up with the assertion that the Jewish people in Europe can't be saved," they told him.[66]

But what could be done? How could the Allied powers save the Jews behind Hitler's lines? Bomb German cities, the Bund representative told him, and drop leaflets during the raids telling the Germans about what is being done to the Jews. "We know," he said, "that possibly this plan cannot be carried out, that it cannot fit into Allied military strategy, but we can't help that. The Jews, and those who wish to help them, cannot afford to approach this war from a purely military standpoint. Tell the Allied governments, if they want to help us, to issue official declarations to the German government and people telling them that the consequences of continued persecution will be mass reprisals, the systematic destruction of the entire German nation." [67]

It was the hope of the Jewish representatives that the plea would get through to the Jewish populations in America and Britain, and that they would then put pressure on their governments. The message went on:

> Tell the Jewish leaders [in the United States and the United Kingdom] that this is no case for politics or tactics. Tell them the earth must be shaken to its foundations, the world must be aroused. Perhaps then it will wake up, understand, perceive. Tell them they must find the courage to make sacrifices no other statesmen have ever had to make, sacrifices as painful as the fate of my dying people; and as unique. This is what they do not understand. German aims and methods are without precedent in history. The democracies must react in a way that is also without precedent, choose unheard-of methods as an answer. If not, their victory will be only partial, only a military victory. Their victory will not preserve what

[66] Karski, *op. cit.*, p. 327.   [67] *Ibid.*, p. 326.

the enemy includes in his program of destruction. Their methods will not preserve us.

You ask me what plan of action I suggest to the Jewish leaders. Tell them to go to all the important English and American offices and agencies. Tell them not to leave until they have obtained guarantees that a way has been decided upon to save the Jews. Let them accept no food or drink, let them die a slow death while the world is looking on. Let them die. This may shake the conscience of the world.[68]

The courier brought the message to Zygelboym in London. The Bund leader was despondent; he saw that the suggestions of the Warsaw Jewish leaders could not be carried out, that British and American leaders would refuse for military and political reasons. To the suggestion that the Jews go on a sit-down hunger strike in British and American government offices he replied: "It is impossible, utterly impossible. You know what would happen. They would simply bring in two policemen and have me dragged away to an institution. Do you think they will let me die a slow lingering death? Never . . . they would never let me." [69]

Zygelboym was losing hope. His pleas for action to save Poland's Jews fell on deaf ears: "Our actions and protests have no practical value," he wrote the American representative of the Bund. Moreover, he was losing faith in the Polish Parliament; he found it more rewarding to speak before an audience of dock workers in Hull than to the Parliament of the Polish government.[70]

By the end of April the Bund was receiving reports in London on the tragically heroic struggle in the Ghetto. Zygelboym commented on the last dispatch from the Ghetto: "It breathes with the fact that all is ending . . . It is impossible to work or to live with this knowledge." On the night of May 11, Zygelboym registered his personal protest against the

[68] *Ibid.*, pp. 327–328.   [69] *Ibid.*, p. 334.
[70] From "Arthur" [Zygelboym] to American Representation of the Bund, New York, January 1, 1943; May 3, 1943.

destruction of the Jews while the rest of the world callously looked on: he committed suicide.[71]

Zygelboym left a letter of farewell to the Polish president and prime minister; it read in part:

> I cannot remain alive while the remnants of the Jewish people in Poland, whom I represent, are being murdered. . . .
>
> With my death I hope to express the sharpest protest against the passivity with which the world looks on and permits the extermination of the Jewish people.[72]

CONCLUSION

There was no longer a Jewish constituency in Poland; the Bund's mission had ended.

> Fallen and broken in prison,
>   you died victoriously;
> In fighting for the working class,
>   you died so gloriously.[73]

[71] From "Arthur" [Zygelboym] to American Representation of the Bund, April 30, 1943. Copy in Bund Archives; see also *Zygelboym Bukh*, p. 40.

[72] From S. M. Zygelboym to General Wladislaw Sikorski, Prime Minister of Poland, May 11, 1943. Copy in Bund Archives.

[73] Dirge of the Russian Social Revolutionists, 1905.

XI

An Appraisal

THE Polish Bund was a political failure.

It did not become a significant force in interwar Poland. Not a single Bundist ever sat in the Sejm; nor had the Bund influenced the direction of independent Poland. The Poland Hitler conquered was little changed from the Poland Pilsudski had created in 1918. The Jews were still persecuted; the political system was, if anything, less democratic. Socialism had failed to win over the mass of the workers, peasants, and intellectuals. Poland was the same backward, authoritarian republic.

Obviously, all this cannot be blamed on the Bund. But neither can the Bund be absolved of failure to play its own part more effectively in developing an alternative.

Postwar changes in the areas that most interested the Bund were likewise little influenced by it. The Communist state that emerged in Poland after 1944 was created by the conquering Red Army. It was politically antithetical to the state envisioned by the Bund's leaders before and during the war. With establishment of the State of Israel, the debate over the Jewish question was settled along exactly the lines suggested by the Zionists, which the Bund had vigorously opposed.

The Bund could not have prevented the final destruction of the Jewish community in Poland by the Nazis, whatever policies it pursued; nor could it have influenced the postwar developments in the wake of the catastrophe of 1939–1943. The Bund's base had been destroyed in the war; its leaders had been slain by the Nazis or the Soviets, or had fled into exile, and its constituency had been exterminated in the

Ghetto. These death-blows and the postwar aftermath were caused by outside forces. But the failure of the Bund to exert a greater influence in interwar Poland was the result of internal rather than external factors.

The Bund failed because its members were unable to recognize political reality. They looked upon a political party as a sanctified debating society in which fine points of dogma were argued. They did not recognize the party's true role, that of a seeker after state power.

As a party whose minority status made it unable to assume power by itself, it was obliged to find an ally whose views were reasonably similar to its own, and which was not confined to the role of a permanent minority.

The PPS was the potential ally; it was a Socialist party, and its constituency was of the major nationality in Poland. Although the PPS did not rule Poland, except for a brief period immediately after independence, it had the potential for becoming the ruling party.

The Bundists recognized that their party was destined for permanent minority status, but they failed to accept the implications of that fact. Faced with four possible solutions to their dilemma, the Bundists refused to take the necessary action to effectuate any of them.

The possibility that the Bund might have united with the Communist Party was more apparent than real. Although the Bundists for two years did seriously consider such a merger—which a majority favored—it was an impossibility; the differences between the Bund and the Communists were too great. The Communists were enemies of the democratic parliamentary system on which the Bund based its political principles. The issue of proportional representation, which the Bund raised in the Polish Government–in–Exile, may have been based upon erroneous assumptions, but it emphasized the degree to which the Bund was wedded to parliamentary government. The Communists' opposition to parliamentary democracy is a matter of common knowledge; they consider it to be a vestige of capitalism. Communists in power have invariably destroyed parliamentary government; and they have generally come to power by armed uprising or foreign intervention.

Had the Bundists actually gone into the Communist Party in Poland, their leaders would undoubtedly have met the same fate as the Polish Communists who were liquidated by the Soviet regime in 1938.

Merger into a federated PPS would probably have won the approval of most of the Bundists, particularly after 1928. Historical and theoretical considerations made this impossible. The PPS and the Bund had a history of animosity dating back to the late 1890's, when the PPS was closely linked with Polish nationalism. The PPS then considered Polish independence a prerequisite to socialism. The Bundists, on the contrary, did not believe that independence would solve Poland's national or economic problems. This hostility continued long after Poland had won its independence; vestiges remained until 1939.

Since the PPS was not interested in federation as the basis for merger with the Bund, and since the Bund needed the PPS more than the PPS needed the Bund, the proposal was academic at best.

The third possibility, the dissolution of the Bund so that its members might enter the PPS on an individual basis, would probably have met with the approval of the PPS; but it was not acceptable to the Bundists. They could not be convinced that it might be necessary to dissolve the party they had fought so long to build, nor could they be expected to disavow one of their chief rallying calls—that for national cultural autonomy, which the PPS did not support. The idea of dissolution was thus never discussed seriously.

A strong case for dissolution could have been made. A

single party of Socialists would have been considerably more influential than was the proliferation of Socialist parties in interwar Poland. A united party could on several occasions have elected larger Socialist delegations to the Sejm. The PPS would probably not have become quite as revolutionary as the Bundists said they desired to be; but there can be little doubt that the Bundists' influence on the PPS would have been considerably greater if they had been in the Polish party rather than on the outside.

The fourth possibility would have been the easiest to achieve. No argument can be raised against the idea of a working electoral coalition between the Bund and the PPS. That such a coalition failed to develop is further proof of the futility of the Bund's position. Although the PPS may be held partly at fault, it is the Bund that must accept the greater part of the blame. When, in 1930, the PPS formed a coalition of democratic parties against the Pilsudski dictatorship, the Bund was invited to join. The Bundists refused the invitation. The PPS recognized the weakness of its individual position; aware that it could not gain power alone, it formed an *ad-hoc* coalition aimed at ending the dictatorship. Perhaps the coalition could not have effectuated a major social revolution, but it might have brought democratic government to Poland.

The Bundists' reaction was typical of the air of unreality that permeated the movement. They had always opposed coalition with non-Socialists, and therefore they rejected it once again. That becoming part of this coalition might have been an opening through which the Bund could have become part of the Polish body politic was ignored; that it might have meant a more effective movement aimed at democratizing Poland was ignored. The Bundists insisted on being true to their dogmas despite the obvious fact that they might thus help perpetuate a system which was anathema to them. It was this all-or-nothing approach by the Bundists that prevented the formation of a coalition with the PPS.

It is apparent that a party like the Bund cannot hope to

rule by itself. But this does not prevent it from exerting influence upon the politics of the state in which it exists. It can do so by merger or alliance with a larger party which has the potential of forming the government of the country. To accomplish such a merger or alliance, however, requires compromise; and this fact the Bund refused to accept.

A minor party with no possibility of seizing the reins of government can serve only as an influence upon a party capable of assuming power; no other role is available to it except, perhaps, that of a political Don Quixote.

THE NATIONALITY QUESTION

The failure of Marx to understand the importance of the nationality question had serious consequences for the Bund. Since it was a self-proclaimed Marxist party, its members felt constrained to argue most issues in terms of Marxism.

National cultural autonomy was a proposal designed originally by Renner and Bauer to solve the peculiar conditions in the Austro-Hungarian empire. The Socialists in that empire were seeking a solution to a particular problem that confronted them, the multiplicity of nationality-based parties. It was rejected by the non-German Socialists in the empire because it obstructed their aspirations. They wanted territorial independence in order that they might shape their own destinies.

Cultural autonomy failed as well to meet the needs of most of the non-Russian minorities in the Czarist empire, who also wanted territorial independence. The Socialists were at the forefront of the independence movements, particularly among the Poles.

But the Bund's position was peculiar. It represented the only nationality that could have accepted national cultural autonomy. The Jews were dominant in no specific geographic area, but were scattered throughout the Pale. After Poland's liberation they were spread throughout the urban centers of that country. All they could hope for, under those conditions, was equality and cultural autonomy. The other nationalities believed they could achieve political as well as cultural autonomy, but this was not possible for the Jews.

The Zionists came to grips with this problem by insisting that Jews could never hope for equality in an alien land—and that any land would have to be alien to the Jews except Palestine, the historic homeland.

The Bund tried to evade the fundamental issue: Could the Jews exist in Poland as a separate ethnic or national group? National cultural autonomy would, on the face of it, have meant recognition that the Jews were a distinct cultural and national group in Poland. It should have been obvious from the outset that the Poles were not ready to concede this recognition. No Polish party supported the Bund's view, and any hope at making it a reality required the support of a major segment of the Polish population.

The Bundists, as is obvious from their party's role in the late 1930's, considered themselves a part of Poland. As members of the Jewish nationality in Poland, they believed they owed a joint loyalty: culturally to their Jewish heritage, politically to Poland. Yet this turned out to be an untenable position.

It was an untenable position so long as the majority population of Poland refused to allow the Jews equality and some degree of autonomy. The cry for national cultural autonomy thus became a self-perpetrated ruse by which the Bundists were able to avoid coming to grips with the essential problem: Could the Jews live as equals in Poland? On the basis of historical evidence, the answer had to be No.

It can be argued that the establishment of the State of Israel in 1948 did not come about because the Zionists wished it. It can be argued that Israel's statehood was born of necessity—that the Nazi slaughter of the Jews, which caused it to be established could not have been foreseen. But the fact remains that the Zionists, when the solution they had proposed became imperative, were in a position to effectuate it. The tragic truth is that when the Jewish problem could no longer be sidestepped, the Bund's proposed solution was no longer viable.

The Bundists erred for three reasons. First, they assumed that a solution had to be found that would not contradict Socialist internationalism. They refused to admit that an answer to a particular problem might require a modification of Socialist doctrine. Second, they failed to realize that in a country such as Poland it might be impossible to achieve cultural autonomy. They refused to recognize the deep-seated attitude among the Poles toward the Jews, as an alien minority whose ways were different from their own. The Bundists could not accept the fact that they were considered aliens precisely because their culture *was* different; and cultural autonomy would have underscored that difference. Finally, the Bundists erred because they refused to allow themselves room for maneuver should it become necessary to accept all or part of the Zionist solution. The Bundists' opposition to Zionism was so intense that they still could not accept it as late as 1942, when it was evident that there could no longer be any hope for a Jewish community in Poland, and that a refuge had to be found outside its borders.

THE MYTH

For the Bund to have existed for twenty-six years as a separate organization in a hostile Poland is attributable to the power of its myth. Bundists undoubtedly realized that their party had no hope of influencing the Polish state except as part of a larger all-nationality Socialist party of Poland. Yet they almost invariably refused to give up their separate existence and insisted on remaining a distinct party—or at least an independent unit in a federated party. Why? This must be attributed to the myth which permeated the Bund.

When in 1921 the members of the Bund rejected the

twenty-one conditions for affiliation with the Comintern, and decided instead to remain outside all world organizations, they gave their most convincing proof of the strength of the myth. A great majority—almost 70 percent—supported a faction that favored a left-wing stance similar to that adopted by the Comintern. Yet almost 90 per cent of the Bundists refused to join the Comintern, if joining meant ousting leaders who vehemently opposed the Comintern's principles (leaders, many of whom had openly opposed the seizure of power in Russia by the founders of the Communist International). Why did the vast majority of the Bundists prefer their leaders, with whom they disagreed on principle, to the Comintern, with which they apparently agreed? Obviously, the only explanation must be the myth of the Bund itself.

Similarly, during the periods of oppression that were numerous in interwar Poland, the myth kept the Bund from disintegrating. When the Polish regime of 1922–1926 closed down Bund organizations in all parts of Poland and made their very existence almost impossible, it was the myth—that indefinable mystique—that kept the party alive. Similarly, during the post-Pilsudski reign of persecution (1935–1939), the myth allowed the Bundists to oppose the government openly, and to emerge as the leading voice of Polish Jewry immediately prior to World War II.

Finally, in the face of a Nazi invader intent on exterminating the entire Jewish people, the myth permitted the Bund to lead a resistance movement and to keep alive some semblance of dignity in the Polish ghettos. No one could have assumed that the small Ghetto resistance force, in which the Bundists played a leading role, could prevent the extermination of Poland's Jewish population. That such a force was formed at all—and that it fought so heroically against impossible odds —must be attributed to the myth which permeated the Bund.

To call the Bund an *ecclesia militanta* is not to denigrate it; faced with insuperable obstacles, it had of necessity to be a devout band, permeated by a myth for which its members would be willing to face persecution and death.

Sorel's theory of the myth is buttressed by the experience of the Bund.

IN DEFENSE OF THE BUND

The Bundists are open to criticism for their failure to realize the role of a party precluded from power. But this is citicism *ex post facto;* through hindsight it is possible to see the Bundists' errors. Yet those errors should not tend to an assumption that the Bundists had no positive political attributes.

Their leaders' analysis of the Russian Bolshevik Revolution and of the Soviet regime—an analysis which by 1930 almost all of the Bundists accepted—was far more sophisticated than the views of most other Socialists and many non-Socialists. The Bund leaders, with few exceptions, saw in the Soviet regime a totalitarianism that could not lead to a Socialist state except as the definition of socialism was revised to fit. Alter's highly critical analysis of the Five-Year-Plan, and his warning that the Stalin purges were a threat to world socialism, showed a clarity of perspective that was lacking in many Socialist leaders and non-Socialist intellectuals during the 1920's and 1930's.

The Bundists' warning to the German Social Democrats (SPD) that their policies were failing to prevent the rise of Hitler was ignored by that party's leadership. It is apparent that the Bundists had a better understanding of German conditions than did the leaders of the German Socialists.

Likewise, the warning made by the Bund's leaders to the rulers of Poland as early as 1933, that Hitler planned to seize their country, was ignored. The Bundists' analysis proved, unfortunately, to have been accurate. Had the warning been heeded, the history of Poland from 1939 to 1945 might have been different.

Moreover, during the Nazi attack and occupation the Bundists showed that the Jews of Poland could have been its patriotic citizens and could have contributed greatly toward its success had they been allowed the opportunity. The Bund and the PPS were the two political organizations which alone opposed—and thus prevented—the surrender of Warsaw to the Nazis without a battle. Bundists fought heroically at the barricades in Warsaw and in the underground battles against the Nazis all through the occupation.

THE POLITICS OF FUTILITY

The Bund did serve a function in interwar Poland but not as a political party. That function was one concerning culture and welfare, which was the responsibility of the state but which the Polish state refused to perform.

The schools that the Bundists organized were of great value for the Jewish population in Poland. Excluded generally from the public schools, or relegated to ghetto benches, the Jews required a separate system to meet their needs. The refusal of the Polish state to meet that need led the Bundists to accept that responsibility for their party. But the organization of a school system was not a function of a political party; it was rather an extralegal responsibility, which was incidental to the Bund's basic task.

Despite the importance of the tasks undertaken by the Bund on behalf of culture and relief, the question can be asked: Was this a responsibility the Bund should have undertaken? If we define the Bund as a political party, the answer must be in the negative. But it must be acknowledged that the Bund saw itself as more than a party; it saw itself also as a protector and disseminator of Jewish culture. It accepted for itself the role of legislator and executor of Jewish national cultural autonomy. Bundists saw their party, in effect, as an extralegal authority for putting many of their policies into practice.

It was not as a cultural or a relief organization that the Bund failed, but rather as a political force. And its acceptance of the responsibilities which it could not induce the state to accept is further proof of this failure. A successful political party would have forced the state to recognize its task. The Bund's failure as a political organization obliged it to undertake such responsibilities.

The failure of the Bund is further accentuated by the unreality that dominated the national conventions of the party. Almost invariably, Bundists faced with critical Polish issues such as anti-Semitism or the repression of labor would debate at length the question of international affiliation. This flight into the world where brave pronunciamentos took precedence over crucial realities was partly the result of the Bund's inability to influence the direction of Poland. But the flight was, as well, a cause of that same incapacity.

Faced with preclusion from an actual role in the government of the state, individual Bundists could assume a certain importance by directing the destiny of the party itself. The factional struggles within the Bund allowed the Bundists to become involved in political activity in which victory was possible, even if the victory was within a powerless party. The politics within the Bund—primarily on the question of internationals—replaced the politics of the state. The political animal was thus able to participate in the decision-making process. Internal politics was in effect an escape mechanism for alleviating the frustration the Bundists experienced in Polish state politics.

The debates within the Bund, and the polarization of factions into left, center, and right wings, rendered the Bund almost totally unable to make the adjustment necessary to work within the context of Polish politics. Unity with the PPS, either by merger or by coalition, was impossible so long as the Bundists considered the internal struggle an end in itself.

The failure of the Bund as a political party can thus be

attributed to its members' failure to recognize their role. Where the Bund should have been attempting to influence the direction of the Polish state, as part of the Socialist party of Poland, it was busy evading that role while it kept its revolutionary posture unsullied.

The politics of the Bund was the politics of futility.

Bibliography

CHRONICLES, MEMOIRS, AND COLLECTED
SOURCE MATERIALS

A Clorer Entfer [A Clear Answer]. London: Polish Socialist Party, 1904.

Abramovitch, Raphael. *The Soviet Revolution, 1917–1939.* New York: International Universities Press, 1962.

Alter, Victor. *Antysemityzm Gospodarczy w Swietle Cyfr* [The Economics of Anti-Semitism in the Light of Statistics]. Warsaw: Mysl Socjalistyczna, 1937.

————. *Czlowiek w. Spolecenstwie* [Man and Society]. Warsaw: Swiatlo, 1938.

————. *Tsu der Idn Frage in Poyln* [On the Jewish Question in Poland]. Warsaw: Monografja, 1937.

American Jewish Yearbook, 1900–1901. Philadelphia: Jewish Publication Society, 1901.

American Jewish Yearbook, 1928–1929. Philadelphia: Jewish Publication Society, 1929.

Arcady. New York: Ferlag Unser Tsait, 1942.

Ausubel, Nathan. *Pictorial History of the Jewish People.* New York: Crown Publishers, 1953.

Barikht fun der VIII Konferents fun Bund [Report on the Eighth Conference of the Bund]. Geneva: Algemajner Idisher Arbeiter Bund fun Poyln, Litte, un Russland, 1910.

Barnett, Clifford R. *Poland: Its People, Its Society, Its Culture.* New York: Grove Press, 1958.

Bauer, Otto. *Die Nationalitätenfrage und die Sozialdemokratie* [The Nationality Question and the Social Democracy]. Vienna: Wiener Volksbuchhandlung, 1924.

Bernstein, Eduard. *Evolutionary Socialism.* New York: Schocken Books, 1961.

Bor-Komarowski, Tadeusz. *The Secret Army.* London: Gollancz, 1950.

Buell, Raymond L. *Poland: Key to Europe.* New York: Alfred A. Knopf, 1939.

Bunyan, James, and H. H. Fisher. *The Bolshevik Revolution, 1917–1918: Documents and Materials.* Stanford, California: Stanford University Press, 1934.

Burke, Edmund. *The Works of the Right Honorable Edmund Burke.* Boston: Little, Brown and Co., 1865.

Carr, E. H. *The Bolshevik Revolution, 1917–1923.* London: Macmillan, 1950.

Chmurner Bukh [Chmurner Book]. New York: Ferlag Unser Tsait, 1958.

Cole, G. D. H. *A History of Socialist Thought: Communism and Social Democracy, 1914–1931.* London: Macmillan, 1958.

Concise Statistical Yearbook of Poland, I, 1930. Warsaw: Chief of the Bureau of Statistics, 1930.

Concise Statistical Yearbook of Poland, II, 1931. Warsaw: Chief of the Bureau of Statistics, 1931.

Der Bund in Der Revolutsie fun 1905–1906 [The Bund in the Revolution of 1905–1906]. Warsaw: Ferlag Di Welt, 1930.

Der Jidiszer Arbeiter Klas in Jor 1936 [The Jewish Working Class in the Year 1936]. Lodz: J. Kiersz, 1937.

Di Geshikhte fun Bund [History of the Bund]. New York: Ferlag Unser Tsait, 1963.

Di Geshikhte fun Idisher Arbeiter Bavegung in Rusland un Poyln [History of the Jewish Labor Movement in Russia and Poland]. Geneva: Algemajner Idisher Arbeiter Bund fun Rusland un Poyln, 1900.

Di Milkhome fun P.P.S. Kegn Bund [The P.P.S. War Against the Bund]. Bobruisk (?): Algemajner Idisher Arbeiter Bund, 1898.

Documents on Polish-Soviet Relations, 1939–1945. London: Heinemann, 1961.

Drohojowski, Jan. *Brief Outline of the Jewish Problem in Poland.* Brooklyn: Polish National Alliance, 1938.

Duverger, Maurice. *Political Parties.* New York: John Wiley and Sons, 1963.

Dziewanowski, M. K. *The Communist Party of Poland.* Cambridge: Harvard University Press, 1959.

Elbogen, Ismar. *History of the Jews After the Fall of the Jewish State.* Cincinnati: Union of American Hebrew Congregations, 1926.

Erlich, Henryk. *Der Icker fun Bundism* [The Basis of Bundism]. Warsaw: Algemajner Jidiszer Arbeiter Bund, 1934.

——. *The Struggle for Revolutionary Socialism.* New York: The Bund Club, 1939.

Frolich, Paul. *Rosa Luxemburg: Gedanke und Tat* [Rosa Luxemburg: Thought and Deeds]. Paris: Editions Nouvelles Internationales, 1939.

Gay, Peter. *The Dilemma of Democratic Socialism.* New York: Columbia University Press, 1952.

Gillie, D. R., ed. and trans. *Joseph Pilsudski, Memories of a Polish Revolutionary and Soldier.* London: Faber and Faber, 1931.

Goldfinger, H., M. Mirsky, and S. Zachariasz, eds. *Unter der Fon fun KPP* [Under the Banner of the Communist Party of Poland]. Warsaw: Ksiaszka i Wiedza, 1959.

Goldstein, Bernard. *The Stars Bear Witness.* New York: Viking Press, 1949.

——. *Tsvantsik Yor in Varshever Bund* [Twenty Years in the Warsaw Bund]. New York: Ferlag Unser Tsait, 1960.

Heller, Joseph. *The Zionist Idea.* New York: Schocken Books, 1949.

Henryk Erlich un Victor Alter. New York: Ferlag Unser Tsait, 1951.

Henryk Erlich un Victor Alter, Gedank Bukh [Henryk Erlich and Victor Alter, Book in Memoriam]. Buenos Aires: Agrupacion Socialista "Bund," 1943.

Hertz, I. S. *Geshikhte fun Bund in Łodz* [History of the Bund in Łodz]. New York: Ferlag Unser Tsait, 1958.

Hertzberg, Arthur. *The Zionist Idea.* Cleveland and New York: World Publishing Co., 1959.

Hilsberg, Raul. *The Destruction of the European Jews.* Chicago: Quadrangle Books, 1961.

Humphries, Grace. *Pilsudski: Builder of Poland.* New York: Scott and Moore, 1936.

In di Yorn fun Idishn Khurbn [In the Years of the Jewish Catastrophe]. New York: Ferlag Unser Tsait, 1946.

Jewish Encyclopaedia. New York: Funk and Wagnalls, 1909.

Kallen, Horace M. *Frontiers of Hope.* New York: Liveright, 1929.

Karski, Jan. *Story of a Secret State.* Boston: Houghton Mifflin, 1944.

Keep, J. L. H. *The Rise of Social Democracy in Russia.* London: Oxford University Press, 1964.

Key, V. O. *Politics, Parties, and Pressure Groups.* New York: Crowell, 1964.

Konavlov, S. *Russo-Polish Relations.* Princeton, N.J.: Princeton University Press, 1945.

Korbel, Josef. *Poland Between East and West.* Princeton, N.J.: Princeton University Press, 1945.

Labor Zionist Handbook. New York: Poale Zion-Ziere Zion, no date.

Lenin, V. I. *The Right of Nations to Self-Determination.* Moscow: Foreign Language Publishing House, 1947.

Lichtheim, George. *Marxism: An Historical and Critical Study.* London: Routledge and Kegan Paul, 1961.

Lloyd George, David. *War Memoirs of David Lloyd George, 1914–1915.* Boston: Little, Brown and Co., 1933.

Machray, Robert. *Poland, 1914–1931.* London: George Allen and Unwin, 1932.

McKenzie, Kermit E. *The Comintern and World Revolution, 1928–1943.* New York: Columbia University Press, 1964.

Martov, Lev [pseudonym of Iulii Ossipowich Tsederbaum]. *Der Nayer Epoche in der Idisher Arbeiter Bavegung* [The New Epoch in the Jewish Labor Movement]. Geneva: Algemajner Idisher Arbeiter Bund fun Poyln, Litte, un Rusland, 1904.

Marx, Karl. *A World Without Jews.* New York: Philosophical Library, 1959.

———. *Historische-Kritische Gesamtausgabe, Erste Abteilung.* Berlin: Marx-Engels Verlag G.M.B.H., 1927.

———, and Friedrich Engels. *The Communist Manifesto* (Centenary Edition with Introduction by Harold Laski). London: George Allen and Unwin, 1961.

Memorandum fun der Delegatsie fun Idishn Kommunistishn Arbeiter Bund in Poyln (Combund) Tsum Oysfir Komitet fun III Kommunistishn International [Memorandum from the Delegation of the Jewish Communist Workers Bund in Poland (Combund) to the Executive Committee of the III Communist International]. Warsaw: Land Eksekutiv fun Idishn Kommunistishn Arbeiter Bund in Poyln, 1922.

Menes, A., Raphael Mahler, Jacob Shutsky, and Victor Shulman. *Di Idn in Poyln* [The Jews in Poland]. New York: Committee for Publication of "The Jews in Poland," 1946.

Minc, P. [Alexander]. *Di Geshikhte fun a Falshe Iluzie* [The History of a False Illusion]. Buenos Aires: Union Central Israelita, 1954.

Neumann, Sigmund. *Modern Political Parties.* Chicago: University of Chicago Press, 1956.

Pares, Bernard. *The Fall of the Russian Monarchy.* New York: Alfred A. Knopf, 1939.

Pat, Jacob. *Der Oysveg in Poyln* [The Solution in Poland]. New York: Jewish Labor Committee, 1938.

Patkin, Abraham. *The Origin of the Jewish Labour Movement.* Melbourne: F. W. Cheshire Pty., 1947.

Penniman, Howard R. *Sait's American Parties and Elections.* New York: Appleton-Century-Crofts, 1952.

Pinkus, Oscar. *The House of Ashes.* Cleveland and New York: World Publishing Co., 1964.

Price, John. *The International Labour Movement.* London: Oxford University Press, 1945.

Reddaway, W. F. *Marshal Pilsudski.* London: George Routledge and Sons, 1939.

Resolutsie fun Comintern Vegn Anshlus fun'm Combund in Comintern [Resolution of the Comintern Regarding the Affiliation of the Combund in the Comintern]. Warsaw: Land Eksekutiv fun Idisher Kommunistisher Arbeiter Bund, 1922.

Sachar, Howard M. *The Course of Modern Jewish History.* Cleveland and New York: World Publishing Co., 1958.

Segal, Simon. *The New Poland and the Jews.* New York: Lee Furman, 1938.

Sorel, Georges. *Reflections on Violence.* New York: Collier Brooks, 1961.

Trotsky, Leon. *History of the Russian Revolution.* New York: Simon and Schuster, 1937.

Tsvai Konferentsn [Two Conferences]. Warsaw: Algemajner Jidiszer Arbeiter Bund, 1918.

United States House of Representatives Select Committee on Communist Aggression. *Third Interim Report.* Washington: Government Printing Office, 1954.

Vegn Bund in Poyln [About the Bund in Poland]. Bund Club of New York, 1937.

Vladimir Medem: Tsum Tsvantsikstn Yortsayt [Vladimir Medem: On the Twentieth Anniversary of His Death]. New York: Amerikaner Representants fun Algemajner Idisher Arbeiter Bund in Poyln, 1943.

Vlavianos, Basil J., and Feliks Gross. *Struggle for Tomorrow.* New York: Arts, Inc., 1954.

Von Oertzen, F. W. *So This Is Poland.* George Allen and Unwin, 1932.

Vtoroii Vserosiiski Sezd Sovetov Ri. S.D. [Second All-Russian Congress of Soviets of Workers and Soldiers Delegates]. Petrograd, 1917.

Zachariasz, S. *Di Kommunistishe Bavegung Tsvishn der Idisher Arbeiter Bafelkerung in Poyln* [The Communist Movement Among the Jewish Workers in Poland]. Warsaw: Ferlag Idisz Bukh, 1954.

Zhitlowski, Chaim. *Tsionism Oder Sotsialism* [Zionism or Socialism]. Geneva: Idisher Arbeiter, 1899.

Zygelboym Bukh. New York: Ferlag Unser Tsait, 1947.

MANUSCRIPTS, LETTERS, CIRCULARS, AND HANDBILLS

Except as otherwise stated, all unpublished materials listed here are in the Bund Archives at 25 East 78th Street, New York, New York. The collection is quite extensive and covers the Jewish Socialist and Labor movements from the mid-nineteenth century to the present. It is particularly rich in material relating to the Eastern European Jewish labor movement, but also includes a number of rare and valuable materials relating to the American movement. Included in the collection are invaluable holdings on the Polish Bund.

Barikht fun Tsentral Komitet [Report of the Central Committee]. Warsaw: Algemajner Jidiszer Arbeiter Bund in Poyln, 1935. Mimeographed.

Barikht fun Tsentral Komitet fun Untererdishn Bund Vegn Lebn in Ghetto [Report by Underground in Poland on Life in the Ghetto]. March 16, 1942.

Barikht fun Virtshafts Komitet fun Idishe Arbeiter in Varshe [Report of the Economic Committee of Jewish Workers in Warsaw]. 1917. Mimeographed.

Circular Number 36. Central Komitet, Algemajner Jidiszer Arbeiter Bund in Poyln. March 13, 1936.

Die Judenfrage. Resolution of International Socialist Congress in Berne, Switzerland, 1919, on the Jewish Question.

Do Ogolu Zydowskiej Inteligencji Pracujaci. Bund Appeal to Jewish Intelligentsia in 1928 Election.

Fishman, I. Report on Lublin Conference, 1917. Untitled typescript in Yiddish.

Materialn tsum Diskusie farn V. Tsusamenfor [Materials for the Preconvention Discussion of the Bund]. Mimeographed, 1934.

Memorandum der Wilner Judischer Socal demokratischen Organisation Bund [Memorandum of Vilno Bund]. 1917. Typescript.

Meyer, David. Barikht fun Lubliner Konferents [Report on Lublin Conference]. 1917. Yiddish typescript.

Millman, A. Barikht fun der Lubliner Konferents [Report on the Lublin Conference]. 1917. Yiddish typescript.

Nider Mit Der Milkhome! Zol Lebn der Sotsialism! [Down with the War! Long Live Socialism!]. Handbill of Bund, SDKPiL, Lewica, August 1914.

Oyfruf Vegn Der Mobilizatsie [Proclamation Against the Mobilization]. Handbill of Bund, SDKPiL, and PPS Lewica, July 1914.

Shukman, H. "The Relations Between the Jewish Bund and the Russian Social Democratic Workers Party, 1897–1903." Unpublished D. Phil. dissertation, Oxford University, 1961. Copy in Bund Archives.

Tezn un Referat an Der Teme "Folks Front Oder Proletarishe Klasn Front" [Theses and Discussion on the Question "People's Front or Proletarian Class Front"]. Internal Membership Bulletin of the Bund, 1936.

Tsu Alle Idishe Arbeiter in Poyln. Handbill addressed "To All Jewish Workers in Poland," signed by Algemajner Jidiszer Arbeiter Bund, Warszawa, November 10, 1931.

Tsu di Idishe Arbeiter un Folksmassn fun Varshe. Handbill addressed to "The Jewish Workers and Common People of Warsaw," signed Warszawer Komitet, Algemajner Jidiszer Arbeiter Bund, October 1937.

DOCUMENTS IN OTHER COLLECTIONS

Secret Police Files, Elias Tcherikower Archives, YIVO-Institute for Jewish Research, New York.

Trial of Major War Criminals. Transcripts in Library of Congress, Washington, D.C.

ARTICLES AND PERIODICALS

"A Blik in Varshe" [A Look at Warsaw], *Der Wecker*, II (February 25, 1922).

A. G. W. "Fomentations in Poland," *The Nation*, CXVI (February 28, 1923).

Alter, Victor. "Farvos Ikh Hob Nisht Gevolt Shraybn" [Why I Did Not Want to Write], *Socialistisze Bleter*, I (June 1931).

A——n. "A Por Bamerkingen Tsum Artikl fun Altern, 'Di Internatsionale Diskusie Vegn Ratn Ferband'" [A Few Comments on Alter's Article "The International Discussion About the Soviet Union"], *Uncer Cajt*, V (April 1931).

"Are Bolsheviks Mainly Jewish," *Literary Digest*, LIX (December 14, 1918).

Aronson, Gregory. "Der Bund in Rusland" [The Bund in Russia], *Unser Tsait*, XVII (November–December 1957).

Barbusse, Henri. "Jailing Workers in Poland," *The Nation*, CXX (March 11, 1925).

Buell, Raymond L. "Political Conflicts in Poland," *Virginia Quarterly Review*, XV (April 1939).

Chernov, Victor. "Joseph Pilsudski: From Socialist to Autocrat," *Foreign Affairs*, XIV (October 1935).

Chmurner, Joseph [pseudonym of Joseph Lestchinsky]. "An Enderung?" [A Change?], *Uncer Cajt*, III (January 1929).

D. M. "Der Bund in di Iberkerenishn in Poyln" [The Bund and the Revolution in Poland], *Der Wecker*, IV (July 3, 1926).

Dar, Yaakov. "Ver iz Niderik Gefalln?" [Who Has Fallen Low?], *Letste Nayes*, Tel Aviv, January 25–29, 1959.

"Degeneratsye fun a Partei" [Degeneration of a Party], *Uncer Cajt*, V (March–April 1932).

"Dekleratsye fun Bund in Poylishn Golos-Parliament" [Declaration by the Bund in Polish Parliament-in-Exile], *Unser Tsait*, II (June 1942).

"Der IIIer Tsuzamenfor fun Algemajner Idishn Arbeiter Bund in Poyln" [The Third Convention of the General Jewish Workers Bund in Poland], *Arbeiter Luakh*, VI (Warsaw, 1925).

"Der Ekstra Tsuzamenfor fun Bund in Poyln" [The Special Conference of the Bund], *Der Wecker*, IX (June 28, 1930).

"Der Erfolg fun di Royte in Poyln" [The Victory of the Reds in Poland], *Der Wecker*, II (July 15, 1922).

"Der Ershter Mai Pogrom Oyf Idishe Arbeiter" [The May Day Pogrom on Jewish Workers], *Der Wecker*, II (June 3, 1922).

"Der Letster Tsuzamenfor fun 'Bund' " [The Latest Convention of the Bund], *Der Wecker*, II (March 18, 1922).

"Der Poylisher Bund" [The Polish Bund], *Der Wecker*, IX (June 14, 1930).

Dunai, A. "Der Ferter Konferents fun Bund" [The Fourth Conference of the Bund], *Der Wecker*, VIII (March 23, 1929).

Easterman, A. L. "Poland, Land of Whispers," *Living Age*, CCCL (January 1938).

Erlich, Henryk. "An Enderung?" [A Change?], *Uncer Cajt*, III (January 1929).

——. "Der Muser Hashakel" [The Moral of the Story], *Uncer Cajt*, III, Number 3 (1929).

——. "In Kampf Kegn Reformistishe Ilusies" [The Struggle Against Reformist Illusions], *Uncer Cajt*, III (March–April 1929).

——. "Politishe Perspektivn" [Political Perspectives], *Uncer Cajt*, VI, Number 2 (1932).

——. "Tsi iz der Sovetn Regirung an Arbeiter Regirung?" [Is the Soviet Government a Workers' Government?], *Uncer Sztyme*, III (November 1918).

Goldfarb, Max. "Di Poylishe-Idishe Betsiyungen un der Bund" [Polish-Jewish Relations and the Bund], *Zukunft*, XIX (1914).

Grywicz, Karol. "Dyktatura" [Dictatorship], *Walka*, III (July–August 1926).

Halpern, I. "Di Sotsiale Trayb Koikhes fun Sanacia Regime" [The Social Forces Driving the Pilsudski Regime], *Uncer Cajt*, II (May 1928).

Hertz, S. "Aynike Shtrikhn Vegn der Idisher Arbeiter Bavegung" [Certain Factors Regarding the Jewish Labor Movement], *Socialistisze Bleter*, I (June 1931).

Holtz, Aaron. "Der Grosser Klub in Varshe un di Kommunistishe Bavegung in Amerika" [The Grosser Club in Warsaw and the Communist Movement in America]. Letter, *Jewish Daily Forward*, February 18, 1954.

"In Poyln" [In Poland], *Der Wecker*, IV (July 31, 1926).

Kazhdan, Sh. "Es Vilt Zikh un Es Shtekht Zikh" [There Is a Desire and a Drive], *Socialistisze Bleter*, I (June 1931).

"Kh'Arthur Zygelboym in Poylishn Natsional Rat" [Comrade Arthur Zygelboym in Polish National Parliament], *Unser Tsait*, II (March 1942).

Kligsberg, M. "Sotsialism un 5–Yor Plan" [Socialism and the Five-Year Plan], *Socialistisze Bleter*, I (June 1931).

Kossofsky, Vladimir. "Farvos un Vi Azoy der 'Bund' hot Zikh Tseshpoltn" [Why and How the Bund Split], *Zukunft*, XXIV (1921).

Krishtof, P. "Fun 'Goldenem Mitn' tsum Shvartsn Rand" [From the 'Golden Mean' to the Black Extreme], *Jugnt Vecker*, V (December 1926).

Lestchinsky, Jacob. "Di Revolutsionere Iberkerenishn in Poyln" [The Revolutionary Upset in Poland], *Der Wecker*, IV (June 12, 1926).

Lezgin, H. "A Shedlekher Tuml" [A Harmful Tumult], *Unser Tsait*, II (April 1942).

Lipson, Leslie. "The Two-Party System in British Politics," *American Political Science Review*, XLVII (June 1953).

Litauer, Stefan. "Poland's Problems in 1939," *Fortnightly Review*, CLI (February 1939).

Litvak, A. [pseudonym of Haym-Yankl Helfand]. "Lederbour's Internatsional un der Poylisher Bund" [Lederbour's International and the Polish Bund], *Der Wecker*, II (August 2, 1922).

———. "Varum Ikh Bin Kegn Poylishn Bund" [Why I Oppose the Polish Bund], *Der Wecker*, II (August 2, 1922).

Medem, Vladimir. "Der Goirl fun der Russishe Revolutsie" [The Fate of the Russian Revolution], *Uncer Sztyme*, I (August, 1918).

———. "Di Idishe Shul-Bavegung in Poyln" [The Jewish School Movement in Poland], *Der Fraynd*, October–November, 1921.

———. "Farvos Ikn Bin Kegn Tsionism" [Why I Oppose Zionism], *Naye Velt*, X (July 2, 1920).

———. "Farvos iz der Bund in Poyln Nit Farnandergefaln" [Why the Bund in Poland Was Not Torn Asunder], *Zukunft*, XXVI (1921).

Mendelson, S. "A Nayer Kurs" [A New Course], *Unser Tsait*, II (March 1942).

———. "Es Muz Kumen Maysim" [Miracles Must Come], *Unser Tsait*, II (November 1942).

———. "Vuhin Geht di Sikorski-Regirung?" [Where Is the Sikorski Government Going?], *Unser Tsait*, II (June 1942).

Meyer, David. "Der Itztiger Tsushtand fun der Arbeiter Bavegung in Poyln" [The Present Condition of the Polish Labor Movement], *Der Wecker*, III (August 16, 1924).

Michalewicz, B. "Di Sotsiale Revolutsie un der Marxism" [The Social Revolution and Marxism], *Uncer Sztyme*, II (October 1918).

Mus, E. "Der Bund un di Sejm Vahln" [The Bund and the Sejm Election], *Uncer Cajt*, II (March–April 1928).

Nayer, A. "Brief fun Varshe" [Letter from Warsaw], *Naye Velt*, X (October 8 and 15, 1920).

———. "Der Bund in Poyln" [The Bund in Poland], *Naye Velt*, X (October 25, 1921).

Niedzialkowski, M. "Di Revolutsie in Poyln un di Poylishe Sotsialistn" [The Polish Revolution and the Polish Socialists], *Der Wecker*, IV (June 26, 1926).

"Nokh di Mai Iberkerenishn" [After the May Revolution], *Jugnt Vecker*, V (June 1926).

Novogrodsky, Emanuel. "Der Bund in Irushelayem de Litte" [The Bund in Jerusalem of Lithuania], *Forois*, XVIII (October 1957).

———. "Der Bund in Kovner Litte" [The Bund in the Kovno Area of Lithuania], *Forois*, XVIII (October 1957).

———. "Der Bund in Umophengign Poyln Tsvishn Bayde Velt Milkhomes" [The Bund in Independent Poland Between the Two World Wars], *Unser Tsait*, XVIII (November–December 1957).

———. "Ha Bund Bain Shatai Milkhoma Ha Ellem" [The Bund Between Two Wars] (Hebrew), *Encyclopaeda of Jewish Life in the Diaspora* (Tel Aviv, 1959).

———. "Mai Blumen Iber di Ghetto-Vant" [May Flowers Over the Ghetto Wall], *Unser Tsait*, II (May 1942).

Ohler, Leon. "Di Tsvayner in Poylishn Bund" [The Second Faction in the Polish Bund], *Unser Tsait*, XVII (November–December 1957).

Ozher, Mauritzi. "Di Daytshe S.D. un di Presidentn Valhn" [The German Social Democrats and the Presidential Election], *Uncer Cajt,* V (July 1931).

——. "Unser Tog Ordnung: Sotsialism" [Our Order of the Day: Socialism], *Socialistisze Bleter,* I (June 1931).

Pizyc, H. "Mir un der P.P.S." [We and the P.P.S.], *Socialistisze Bleter* I (June 1931).

"Proklamacia Antysemicka z Czasow Okupacji Niemieckiej, 1918" [Anti-Semitic Proclamation During the German Occupation, 1918], *Dziennik Poranny* January 19, 1919.

"Protest fun Algemajnem Idishn Arbeiter Bund Kegn dem Anti-Semitishn Bashlus fun Poylishn Natsional-Rat Vegn a Idisher Milukhe" [Protest of the General Jewish Workers Bund Against the Anti-Semitic Action of the Polish Parliament About a Jewish State], *Unser Tsait,* II (July 1942).

Ratman, A. [pseudonym of Gershon Ziebert]. "Der Bund in Poyln" [The Bund in Poland], *Naye Velt,* VII (September 30, 1920).

——. "Der Ershter Idisher Shul Tsuzamenfor in Poyln" [The First Yiddish School Convention in Poland], *Der Fraynd* September 1921.

"Reaction in Poland," *The Nation,* CXVIII (May 11, 1924).

"Report of the International Missionary Council," *Commonweal,* XXVI (September 3, 1937).

Sherer, Emanuel. "A Brik Tsum Morgen Oder a Shtrik Tsurik?" [A Bridge to Tomorrow or a Road Back?], *Unser Tsait,* II (April 1942).

——. "Primo-Secundo-Terzio" [First-Second-Third], *Socialistisze Bleter,* I (June 1931).

Smogorzewski, Casimir. "Poland's Crisis and Its Background," *Living Age,* CCXXIX (June 26, 1926).

Smolar, Boris. "What Polish Jews Are Facing," *The Nation,* CXXIV (January 27, 1932).

"To All Members of the All-Jewish Workers' Union (The Bund) of Poland," *Bulletin of the Executive Committee of the Communist International,* II (September 20, 1921).

"Vaygeshray fun der Idisher Bafelkerung in Poyln" [Cry of Pain of the Jewish Population in Poland], *Unser Tsait,* II (October 1942).

Werder, Aleksandr [pseudonym of Emanuel Sherer]. "Ostatnie Wypadki w Polsce" [Latest Occurrences in Poland], *Walka,* II June 1926).

Zachariasz, S. "The Ghetto Was Not Alone," *Jewish Life,* IV (April, 1951).

"Zay Hobn Zikh Tsusamengetrofn" [They Have Joined Together], *Jugnt Vecker,* V (July 1926).

Zukerman, William. "Jews and the Fate of Poland," *The Nation*, CXLVI (April 2, 1938).
——. "The Polish Election," *The Nation*, CXXVI (March 7, 1928).
Zygelboym, Shmuel Mordecai (Arthur). "In Kampf far Veltlakhe Kehillas" [In Struggle for Secular *Kehillath*], *Uncer Cajt*, III (April 1929).
Zylberfarb, M. "A Por Kritishe Bamerkungen Tsu der Vahl Kampanye fun Bund" [A Few Critical Remarks About the Bund's Election Campaign], *Uncer Cajt*, II (March–April 1928).

PERIODICALS

Arbeiter Luakh [Worker's Calendar]. Bund Annual in Warsaw, 1919–1926.
Arbeiter Sztyme [Worker's Voice]. Bund Daily, Warsaw, 1920–1921.
Bulletin of the Executive Committee of the Communist International.
Cummunist International. Organ of the Communist International.
Czerwony Sztander [Red Flag]. Communist organ, Warsaw, 1931.
Der Emes [The Truth]. Yiddish Daily organ of the Communist Party, Moscow, 1920–1939.
Der Fraynd [The Friend]. Organ of the Workman's Circle in New York.
Der Gedank [The Thought]. Organ of the Combund. Only known issue dated February 1922.
Der Moment [The Moment]. Popular pro-Zionist Yiddish daily, Warsaw.
Der Wecker [The Guardian]. Organ of the Jewish Socialist Alliance, New York, 1921—.
Dos Fraje Vort [The Free Word]. Vilno Social Democratic Bund organ, 1920–1924.
Dziennik Lodowy [People's Paper]. Short-lived joint Polish language daily of the Bund and PPS, 1937.
Folscajtung; also Uncer Folkscajtung, Najer Folkscajtung [People's Paper, Our People's Paper, New People's Paper]. Bund daily, 1921–1939.
Forois [To the Front]. Bund monthly, Mexico City, 1940—.
Freie Wort [Free Word]. Yiddish Socialist biweekly, London, 1920(?)–1940.
Gazeta Polska [Polish Gazette]. Voice of the Pilsudski regime in Warsaw.
Glos Bundu [Voice of the Bund]. Bund weekly in Polish, 1919–1920.
Glos Komunisticzny [Communist Voice]. Communist organ.

Bibliography 283

Hajnt. Popular Warsaw Yiddish daily.

Jewish Daily Forward. Popular New York Yiddish daily with Socialist leanings, 1897—.

Jugnt Vecker [Youthful Guardian]. Organ of Bund Youth in Warsaw, 1922–1939.

Kegn Shtrom [Against the Current]. Left-wing Bund organ, 1930–1935.

Lebnsfragn [Life Questions]. Warsaw Bund organ, 1916–1920.

Morgenshtern [Morning Star]. Bund organ, Warsaw, 1920–1921.

Naye Velt [New World]. Socialist Yiddish weekly, New York, 1912–1921.

Pravda [Truth]. Daily organ of the Soviet Communist Party, Moscow.

Robotnik [Worker]. Daily organ of the PPS, Warsaw.

Robotnik Zydowski [Jewish Worker]. Pro-Bund Polish monthly, 1920.

Socialistisze Bleter [Socialist Leaves]. Right-wing Bund factional organ, 1931.

Svoboda Rossiia [Russian Freedom]. Russian daily, 1917.

Sztandar Socializmu [Socialist Standard]. Communist weekly, Warsaw, 1918.

The New York Times.

The Times, London.

Uncer Cajt [Our Times]. Bund monthly, 1927–1939.

Unser Tsait [Our Times]. Bund organ, New York, 1940—.

Uncer Sztyme [Our Voice]. Warsaw Bund monthly, 1918.

Unzer Gedank [Our Thought]. Vilno Bund weekly, 1921–1924.

Walka [Struggle]. Polish language Bund monthly, Cracow, 1924–1928.

Warszawer Radio [Warsaw Radio]. Popular daily.

World Views and News. Official Comintern organ, 1939.

Zukunft [Future]. Yiddish intellectual monthly, New York, 1895—.

Index